Investing in Enchantment

Investing in Enchantment

Memory, Market, and the Family Vacation Home

Michelle Janning

ROWMAN & LITTLEFIELD
Lanham • Boulder • New York • London

Published by Rowman & Littlefield
An imprint of The Rowman & Littlefield Publishing Group, Inc.
4501 Forbes Boulevard, Suite 200, Lanham, Maryland 20706
www.rowman.com

86-90 Paul Street, London EC2A 4NE

British Library Cataloguing in Publication Information Available

Library of Congress Cataloging-in-Publication Data

Names: Janning, Michelle Yvonne, author.
Title: Investing in enchantment : memory, market, and the family vacation home / Michelle Janning.
Description: [Lanham] : [Rowman & Littlefield], [2024] | Includes bibliographical references and index.
Identifiers: LCCN 2024010900 (print) | LCCN 2024010901 (ebook) | ISBN 9781538182673 (cloth) | ISBN 9781538182680 (paperback) | ISBN 9781538182697 (epub)
Subjects: LCSH: Vacation homes--History--21st century. | Vacation rentals--History--21st century.
Classification: LCC HD7289.2 .J36 2024 (print) | LCC HD7289.2 (ebook) | DDC 333.33/8–dc23/eng/20240613
LC record available at https://lccn.loc.gov/2024010900
LC ebook record available at https://lccn.loc.gov/2024010901

For Jeff and Cheryl Bloom, neighbors I'd choose again and again

Contents

Acknowledgments

This has been the longest research project I've ever conducted, and the collection of supportive people is itself lengthy. I'm grateful, of course, to my small "team" within my extended family: Neal and Aaron (along with Pluto the dog). You know me well, you always ask me the right questions, and you make going on vacation especially memory-filled and easy. Thanks for being my home.

To my friends and extended family—including the ones who actually have family vacation homes—thanks for the stories, the family fun, the frank conversations about money, and the support for me and my work. I've been talking about this stuff for so many years, and you all just kept listening. Thank you for that. Mom, I'm especially grateful for your stories about Hawaii. Diane, I'm especially grateful to you for teaching me how to fish, literally and figuratively.

My Whitman College sociology colleagues always inspire me, with particular inspiration for this project about methods and research ethics from Rachel Nickens and Alissa Cordner, culture and inequalities from Helen Kim, economic sociology from Gilbert Mireles, and the significance of history and technology from Alvaro Santana-Acuña. I'd like to also extend my gratitude to my psychology colleague Matthew Prull, who provided conceptual help on the topic of memory. Speaking of social sciences, the administrative work associated with social science faculty research is never a tiny thing, so I'm forever indebted to Richele Heilbrun for help with all things related to receipts, three-hole punches, and Trapper Keepers. While I enjoy working with this whole bunch on a daily basis, I suspect a vacation with them would be fun, too.

My institution—Whitman College—supports interdisciplinary research both rhetorically and financially. I am thankful to be at a place where I could ebb and flow with a project interrupted by the pandemic and continue to get financial support from the Sociology Department, the Raymond and Elsie Gipson DeBurgh Endowment, and the provost and dean of the faculty office. This support allowed me to involve students every step along the way. I could not have done this research without these stellar Whitman College student collaborators: Grant Yeatts, Tate Kautzky, Michelle Zhang, Hannah Bashevkin, Nate Raphael, and Bridget Kennedy. I'd also like to include the eleven students in my fall 2023 Sociology of the Family class from my time as a visiting scholar at the University of Minnesota Morris in this collection of wonderful student collaboration. It is their insights, observations, questions, and hard work that motivated me all along. All these students—and my wonderful U of M Morris colleagues—deserve a vacation.

People who reviewed my work have made it much better than it would be if I were doing this alone while stranded on an island. These include my wonderful Rowman & Littlefield editor Alyssa Palazzo, who helped me figure out that this is—in the end—a book about families. I'm also grateful for helpful tips from Samantha Delwarte and the entire Rowman & Littlefield team; for the wise feedback on my proposal from Mirelle Cohen, Arielle Kuperberg, Katie Pridgen, and Jill Sturges; and for a bit of narrative review from Philip Cohen. And thanks to Allison Pugh for really understanding my sociological voice.

I cannot say enough good things about the person who provided professional editorial help in the writing of this book: Daniel LeRay. While I never did find a way to include "Island Niles" in the text (Oh, wait! I did it here!), your comments continue to make me smile to this day. Thank you for your kindness, cleverness, and swiftness. I owe you an Aloha shirt.

The people who agreed to be interviewed deserve a lot of thanks for taking time to talk about their families and homes, showing me around their neighborhoods (or showing me pictures), and sharing insights about the broader social world as we talked about our smaller ones. I learned so much about families, vacations, and homes from you all. I also learned a lot about vacation rental regulations through conversation and by watching the thorough and careful work of Walla Walla city manager Elizabeth Chamberlain.

To friends I get to see often, including our Walla Walla peeps and especially Joshua and Lisa: thanks for the weekly food and ridiculous reality TV data analysis. I'll let you know when I've drafted the pitch for a family vacation home/dating reality TV show so we can make a game of it. To my longtime friends Angela Bina, Melissa Alcorn, Amy Johnson, Jennifer Steffens, Erica Anaya, and Jennifer Burke—thanks for always talking and laughing with me as if no time has gone by since the last time. When's our next fun vacation?

Finally, I want to acknowledge the two trivia teams with whom I've had the recent honor of answering questions about pointless things on a weekly basis: ÖBTT and Yikes! Thanks for supporting me as I work toward finding answers, even if I get things wrong sometimes—a treasure for anyone who has decent ideas but needs support from others to get them on paper. I have an idea for a trivia category for next time: world's most obscure vacation home spots.

Chapter 1

Unpacking Family, Vacation, and Home in the Family Vacation Home

I recently stumbled across a photo of me as an eleven-year-old holding a fishing rod with a tiny sunfish dangling from the hook. It is one of those Kodachrome photos from the 1980s that has faded over time. I had caught the fish at a family friend's lake cabin in northern Minnesota, a place I got to visit a couple of times each summer as a child. I was so proud of this catch, evidenced by my huge smile. That lake cabin was enchanted, in my estimation. I have our family friend Diane to thank for these happy memories, since—aside from our backyard—my family didn't have our own vacation spot. She let me stay at the cabin without asking for anything in return. To this day, I consider her a part of my family.

When I look at the picture from time to time, I take a second glance at the popped lavender polo shirt collar around my neck and the thick glasses on my face and am transported back to a magical and carefree time when I had fewer responsibilities. But I also think back to how I *really* was at that age: excessively nervous about having friends and intensely dedicated to academic and musical achievement, to a point that I suffered from daily stress-induced headaches that necessitated months of therapy and stress management skill development. It makes sense that I was happy to go to a magical place where my very real preteen anxieties faded away. While my family life was incredibly supportive and nurturing, my ailments made home and school feel far from magical.

You could say this tiny cabin on this tiny lake in Minnesota remains a magical place in my mind, and that my memories of that tiny sunfish from that place and time are filled with wonder and awe. Anyone looking at the picture could see this. But, of course, the anxieties that plagued my mind are invisible in this picture. You could say this family vacation home experience—even though it wasn't with my legal family or within a vacation home that belonged to us—was enchanting. But you could also say the not-so-magical realities of life are easy to hide in a memory captured in a snapshot. You could say that the enchantment of family life is alive and well, while at the same time the realities of life may not feel very magical.

Digital design expert David Rose begins his book *Enchanted Objects: Innovation, Design, and the Future of Technology* with the question, "What makes something magical? Enchanted?"[1] Rose, whose intended audience includes design, business, and technology professionals, says that enchanted objects are ones that engage with people in such a way that they "resonate with the latent needs of those who use them" and "create an emotional connection with us human beings."[2] Put simply: to enchant an object is to make an ordinary thing extraordinary.[3] And for Rose, the root of enchantment lies in the fairytales and myths that make up our childhood fantasies. Enchantment is "a realization of our fondest fantasies and wildest dreams. A reimagining of flying carpets, talking mirrors, protective cloaks, animated brooms, and omniscient crystal balls—as well as cherished everyday objects of our past lives. . . . Things we have always loved, dreamed about, and wanted in our lives."[4]

This definition implies that objects that carry out our nostalgic fantasies allow us to deeply connect with our emotional selves and make our dreams come true. But is that entirely realistic? Further, does being realistic ruin the fantasy?

The boundary between reality and escape intrigues me, as does the idea of enchantment in the form of a material object or place. I suppose if an enchanted object were created that would allow me to escape my everyday life, it would need to somehow encapsulate that sunfish, the tiny cabin on the lake, and, of course, my fabulous 1980s outfit. Similarly, if a family wanted to escape the stresses of everyday life, it'd be helpful to find a place to escape to that is enchanted, perhaps even a "home away from home," as historian John Gillis called it,[5] that would allow for the easy creation of happy, stress-free memories.

Enter family vacation homes.

Whether browsing vacation rental websites or real estate listings in tourist locales, it is clear that family vacation homes are purported to be escapes from reality, even while we increasingly recognize that we cannot fully escape "reality." If people believe that real life (and accompanying objects or spaces) can be enchanted and that homes may actually be places filled with stress, what do we make of yet another space where people pursue enchantment: the family vacation home? What purpose does this kind of place serve, what does it look like, and what does it tell us about larger social patterns surrounding families, homes, leisure, and the economy?

For the last several years, I have been gathering and analyzing diverse types of data related to family vacation homes in the United States. The findings presented in this book are based on a review of relevant interdisciplinary research, news items, and real estate resources, along with sociological analysis of these interconnected data sources:

- Phone and in-person interviews with and surveys of homeowners in forty-five households across fourteen US states who own properties that are used for family getaways (their own, and/or rented to other families using online platforms or property rental companies)
- Physical and virtual home and neighborhood "windshield and walking surveys"[6] of the locations where interviewees have vacation homes
- Interviews with and surveys of stakeholders in positions connected to vacation home and family tourism markets and industries (e.g., real estate, lending, tourism, community organizing, city government, property management, and home remodeling)
- Participant observation at hospitality design and vacation rental owner conferences
- Participant observation at public meetings about short-term rental regulations and controversies in an amenity-rich tourism community
- Content analysis of video and transcripts of lifestyle television shows about vacation properties that are aimed at families
- Content analysis of text from news articles about vacation home controversies during COVID-19 lockdowns in communities in the geographic areas near interviewees' homes
- Content analysis of vacation rental company webinars on how COVID-19 has shaped the vacation rental marketplace

Each chapter contains evidence gathered in the form of data and stories from any of the aforementioned sources that help demonstrate and corroborate patterns, but the bulk of analysis throughout the book is based on homeowner interviews. I use a mixed-method qualitative approach to analyze these diverse and rich data sources, triangulating my analysis to highlight patterns that are evident across data sources and across time (including ways that patterns emerging before the pandemic do or do not continue today). I use pseudonyms for all individuals, and I rename geographic locations into fictitious regional names (e.g., Northern Lake Country or Western Desert). Information about research sites and my approach to qualitative data gathering, triangulated analysis, and ethical considerations about people and place confidentiality and beyond is elaborated in the appendix.

I am a family sociologist, which means I am dedicated to finding patterns that demonstrate cultural values, conflicts, and trends that move beyond individual experience in order to help describe and explain what is actually going on with families today. I study the family at both the interactional and institutional levels, which means I look at people's within-family (and even within-self) experiences alongside broader neighborhood, community, and societal structural and cultural patterns that shape and are shaped by everyday family dynamics. I combine stories I gathered from interviewees and at varied research sites with rigorously analyzed and sociohistorically contextualized data. In doing this, I aim to demonstrate my use of the *sociological imagination*, a concept sociologist C. Wright Mills coined to describe the capacity to understand any phenomenon by considering both individual stories and broader social and historical contexts.[7] The family vacation home is assuredly a site that allows for a gathering of individual family vacation home memories and stories. It also allows for a playful and surprising analysis of the porousness of boundaries surrounding family, home, work, and leisure. Further, it reveals rich and deep patterns relating to social inequalities, cultural values about family inclusion and exclusion, changing conceptions of retreat from stress, and complex and competing definitions of citizenship in a marketplace meant to foster family connectedness.

In this book, I focus on the ways that family memories and nostalgia become social strategies meant to "enchant" the family vacation home as a magical place removed from both the marketplace and the headaches of everyday work, family, and politics. I examine the perceptions and practices of homeowners who use their vacation homes for personal family use, who rent their homes to others, or both. I ask and answer how the specific case of family vacation home ownership tells the general story of what's happening in contemporary families and neighborhoods. Specifically, I uncover patterns about how the type of property ownership and property use shape the material, spatial, and social manifestation of (a) family, vacation, and work identities; (b) the social construction of family relationships and boundaries; (c) definitions of neighborhood and community connection; (d) moral and legal designations of "right" and "wrong" constructions of home and neighborhood; and (e) generational change relating to property and family roles. As I discuss findings in each of these areas, I uncover broader patterns relating to the sharing economy, cultural values surrounding vacations and families, the commodification of intimate life, the impacts of COVID-19 on families and leisure, and the perpetuation of unequal access to amenity-rich housing options based on race and class.

Below, I discuss the definition of family vacation home used in this research. I then briefly unpack historical and current understandings of families, vacationing, and the vacation home marketplace to contextualize the project, followed by an articulation of the conceptual frameworks that guide my questions and analysis. I conclude this introductory chapter with an itinerary of the remaining chapters and a story.

DEFINING HARD-TO-CLASSIFY PEOPLE AND PROPERTIES

This book is about perceptions, symbols, and everyday practices revealed through rigorous qualitative analysis of diverse data sources. I aim to reveal how much impact people's actual experiences and beliefs have on their understanding and use of a family vacation home. I do *not* aim to present a study of legal definitions of vacation homes, and I do *not* intend to examine mismatches between the actual use of a home and its legal classification. My research approach is informed by housing and urban studies scholar David Clapham's push for an approach to understanding housing and homes.[8] Specifically, he argues for the importance of qualitative inquiry in uncovering meanings, complexities, and subjectivities about housing that cannot be found by analyzing governmental policy or framing homeowners as consistently rational (or even consistent) actors. Clapham proposes that "[i]t is through interaction that individuals define themselves and the world they inhabit, and so it is through interaction that the nature of individuals becomes apparent to themselves and to others."[9] Further, the strategies of homeowners—either ad hoc reactions to external circumstances or proactive plans and pursuits—are crucial to unpack if we want to understand how housing choices are made. In other words, if we want to understand how the experience of home *actually* operates in society—vacation homes or otherwise—we need to go beyond formal classifications of homeowners and toward a study of what homeowners actually think and do. We need to study perceptions and everyday practices of families.

Here I want to articulate what I mean by *family vacation home* as it is conceptualized in this book. Describing my use of this term necessitates a story about how this research has shifted over the last several years. When I started this project, I thought defining family vacation homes would be a straightforward task. I understood the legal term *vacation home* to require an owner to spend a certain proportion of time there annually to distinguish it from a primary residence, and to be very limited in the amount of time it could be rented to others. Vacation homes would carry mortgage rates that were slightly higher than rates for a primary residence. I understood the term *residential investment property* to require an owner to spend much less time there because it would be rented out more; it is a place that—if sold—would carry hefty capital gains taxes. When purchased, investment properties would also carry higher mortgage rates. I understood that, in general, these properties would be situated in residentially zoned neighborhoods. More details about these formal governmental classifications are included in the appendix.

As I started to talk with people about their second properties, however, I realized that the formal classifications of properties based on taxes, zoning, mortgages, and governmental definitions were useful, but were definitely not how people *actually* used or thought about their homes. The homes owned by my interviewees (and by others I came across in my research) were not only hard to classify because sometimes people didn't want to classify them (to save money on taxes, for example, or to not have to report a property as an investment property in any official way); they were also hard to classify because their use and definition changed, even for the families themselves. During the time frame of my research, some families were actually in the process of deciding whether to increase the amount of time they were renting out their vacation home because it wasn't being used by family members as much as they had hoped. Some were shifting the use of an investment property to be a vacation spot for their family to use more often. Some were using portions of their primary residence to rent out as a vacation spot for other people. Some rented their vacation homes to families once or twice and then switched to long-term rental, or the other way around. Others had no idea what the legal or taxation classifications were supposed to be for a property, since they had inherited the property from parents or even grandparents and other family members managed the financial aspects of the property. And still other elements of my research shifted because people changed how they used their homes (and other people's homes) for leisure and paid work during COVID-19 lockdowns.

It became clear as my data collection continued that even the process of defining terms needed for describing the types of properties included in my study was part of the larger issue of changing definitions and boundaries around family and home. Just because the Internal Revenue Service (IRS) sees a property as an investment property doesn't mean owners don't actually use it from time to time for their own family vacations. Just because people allow friends to stay at their vacation home for free (because they're "family") doesn't mean they don't accept gifts or donations for the stay, thus making it more like an investment property. Just because money is not formally exchanged doesn't mean there isn't some kind of currency for using another family's vacation home. Just because a home is defined as a vacation home doesn't mean that people don't telecommute from there when their offices are shut down. Just because families don't like to talk about money doesn't mean these kinds of properties don't have powerful roles in difficult economic decision-making processes. Just because a vacation home is about families doesn't mean the marketplace is absent from its meaning. And just because a vacation home is situated in a real estate marketplace doesn't mean that family memory-making disappears from its valuation.

As my research continued, it became apparent that the family vacation home was more about *place* than it was about *space*. As sociologist Karen Stein notes,

> Space is made up of structures and forms. It is the distance between objects, the location of things, and the directions between them. Place is a location that has been provided with meaning by the people who inhabit it or visit it. Rather than a geometric abstraction, place is invested with values. Place can be as small as a corner of the room with a favored chair or as large as a city. Space becomes place as people get to know it and give it value.[10]

Because of all of this, I study family vacation homes as distinct from formal classificatory schemes. In fact, I have created my own classifications based on the experiences of people included in my research, detailed below. While one could argue that this limits any capacity to map my research onto other studies using formal classifications, I see this as a project dedicated to people's meaning-making about the significance and strategies associated with identity, family definitions, and relationships with neighbors and communities. This book fills a gap in current understandings about family vacation homes because it is about how families perceive and experience their properties, rather than how their properties are classified by formal institutions.

Ultimately, I decided to include family vacation homes that meet the following criteria: they are defined by homeowners as second home spaces that are used by family, rented to others, or a mixture of both—all for the purpose, for the most part, of vacation stays; they are dwellings in which the homeowners have control over the purchase and potential sale of the property and its furnishings; and they are among one or two places owned by homeowners. What am I excluding from this definition? It is already the case that family vacation homes are only one type of vacation, and they are also only one type of home. But even this definition could include spaces and places that fulfill the leisure goals of a traveling family at the same time they can be defined as a home. These places, which I have excluded from my research, run the gamut from timeshares to hotels and resorts that have regular visitors and vacation rentals that are part of a large portfolio of properties managed and owned by corporations or what some people call the "professional landlord class."[11] I also exclude investment properties that are primarily rented to others for nonvacation travel or for long-term lease. I do not include these types of properties in this research because they do not reveal patterns about how families use vacation homes for themselves as small-scale enterprises meant to provide escapes for themselves or for other families. They do not tell a clear enough story about families and leisure in the sharing economy, which ultimately is what I am trying to do here. I study quintessential family vacation homes that are at a historical crossroads, part of a decades-old pattern of homes away from homes that are not technically part of growing massive corporate investment property portfolios but that cater to family escapes that may be desired by one's own family or by other families that may use the space for a formal or informal fee.

The type of dwelling varies in my research. I focus on homeowners who own and/or rent condos, cabins, rooms in their homes, *accessory dwelling units* (ADUs) such as cottages or mother-in-law suites, small and large single-family homes, and even recreational vehicles (RVs) like campers and tents that fit atop a truck. As I continued with my research, it became apparent that type of dwelling mattered less than other dimensions of families and neighborhoods, elaborated throughout the book. It also became apparent that spaces *within* a homeowner's primary residence could come to be defined as vacation spots, especially when rented out to others. So those are included here as "vacation homes," too.

As my data collection shifted my understanding of what a family vacation home is, it also led me to delineate three subgroups of property owners: families that have a vacation home that is meant entirely or predominantly for their own personal use are included—the *Personal Property group*; those who use a family vacation home for themselves but also rent it to others for a significant amount of time—the *Mixed Property group*; and finally, those who have a vacation home that they entirely or predominantly rent out to others in order to make money—the *Investment Property group*. One of the puzzles of sociology is to use categories at the same time as we complicate or dismantle them. In this way, I provide working definitions of the types of properties I'm talking about. But throughout the book, I also show ways that families' use and definitions shift depending on motivation and circumstances. How I arrived thoughtfully at these homeowner classifications is detailed in the appendix.

Like Stein, who points out that similar strategies and mechanisms can be present across different types of vacations (relaxing, adventurous, and staying home),[12] I argue throughout this book that while owning a family vacation home for others' use, for personal use, or for both can differentially shape many outcomes for families, it is also clear that patterns of identity formation, boundary making, and conceptions of home, neighborhood, and community persist across property groups. Changing conceptions of families, vacations, and vacation homes in the sharing economy—discussed in the next section—have shaped these patterns.

HISTORICAL CHANGE IN FAMILIES AND THE VACATION HOME MARKETPLACE

Changing Families and Homes

The definition of *family* (and who counts according to this definition) has diversified over the past few decades to include varying household arrangements, relationship types, and degrees of legal recognition.[13] At the same time, the concept of "the family" is a powerful force in the modern imagination in terms of its ability to sustain the economy and dominate political and cultural debates, from reproductive rights to emotional appeals about "family values." But the use of "the family" or "family values" to reference some kind of monolithic view of what a family is "obscures the diversity of family forms and inflicts real pain on those who do not conform to a single, narrowly defined notion of family"[14] that people presume thrived in the past. Or, as historian Stephanie Coontz has said, we get stuck in a *"nostalgia trap."*[15]

In reality, contemporary families vary based on any number of factors, such as partners' marital status, number of kids, coresidence, number of generations residing in the same household, sexual orientation, and the presence or absence of biologically related people. As demographers and family scholars note, there is no majority family "type" anymore.[16] As family structures have changed, the paths that people take throughout their family lives have also become less linear, from delayed age at first marriage and childbearing to increases in cohabitation and polyamory, and from late-in-life partnerships to commuter relationships and "living-apart-together" partnerships. And despite some efforts to posit a singular family form that serves as an ideal in contemporary society, Americans are increasingly likely to approve of diverse family forms.[17]

Acknowledging that family can take many forms does not necessarily mean that people think "anything goes" when it comes to family. A definitive version of family may emerge even among those who acknowledge the diversification of family forms. This is, in part, due to a continued longing for home as a desirable and comfortable place removed from the public realms of work and politics. Home, whether evoked as a place, an idea, or a group of people, is still intimately connected to a conception of family. People in the United States still disproportionately believe that a single-family detached dwelling with a yard is an ideal place to live, even as homeownership becomes harder to obtain for large swaths of the population.[18] And they still have images of certain elements of relationships in mind when they think of family: people who are emotionally connected to each other, who support each other, who feel an obligation to each other, and who can be entitled to legal or social benefits associated with these relationships. This set of definitions usually includes time for family togetherness and entitlement to property.[19]

Families (and homes) have always intersected with other parts of life, suggesting that the boundary around family (and home) is porous. Primarily because of technological innovation, family life has become more visibly intertwined with other *social institutions* (i.e., the long-lasting patterns in society that meet and serve as a framework for our basic needs) such as the economy and education. We have seen drastic increases in online learning and working from home, as well as greater likelihood to share family stories via social media and shop online from the couch.[20] The blurring of family life with other institutions became vividly apparent during COVID-19 lockdowns, with kids attending school in one room while parents worked from home in another. This blurring of lines certainly came with added stress, especially for working mothers with young children[21] and for families of color or those with limited access to financial or digital resources on account of their precarious financial standing.[22] Being at home during the pandemic brought some families closer together; however, it also revealed some harsh realities about family relationships, work stress, and unequal access to spaces and the digital means necessary for blurring life realms in a satisfactory way.[23]

Family togetherness is not an issue reserved for research and theorizing only about the coronavirus pandemic. In fact, over the last few decades, an increasing desire for quality time with family at home has been accompanied by a decreasing amount of time and space at home to meet this desire. The solution: an increase in the reimagining of family quality time (and space) in the form of a second home, with the result that "new myths and rituals have begun to emerge, challenging the old without wholly displacing them."[24]

The appeal of family vacation homes, then, is part of a historical pattern wherein people increasingly recognize a diversification of family forms, understand that home life can be as stressful as work life, blur boundaries between life realms that make defining a home as a haven removed from everything else hard to do, yearn for family quality time, and long for home.

Changing Vacations

Beyond snapping up a great family package deal at Legoland, why are vacation locations a useful and interesting place to explore families? While I don't discuss vacationing as a whole in this book (since that would include a vast repertoire of research on anything from Disney cruise ships to KOA campgrounds), it is important to situate family vacation homes in the larger story of vacationing.

Stein provides a helpful definition of *vacation*, especially in terms of how it is culturally constructed as both "freedom from" and "freedom to."[25] To elaborate, a vacation has two possible features: it can mean a getaway, or freedom from stressful everyday work and family roles and identities; and/or it can mean adventure, or freedom to try something new that seems different from everyday life. In both cases, a vacation is a contrast to everyday life that is presumably uninteresting yet stressful.

Vacationing became prevalent for middle-class American families after World War II, signaling affluence to other families, providing opportunities to educate children in life skills and citizenship, and serving as a concentrated way to promote family bonding.[26] But as home life has gotten busier over the intervening decades, "the consumer economy taps into our need for homes away from home,"[27] with vacation destinations marketing homelike amenities and accommodations. Today, families on vacation "are looking for not only all the comforts of home but a more authentic version of what they have left behind."[28]

Certainly, the COVID-19 pandemic radically changed people's travel behaviors. From staycations to temporary moves to countries with varying health resources and policies, how families vacationed took several quick turns. Now, as the world has opened up postlockdown, vacations are taking one of two directions: people are either prioritizing visiting loved ones to reconnect with family and affirm family roles and identities that were interrupted, or they are traveling to places with completely different environments from their homes or hometowns, to "take on that no-rules kind of vacation persona," as Stein has put it.[29] In other words, postpandemic—and, in reality, any—travel allows for familial connection as a familiar self or for adventurous exploration of possible new selves. Both are escapes from everyday life and responsibilities.

Family vacations have always been defined as escapes from everyday life, even if the places and forms they take have changed across time and geography. As historian Susan Sessions Rugh outlines, the escapes for families may look different now than in the past, and they vary depending on race, class, and geography.[30] Today, we see fewer summer holidays in the Catskills with dozens of families from a single ethnic or religious affinity group, but more travel to Airbnbs or Vrbos booked online, often with multiple generations from one family.[31] We see fewer celebrity vacationers in condo complexes in Palm Springs and more adventure-rich vacations. We see more geographic mobility and a desire to work from anywhere (even on vacation), alongside greater demand for inclusivity and authenticity.[32] We see family vacations being framed not just as an escape from work (except for those wishing to telecommute) but also as an escape from the stresses of everyday family life, especially since the pandemic.[33]

And what about family vacation homes—how have they changed over time? One of my interviewees, Joseph—who, with his wife, has a family vacation home in a small condominium complex in Western Desert that they both rent out and use themselves—observed what he perceived to be changing historical trends in vacation home real estate, particularly when he compared his current second home to what he saw in his childhood community on the East Coast, and especially for affluent people:

> I think it's gotten a lot more common. I mean, when I think of when I was growing up, it was kind of unusual for people to have a second home. They might have a cabin or something—something really small. Like a little vacation bungalow. But now people have second homes. I mean, this property that we have, it's a home. I mean, we could live there full-time if we chose to, based on the comfort level.

Joseph equated historical changes with an expanded definition of a vacation home as a place that felt like it had the potential to be a more permanent *home*. He based this on his own experience but also on his keen observations about his vacation home community, where he was actively involved in local politics related to homeownership, short-term rentals, and housing affordability.

Family vacation homes, and all that takes place in and surrounding them, are a microcosm of broader social patterns for families and beyond. These homes offer a site to examine how families come to experience and display freedom, class position, and intimate relationships. There is a rich and diverse existing body of research dedicated to understanding family vacation homes and their surrounding communities, to which I am adding my own analysis. Included in this helpful scholarly landscape is Lisa Sun-Hee Park and David Naguib Pellow's *The Slums of Aspen: Immigrants vs. the Environment in America's Eden*,[34] which details historical and contemporary patterns of access and interaction of wealthy vacation home owners and immigrant laborers in a Colorado ski resort area, with a sociological focus on how environmental protection served to perpetuate race and class inequalities. Susan Sessions Rugh's *Are We There Yet? The Golden Age of American Family Vacations*[35] offers a historical analysis of the "magical times" of the family vacation home over time in the United States, focusing on ways that changing conceptions of work and play and evolving diversity of family forms have influenced the popularity of, and access to, family vacations. Corey Dolgon's *The End of the Hamptons: Scenes from the Class Struggle in America's Paradise*,[36] which takes a sociological approach to many issues surrounding social relations in a vacation community, focusing on controversies that split groups with competing moral claims and differential access to valuable resources, also informs this book. Other projects focused on class differences and land use, alongside environmental impacts, also shaped the questions

I asked of my interviewees. These include C. Michael Hall and Dieter K. Muller's *Tourism, Mobility, and Second Homes: Between Elite Landscape and Common Ground*[37] and Norman McIntyre, Daniel Williams, and Kevin McHugh's edited volume *Multiple Dwelling and Tourism: Negotiating Place, Home, and Identity*.[38] Finally, housing studies expert Chris Paris's *Affluence, Mobility and Second Home Ownership*[39] lays a helpful groundwork for a lot of what I aim to do, showing readers how home is socially constructed, the ways second and vacation homes are variously experienced in many places based on affluence, policy, and housing dilemmas as well as connections to more global issues such as transnational second homes.

How much can a book about family vacation homes tell us about *all* families? Property ownership is a demarcation of *socioeconomic status*, or one's social class position; it is a measure of wealth.[40] Research on family vacation homes is, of course, research about people who have plentiful resources. This means that what I write about in this book has limitations in terms of generalizability to all families. In response to this limitation, I frame my approach similarly to that of Ann Swidler,[41] who studies cultural conceptions of love. Swidler notes that her sample of predominantly white, middle- and upper-middle-income people represents mainstream ideals that are not so much a representation but more of a ruler by which most other families measure their experiences. They thus serve as "prototypical" rather than "typical."[42] Focusing on the lived experiences of families with relative *privilege*—having access to benefits that come with high status and often wealth, including being held in high esteem by others—can also offer new details about how their consumption practices, and the rhetoric they use to describe these practices, reveal how privilege operates in terms of a desire to be morally good and "normal," as sociologist Rachel Sherman's study of wealthy homeowners uncovers.[43] Descriptions of the variation in homeowner type across my research sites, including by income and property value, are delineated in the appendix.

My research situates leisure in vacation home settings. These domestic sites are not immune to the labor of everyday home and family relationship management (or to the structural inequalities that come with amenity-rich locations that bring in affluent home buyers), but they are meant to be free from the stresses associated with this labor, meant to free up vacationers to try new things. I study families who, while more privileged than most, shape and are shaped by current conceptions of enchanted family life. This enchantment is vividly and variably represented in family vacation homes as I frame them in this book.

Changing Vacation Homes and the Sharing Economy

Using a family vacation home just for one's own family does not mean that the property is removed from a larger discussion of amenity-rich vacation spots as sites for controversy over short-term rental regulations. In all three property groups in my research, the topic of renting out a vacation home to others came up, either because they were currently doing this, because neighbors were doing this, or because they were thinking about transforming a home used just for family into one that could make some money to help pay the bills. Given that family vacation homes have been around for a long time, how new is the topic of short-term vacation rentals in residential areas, and how does it shape how families view their vacation homes?

Homes serving as commercial spaces is not a new idea, as evidenced in the rich and complex history of boarding houses and home-based businesses in the United States,[44] but today's trends reveal new ways of looking at the intersection between homes and the marketplace, especially in terms of vacation rentals.[45] In addition to the post-COVID-19 patterns that we are still uncovering, there are other patterns in vacation practices and preferences that demonstrate historical change. Many of these are connected to changes in the ways that economic exchange and entrepreneurialism work: namely, the increase in transactions situated in the *sharing economy*, which gives consumers the ability to share "creation, production, distribution, trade and consumption of goods and services."[46]

Airbnb, Vrbo, Vacasa, HomeToGo, and other similar online companies are vivid examples of new marketplaces that allow ordinary people to dabble in business ventures by renting out their primary or second residences or portions of them. Owners and renters serve as "cocreators" of value in the global travel service marketplace,[47] since the economic exchange occurs between peers, not between a person and a company. This exchange is part of a rise in what sociologist Juliet Schor terms "connected consumption,"[48] often referred to as the sharing or gig economy.[49] Sometimes, this is framed as a way to support small businesses rather than corporate hotels, even if the companies sponsoring online bookings of private properties are themselves large corporate entities.

The sharing economy is dubbed as a location for entrepreneurial do-it-yourself (DIY) business success. The fact that the exchange of space for money has become easier and more widespread is a result of the technological platforms on which the exchange takes place.[50] Some academic (and other) voices have taken a critical stance toward the phenomenon. Sociologists have written about the implications of the sharing economy, including a loss of community in neighborhoods with lots of short-term rentals and high rates of tourist turnover that result from "platform capitalism,"[51] and the paradox of the sharing economy (using localized channels and informal exchange of goods and services, such as apartments or car rides, between private citizens) as not technically sharing since the exchanges involve a fee (and a for-profit corporation).[52] Additional topics of scholarly inquiry surrounding the sharing economy include: boosting large for-profits like Airbnb even as individuals are making money; advertising goods and services as localized, friendlier, and more collaborative, even as this process succumbs to larger corporate practices, benefits large (sometimes nonlocal) for-profit companies, and hides the labor and precarious employment involved (dubbing the industry as the "1099 economy"); and the role of technology in mediating interpersonal trust between owners and renters via rating systems.[53] These findings point to the notion that ordinary people, regardless of their occupation, can now more easily delve into the kind of business venture that used to be reserved for hotels, real estate developers, and other corporate entities; researchers continue to uncover whether and how the outcomes are beneficial or detrimental (and for whom).

Primary or second residences turned into vacation rentals, while a big part of the upswing in sharing economy ventures, are impacted by broader economic forces such as housing affordability.[54] Home buying for potential use in the sharing economy has changed as the broader market has changed. For example, COVID-19 shook up the real estate sharing economy industry,[55] causing an increase in vacation home purchases during the pandemic followed by a return to prepandemic levels more recently.[56] Recent trends in upstate New York show that people who are affluent enough to buy homes are not interested in renting them to others. The causes? A glut in inventory with accompanying rental saturation and a lack of desire to put that much money and effort into a property that may not reap the expected benefits.[57]

Some of the ups and downs of the vacation rental industry depend on patterns in the overall economy, and some depend on local regulations. If this kind of home use is not allowed, the homes are not desirable to purchase and rent out. It takes a lot of energy to fight local ordinances and citizens critical of strangers in their neighborhoods. Throughout my years-long gathering of diverse data, I have found hundreds of news articles about changing regulations, many in the communities where my research took place. Highlights of these news stories reveal that the purchase of a first (or any) home is harder for people to afford, which connects to the development of entrepreneurial projects such as renting homes or spaces on Vrbo and Airbnb in order to fund everyday housing costs. These news stories also reveal that neighborhood and community disagreements are increasingly politically charged and polarized.

In addition to historical, economic, and regulatory patterns, it is important to look at how different age groups may be contributing to how family vacation homes may be included in the sharing economy. Generational shifts in values surrounding inclusiveness, formality of social roles, geographic mobility, entrepreneurialism, and the changing significance of spaces and objects in identity formation are uncovered in the family vacation home story. Add to this the fact that younger people are more likely to participate in sharing economy work in general[58]—in part due to preferences and in part due to economic necessity, since the labor market options in traditional economies are stunted—and it becomes clear that we are seeing social change in family vacation home acquisition and desired use.

GUIDING FRAMEWORKS

In this book, I describe and explain specific patterns of family life in vacation homes, expanding on past scholarship related to family vacation homes in amenity-rich communities. Explanation requires embedding my interpretation in existing conceptual frameworks. I employ sociological frameworks surrounding *enchantment* and *memory*. These two frameworks allow me to connect findings about my specific project to larger questions about families, markets, and memory making. They also allow me to test the robustness of conceptual ideas across new sites for sociological study.

Conceptualizing Enchantment

Enchantment, or more accurately, *disenchantment*, is a concept that has filled the minds and writings of sociological thinkers since Max Weber elevated it within the social sciences as *Entzauberung*, a word that translates from German to English as "de-magicization."[59] Weber wrote extensively about the dire consequences of the capitalist-induced bureaucratization and rationalization of every facet of our social worlds, processes that emerged during the Protestant Reformation and continued into the early stages of the development of industrial capitalism.[60] His central argument was that capitalism and bureaucracy, as examples of increased rationalization in society, have "served to undermine what was once an enchanted (i.e., magical, mysterious, mystical) world."[61] In other words, formal systems such as the capitalist "iron cage" marketplace dictate parts of life that ought to remain informal, authentic, and enchanted.[62] As sociologist George Ritzer, who extends Weber's concepts to modern capitalist enterprises that include shopping malls, restaurants, and vacation destinations, notes, "a formally rational world is a disenchanted world."[63] There is no such thing as enchantment when capitalism governs all social life.

Or is there? All this discussion of the powerful infiltration of capitalism into every other institution, and all this focus on economy, religion, and historical change within massive social institutions, may seem disconnected to a project about the intimate life of families on vacation. It may also seem to disallow variation, strategy, or even authentic pleasure if framed as a site ultimately controlled by an "iron cage." So how is Weber's concept of disenchantment connected to interpersonal relationships such as those found in families, especially when the idealized family is supposed to be all about emotional connection, disclosure of our true selves, and retreat from the marketplace and other nonmagical elements of the "real" world? And how might Weber's ideas connect specifically to the family vacation home? The answer: it's complicated, it's wrapped up in consumption and commodification, and it's helpfully elaborated by other scholars who study family relationships.

A book about family vacation homes is not about romance per se, but it is about intimate relationships. Sociologist Eva Illouz's notion that enchantment requires organic and informal social relationships aligns with and extends understanding of enchantment to the realm of intimate relationships, wherein ideal romantic interactions are genuine, relaxed, and reveal people's "true selves."[64] The key word here is "ideal." Illouz defines ideal enchanted love as offering a sense of the sacred, a way to experience feelings that cannot necessarily be rationally justified.[65] But the reality is that romance is deeply entrenched in consumer society. Whether choosing an expensive restaurant to celebrate Valentine's Day or deciding whether to swipe left or right on an online dating app,[66] the fantasy and fairytales fade away when romance is really all about comparing, competing, and consuming. So, because romance is achieved by consuming, and because strong cultural values promote keeping intimate relationships out of the everyday world of financial transactions, people have to strategically construct meaning around romantic consumption practices to distance them from the consumption part—a reconciliation of contradictory things. People have to believe that romance is authentic and not part of a marketplace, even though it may be both. And how might this work? By using consumption that is designed to heighten the affective connection between people so that they can artificially remove themselves from the everyday stresses of family and work life (e.g., via a romantic dinner at a fancy restaurant, or by, well, going on vacation to a romantic getaway).[67]

What about relationships that may not necessarily be about romance? How might enchantment matter for families more generally? As economic sociologist Viviana Zelizer has found, to be priceless often means to be removed from an economic marketplace symbolically, separating whatever is being considered from certain elements of the economy.[68] The marketplace is framed as a place where people are impersonal and cold; the family is all about love. Children are "priceless," for example, even though they cost money to raise and they are "economically worthless."[69] For middle- and upper-income families in particular, children are also meant to be defined as projects that create happiness and a need to have perfect outcomes. Journalist Jennifer Senior, in the aptly titled book *All Joy and No Fun: The Paradox of Modern Parenthood*,[70] articulates that the labor and stress associated with everyday family life needs to be magically hidden behind happy, idealized versions of family. To create treasured moments for the family requires joy. Happiness comes from turning family stress and labor into clear success stories and mementos to signify that success. To have priceless family memories is to personalize the experience out of love, to make it all magical. Thus, the family must be enchanted in order to preserve its story and to protect it from the harsh and impersonal realities of labor and the marketplace. But, of course, it takes work (and often purchases) to create this kind of joy.

The separation of families and the marketplace is artificial, even as it is a powerful cultural value that shapes romance, parenting, and other facets of family life. Sociologist Arlie Hochschild identifies the artificial separation of family and market as part of a "crisis of enchantment."[71] We are faced with a contradictory conundrum of how to view the family in light of consumer society: Is the family the only thing that can be enchanted, or can other things be enchanted, too? On one side of the contradiction, a lot of functions within the family are being outsourced to the marketplace, from personal shoppers to professional organizers. The result is that family-related tasks are increasingly monetized and decreasingly personalized. On the other side of this contradiction is the claim that the family has become framed as enchanted, meaning that it is a "powerful, condensed symbol for treasured qualities such as empathy, recognition, love—qualities that are quintessentially personal."[72] It is a magical life realm, sacred and personalized. The crisis lies in the fact that these are oppositional patterns. Clinging to the notion that family is solely a realm of what theorist Talcott Parsons would have called *expressive* functions[73] is incompatible with believing that the family is also a place for *instrumental*—or task-specific—arrangements. The coexistence of these contradictory trends occurs in what Hochschild calls a *commodity frontier*: a cultural landscape consisting of a strain between the socially constructed assignment of expressive and emotional ideals to families and the assignment of instrumental and seemingly rational ideals to the marketplace.

What do we make of the fact that the stressful and complex realities of family life are idealized or masked by a happy facade while also becoming increasingly visible, both to families experiencing them and to scholars focusing on them? How do we reconcile a need for respite from everyday stresses with the recognition that family life may not be as much of a haven as traditionally thought? Family functions are increasingly relinquished to the marketplace as families get busier and more stressed. At the same time, decreased stability and trust in the economy alongside increased individualism in US society has led to the creation of a need for an escape from the harsh realities of the world. Included in this need has traditionally been a definition of the home as a sacred retreat from the realities of a heartless world,[74] especially among those who wish to preserve a nostalgic vision of American family life. But people across many walks of life have increasingly recognized that home lives are not necessarily havens from a stressful world, because they carry their own stresses,[75] a realization made especially clear during the COVID-19 pandemic[76] and amid housing and economic crises that disproportionately affect low-income families and families of color who cannot afford to buy or keep a home.[77] In other words, we are more aware than ever that the home itself is not necessarily an enchanted escape or a haven from a harsh world.

And yet our everyday actions demonstrate attempts to enchant parts of our intimate world that, according to Weber, have become disenchanted by virtue of them being situated in a capitalist marketplace. We separate the family and the marketplace artificially to preserve the enchanting ideals of family life: emotional connection, irrationality, and authenticity. We succumb to the powerful cultural value of enchantment of the home even as we increasingly realize that family life is far from a fairy tale. As the realities of family-related stresses are increasingly evident, a symbolic separation of home from the marketplace may be harder to achieve. But the ideal of a retreat is still present in people's minds as the powerful concept of home remains a utopian ideal. All of this suggests that a family vacation home as a "home away from home" may come to be defined as a place removed from the everyday stresses of *both* work and family life. When enchantment fades away at home, people look for a second home to (re)create it.

We are mistaken if we think that the family and market are "separate cultural spheres."[78] This puts us at a strained moment—one when we are not sure how to feel about putting a price on the seemingly priceless elements of family life. We are still figuring out what family life is (and should be) after a global pandemic that (temporarily, in some cases) pushed many people further into their private home lives and many others into more hardships than they faced before. Family vacation homes are part of the deeply entrenched cultural story of the romanticization of American family life, a romance with more and more revelation of the real hardships of contemporary family life.

Family Memories and Imagined Future Kinship Nostalgia

If enchantment is *what* people are doing, it begs the question of *how* people are doing it. This brings me to family memory making and the feelings associated with memories—the second conceptual landscape serving as a backdrop for my research. Memory is a powerful tool used in the enchantment of family vacation homes. And memory making is an emotionally laden experience, especially when connected with the powerful cultural influence of enchantment of families and homes. But how might a sociologist focus on memory or emotion, which are seemingly psychological (as well as biological) processes? Sociologists focus on *"the social nature of human emotions, and the emotional nature of social phenomena,"*[79] which means that we move beyond individual emotional responses and toward collective influences and outcomes that signify larger cultural values and processes. In other words, how someone feels demonstrates *"the bodily manifestation of the importance that an event in the natural or social world has for a subject."*[80] The way family vacation home memories connect to emotions emerged in my conversation with Carla, who spelled out why she and her husband Dayton bought their small family vacation home by a river in Northwest Woods:

> To build memories, to keep those memories, to sustain the memories that we had created . . . and then to be able to make sure our children got to know what it was like to be out, away from everything, and to hunt and fish and hike and pick huckleberries and morel mushrooms and just do all those things that we couldn't offer here.

For Carla, being "away from everything" was really about removing her family from the hustle and bustle of everyday work and school life. A few minutes before she said this, she and Dayton detailed their very careful financial decision to buy the house in the first place. They had met with a financial adviser and figured out that they could purchase a second home now as an investment for their eventual retirement. They also knew that they didn't want to wait too many years to decisively carve out a segment of their lives for leisure activities such as berry picking and fishing. For Carla and Dayton, there was a price tag attached to the decision to create family memories in a vacation spot, and they knew that they needed to carefully plan their financial future in order to accomplish their goals. And the entire time they talked about this, they smiled at each other and at me, with numerous animated stories about how they felt happy that they could create these kinds of memories for their children.

How are emotions and memory connected? I'm captivated by people's strategic (though sometimes unconscious) use of spaces and objects to create symbolic representations of family roles and relationships. At times, these symbols and the actions surrounding them showcase a desire to hide a painful family story or share a joyful one. At other times, these actions and symbols demonstrate a way to preserve a particular version of a family story for the future—to save memories of a happy family story. I have spent two decades studying the *curatorial practices of families*—the ways they use, display, save, hide, or remove spaces and objects to symbolize stories about family roles and relationships. In my survey research on love letters, for example, the preservation of a family story was demonstrated (especially by women) by storing letters in a safe and often hidden place.[81] My interview research on family photos revealed that the preservation of a family story was also demonstrated (also especially by women) by sharing the photos with others.[82] On the surface, these two findings may seem contradictory: one demonstrates hiding things and the other demonstrates sharing them. But they both point to the fact that the family story is not only something in need of preservation, it is also necessary to preserve it so that future others can look back at the present as a happy snapshot in time.

I refer to this as *imagined future kinship nostalgia*: projects and curatorial strategies in the present meant to create cherished happy nostalgic memories of today that will be witnessed and referenced by imagined family in the future.[83] These are family stories as they are imagined to be, regardless of reality; they are meant to be seen and heard by imagined future family members who will look back at today with emotions such as happiness, wistfulness, and pride. And the nostalgic view does not necessarily need to capture the actual experiences of an entire event or moment, just the ones that serve to preserve a good family story.

Nostalgia—"a sentimental longing or wistful affection for the past"[84]—is not a new concept in social science research. On a collective level, groups of people may look back fondly (whether this is objectively warranted or not) to a past time period in order to understand or try to compare today's world to some version of yesteryear. On an individual level, thinking about the past in a way that brings up a whole host of emotions can help us understand our current story and enact values that we hold near and dear. For example, Ole and Angela told me a story during their interview about how a large photo of their now-deceased son in their Northwest Woods family vacation home symbolizes cherished memories associated with family vacation home activities. Angela said, "We put a huge picture of him up there with the last buck that he shot just a couple of months before we lost him." In many parts of the interview, hunting served as a key activity in their memories, which instilled a current emotional response and a longing to go back in time.

How do we think about the past, and can we predict the future? Trying to predict future emotion is known in psychology more generally as *affective forecasting*.[85] The idea of imagining a future in which people may look back at today nostalgically is not new, although I apply the concept in ways that contextualize psychological processes in social contexts, specifically the family. Throughout Ole and Angela's interview, hunting was mentioned as a popular past, current, and intended future activity; at several points, they also evoked their hope to be able to look back at current activities in the future.

Sociologist Fred Davis penned a book about the sociology of nostalgia, in which he spent a small section discussing whether people could "feel nostalgia for the future."[86] In cases in which this is possible, Davis noted, it usually takes the form of people imagining themselves in the future looking back nostalgically at today (or any point in the past); the images in that imagining are life events such as marriage, children, or buying a home, which are "the institutional staples which we are socialized to contemplate from an early age and which, indeed, we are required to anticipate if there is to be cultural continuity between generations."[87]

Psychologists studying memory and emotion have examined this process with particular attention to how "the anticipation of feeling nostalgic for life experiences when looking back on them," or "anticipated nostalgia,"[88] may create affective responses to behavior that hasn't happened yet, measured in terms of psychological functioning. Importantly, *anticipated nostalgia* differs from *anticipatory nostalgia*,[89] which is defined as "missing aspects of the present before they are lost in the future"[90] or "missing what has not yet been lost."[91] In other words, anticipated nostalgia is imagining future emotional responses to what's happening today; anticipatory nostalgia is experiencing an emotional response today that is a result of what someone may expect to experience in the future.

My concept—imagined future kinship nostalgia—frames the memory work of people as necessarily sociological and does not require choosing to focus on either a present or future emotional response, nor does it require centering the response on the person imagining it. The "kinship" focus of my concept aligns with Davis's claim that people imagine looking back on usual events that are often associated with family life, but it can include imagining other family members' responses. The "imagined" and "future" focus of my concept aligns with the psychological applications of both anticipated and anticipatory nostalgia. But my concept differs insofar as it decisively situates the memory work in an interactional social context (broader social patterns related to family, vacationing, and the sharing economy), and it allows for both current and future emotional responses to be part of the memory work itself. In other words, my approach does not separate the temporal work of remembering and imagining and the process of having an emotional response as tidily as the psychological literature does, because people in my research do not present any of this with crystal clear boundaries. What did become clear as people discussed their family vacation homes was that they could muster an emotional response now (anticipatory) for what they imagine they or others would feel like in the future (anticipated). I witnessed homeowners showing a quiver of emotion in their voice during the interview thinking about what their kids' emotional response will be in a few months when their family comes to the vacation home for a reunion. I watched people smile and tell cheery stories about their hope that other people's families staying in their vacation home would create fun memories in the future. I also watched these people grumpily imagine what may happen if they are not able to rent out their vacation homes later on, or if they will not be used. I watched people worry now about whether the place will even be able to be used for imagined future family vacations that would create memories five, ten, or fifteen years down the road.

What form does the enactment of imagined future kinship nostalgia take? Families can connect in the same geographic place, but virtual connection across the miles has increased. This is important given how much families have geographically dispersed and found less and less time to gather. Creating family memories in the same place seems to be harder and harder for families to do, although certainly creating memories via activities and events is still a big part of a family vacation experience. Commemorating these still matters, too. From photographs to travel souvenirs, homes are filled with symbols of past experiences. Anthropologist Daniel Miller discusses how objects—not inherently bad or good pieces of *material culture*—come to signify memories of family events and relationships that elicit emotional responses in their possessors.[92] A few photos from a wedding or holiday or "moments when the relationship came closest to its ideal"[93] help families remember someone who has passed away. At the same time, people who wish to have their memory retained by the next generation in their family may select objects—furniture, books, or artwork, for example—that symbolize them as they wish to be remembered. Idealizing family moments and relationships can occur via the saving, storing, displaying, and sharing of symbolic objects. This idealization can also occur via special events. Memories—and therefore imagined future kinship nostalgia—can be represented symbolically and materially.

Modern families rely immensely on remembering, largely because the loss of members via death or moving away from a family home serve to threaten the definition of a family as such. This is different from workplaces, where the departure of members—while having the potential to make those who remain feel loss—does not signal the end of the organization. As a result of the precarity of family continuity (including a squeeze for enough time to spend together in the hectic calendar of daily life), ritualized family events and special occasions—and their accompanying photographic and material souvenirs—are more prominent than ever.[94] The dedication to these occasions is often spent more on the anticipation and remembrance of events than the events themselves. For instance, a photo album of a family reunion from 1997 can be viewed over and over again. Our imaginations and memories can fool us, though, as they compensate for the "short supply of time with which to experience other family members as complex human beings."[95]

So what might all this memory work via activities, objects, and events have to do with a family vacation home? Importantly, as homes have become designed to be more about function or aesthetics that signify minimalism or antimaterialism, people have turned to vacation homes to "offer safer storage for the shared dreams and memories of generations geographically dispersed and constantly on the move from one nondescript domicile to another."[96] Imagined future kinship nostalgia, then, keeps family memories sacred and separate from forces that threaten family togetherness or place family stories in a cold marketplace of impersonal spaces. Imagined future kinship nostalgia, especially via material objects and planned activities and events, becomes a powerful way that families enchant their vacation homes.

Throughout this book I reveal ways that family vacation homes showcase how people actually live their lives in a complicated social world that still tries to separate families and markets, despite all of the apparent ways this is impossible. I uncover emotional and memory-laden strategies used to preserve the enchantment of family life while immersed in places that are obviously market-driven, whether those places are reserved for family use or used to generate income through being rented to other families. In doing so, I offer a new and creative way to understand the power of memory making via imagined future kinship nostalgia, as well as via interactional family and neighborhood processes, in demonstrating deeply held cultural values. I tell the story of how people make meaning of something malleable and emotionally meaningful even as it seems fixed and rational. I tell the story of how the enchantment of property is actually the story of contemporary family life.

JOURNEYING THROUGH THE CHAPTERS:
A FOCUS ON BOUNDARIES

The rest of the book tells the story of changing family patterns as seen in the microcosm of roles, relationships, and practices surrounding family vacation homes and their host communities. I begin with *microsociological* inquiry (identities and group boundaries) and move outward toward *mesosociological* and *macrosociological* inquiry (neighborhoods, communities, demographic groups) in the next several chapters, with a focus on the significance of time in the chapter before the conclusion.

Like many sociologists, I talk a lot about *boundaries* in my work. Boundaries are social constructions, meaning that we create, place, and move them according to what we define as important to include and exclude. They are used to differentiate geographic spaces, as one might do when defining a neighborhood as commercially or residentially zoned, but also to classify people along social groupings and time periods[97] and to delineate different life realms, such as home and work and how we see ourselves in those realms.[98] Boundaries can also be used to differentiate between definitions of right and wrong.[99] The ways that boundaries are socially constructed when it comes to family vacation home possession, use, and potential dispossession serves as an organizational foundation for this book. Boundaries are also used to conceptually demarcate the focus (and title) of each chapter.

In chapter 2, I discuss how family vacation homes showcase boundaries around various conceptions of self, which can also mean changing experiences based on roles and types of labor performed in a family. Chapter 3 includes my findings about the boundaries around who does and does not count as family, as told through spatial and material forms. Moving beyond the family and home, in chapter 4 I focus on the boundaries between vacation homes and the neighborhoods and communities in which they are situated, in terms of geographic, economic, and social connections with communities. In chapter 5, I uncover how family vacation homes tell the larger story of demographic and moralistic boundaries, with attention to class and race inequalities as they relate to who is entitled to live in (or sometimes rent) these spaces, and who is seen as an insider or outsider in amenity-rich neighborhoods and communities that are filled with family vacation homes. Chapter 6 attends to the significance of temporal boundaries, both historical transformations that shape the family vacation home experience and within-family generational change in desires about what to do with the properties. The book concludes with a discussion of how my findings and guiding frameworks are integrated and how family vacation homes tell a larger story about contemporary families, memories, and the marketplace.

Family Vacation Homes: Let's Go!

Imagine the following scenarios:

Four siblings inherit a family cabin in a rural forest in the northwestern United States. One sibling lives nearby. Only three want to continue using it. They figure out a plan to "buy out" the uninterested sibling, which includes allowing one sibling a reduced price because he will take on the role of property and maintenance manager.

A grandmother in a midwestern city has a small lakeside vacation home that her family has used for generations, but now her daughter thinks they should remodel it and rent it out to families on vacation to earn a little extra money. The woman feels uncomfortable about having strangers pay to stay in her home, and she worries that this will mean charging a fee to friends who may wish to stay there.

A mother in wine country enjoys using her ADU as a vacation rental for couples, even though she and her husband built it for an aging parent who never used it. She takes pleasure in hosting and decorating the space with family mementos and pictures of the region's sprawling vineyards. She loves having guests return each year and has become friends with some of them.

A family is trying to decide whether to continue holding holiday events at their family vacation home near the ocean on the East Coast, since the older daughter is finishing graduate school and moving in with her partner, the younger son is starting college, and the parents are planning to downsize into a smaller home closer to both children.

Each of these stories comes from people I interviewed about their family vacation homes. Each tells the story of how vacation property ownership, location, and use may vary from family to family and from person to person. But these scenarios also paint a picture about how family roles and relationships impact that story and point to many shifting family patterns in the United States: increasing geographic mobility among younger generations, generational shifts in beliefs about whether family spaces should be used to make money, a desire to create memorable family moments for people on vacation, changing work and family roles during a marriage, and reconsideration of family rituals in light of changing life stages. In other words, how people use family vacation homes is not just a story about vacations; it is also a story about changing family patterns.

As you read the next chapters, please bear in mind that this entire project is about both individual stories and broader patterns that a systematic study of a diverse and complex data set may reveal. Each chapter will include individual family stories and broader social patterns. To situate my approach to storytelling as a way of revealing patterns in data, I'll close this introductory chapter with a story that connects to several themes throughout the book. I follow a similar format in each chapter's conclusion.

Rich and his husband Marcus spend a lot of their vacations in their second home in Western Desert. They had decided to buy a second home in this community because of their desire to feel welcome as gay men (the annual Pride festival was a good indicator for them) and because they were interested in starting a business there. They told me lots of stories of parties they'd had over the years with their friends, some of whom traveled from afar and some of whom lived there year-round. Most involved lavish dinners and fun pool parties. About half the year, they rented out their home to vacationers using online short-term rental platforms such as Airbnb or Vrbo. Both in their late forties, they bought the house with the thought that they'd retire in the community, though they were not sure they'd stay in this particular house. They planned to spend more time there if their business took off.

Rich told me about his childhood memories at a family cabin in Northern Lake Country, which made me think about my own summer fishing adventures at Diane's cabin. He pondered, "When you live in a place or repeatedly vacation in a place, you build memories there." I remember perking up after hearing his phrasing—"live . . . or repeatedly vacation." He was definitely talking about himself on vacation, including his childhood self and his current self, because in both instances he was thinking about his own repeat vacation memories. And he obviously lives at this second home, at least part time. But implicit in his words and explicit in his practice of renting the home to others for their vacations was the notion that memories created in vacation homes could also be memories for other people's families. This was because he used his home both for his own personal vacations and for investment purposes via short-term rentals.

Rich and Marcus are in the Mixed Property group: they use their second home both for financial gain and for their own family vacations. This puts them in a unique position of noticing how a place can serve multiple purposes for the same person and can serve the same purpose for multiple people. Rich's story also suggests that memories of past vacation experiences may shape current understandings. Importantly, though, as the next chapters detail, people in the Investment and Personal Property categories also shared stories about money and memory that make tidy predictions about motivations based on property category messy.

The family vacation home is not a new topic of study, but we need an updated story about the complicated ways that families today actually use these spaces (theirs or ones they rent from others) and what these family places tell us about contemporary family roles, relationships, and patterns. This book tells that updated story.

NOTES

1. David Rose, *Enchanted Objects: Innovation, Design, and the Future of Technology* (New York: Scribner, 2014), xi.

2. Rose, *Enchanted Objects*, xi.

3. Rose, *Enchanted Objects*, 7.

4. Rose, *Enchanted Objects*, 13.

5. John R. Gillis, *A World of Their Own Making: Myth, Ritual, and the Quest for Family Values* (Cambridge, MA: Harvard University Press, 1996).

6. University of Kansas Center for Community Health and Development, "Section 21. Windshield and Walking Surveys," Community Tool Box, https://ctb

.ku.edu/en/table-of-contents/assessment/assessing-community-needs-and-resources/windshield-walking-surveys/main.

7. C. Wright Mills, *The Sociological Imagination*, 40th anniversary ed. (New York: Oxford University Press, 2000).

8. David Clapham, *The Meaning of Housing: A Pathways Approach* (Bristol, U.K.: Policy Press, 2005).

9. Clapham, *The Meaning of Housing*, 19.

10. Karen Stein, *Getting Away from It All: Vacations and Identity* (Philadelphia: Temple University Press, 2019), 138.

11. Rob Csernyik, "The Professional Airbnb Landlord Class Is Simply the Worst," *Globe and Mail*, December 2, 2023, https://www.theglobeandmail.com/business/commentary/article-the-professional-airbnb-landlord-class-is-simply-the-worst/.

12. Stein, *Getting Away from It All*.

13. Philip N. Cohen, *The Family: Diversity, Inequality, and Social Change*, 4th ed. (New York: Norton, 2024).

14. Gillis, *A World of Their Own Making*, 238.

15. Stephanie Coontz, *The Way We Never Were: American Families and the Nostalgia Trap* (New York: Basic Books, 1993).

16. Cohen, *The Family*.

17. Kim Parker and Rachel Minkin, "Views of Different Family Living Arrangements," in *Public Has Mixed Views on the Modern American Family* (report), Pew Research Center, September 14, 2023, https://www.pewresearch.org/social-trends/2023/09/14/views-of-different-family-arrangements/.

18. Gillis, *A World of Their Own Making*.

19. Pew Research Center, "IV: Family," in *The Decline of Marriage and Rise of New Families* (report), November 18, 2010, https://www.pewresearch.org/social-trends/2010/11/18/iv-family/.

20. Christena E. Nippert-Eng, *Home and Work: Negotiating Boundaries through Everyday Life* (Chicago: University of Chicago Press, 1996).

21. Caitlyn Collins et al., "COVID-19 and the Gender Gap in Work Hours," *Gender, Work and Organization* 28, no. S1 (2021): 101–12, https://doi.org/10.1111/gwao.12506.

22. Irma Mooi-Reci and Barbara J. Risman, "The Gendered Impacts of COVID-19: Lessons and Reflections," *Gender and Society* 35, no. 2 (2021), https://doi.org/10.1177/08912432211001305.

23. Yerís Mayol-García, "Pandemic Brought Parents and Children Closer: More Family Dinners, More Reading to Young Children," US Census Bureau, January 3, 2022, https://www.census.gov/library/stories/2022/01/parents-and-children-interacted-more-during-covid-19. html.

24. Gillis, *A World of Their Own Making*, 228.

25. Stein, *Getting Away from It All*, 15.

26. Stein, *Getting Away from It All*.

27. Gillis, *A World of Their Own Making*, 234.

28. Gillis, *A World of Their Own Making*, 235.

29. Esme Benjamin, "Finding Ourselves: How Travel Shapes Identity," Full-Time Travel, https://www.fulltimetravel.co/ftt_inspirations/finding-ourselves-travel-and -identity/.

30. Susan Sessions Rugh, *Are We There Yet? The Golden Age of American Family Vacations* (Lawrence: University Press of Kansas, 2008).

31. Michael Waters, "The New Family Vacation," *Atlantic*, December 18, 2023, https://www.theatlantic.com/family/archive/2023/12/large-multigenerational-family -vacation-parents-relatives/676382/.

32. Stein, *Getting Away from It All.*

33. Benjamin, "Finding Ourselves."

34. Lisa Sun-Hee Park and David Pellow, *The Slums of Aspen: Immigrants vs. the Environment in America's Eden* (New York: New York University Press, 2011).

35. Rugh, *Are We There Yet?*

36. Corey Dolgon, *The End of the Hamptons: Scenes from the Class Struggle in America's Paradise* (New York: New York University Press, 2006).

37. C. Michael Hall and Dieter K. Muller, *Tourism, Mobility, and Second Homes: Between Elite Landscape and Common Ground* (Clevedon, UK: Channel View Publications, 2004).

38. Norman McIntyre, Daniel Williams, and Kevin McHugh, eds., *Multiple Dwelling and Tourism: Negotiating Place, Home, and Identity* (Wallingford, UK: CABI Publishing, 2006).

39. Chris Paris, *Affluence, Mobility and Second Home Ownership* (Abingdon, UK: Routledge, 2010).

40. Brian J. McCabe, *No Place Like Home: Wealth, Community, and the Politics of Homeownership* (Oxford: Oxford University Press, 2016).

41. Ann Swidler, *Talk of Love: How Culture Matters* (Chicago: University of Chicago Press, 2001).

42. Swidler, *Talk of Love*, 3.

43. Rachel Sherman, *Uneasy Street: The Anxieties of Affluence* (Princeton, NJ: Princeton University Press, 2019).

44. Kari Kohn, "Boardinghouses of Yesterday and What They Mean for Today," NYU Marron Institute of Urban Management, December 30, 2013, https:// marroninstitute.nyu.edu/blog/boardinghouses-of-yesterday-and-what-they-mean-for -today.

45. Host Rooster, "Journey through Time: The Fascinating History of Vacation Rentals," November 1, 2023, https://hostrooster.com/insights/journey-through-time -the-fascinating-history-of-vacation-rentals/.

46. Washington State University Carson College of Business, "How the Sharing Economy Is Transforming Business," November 9, 2023, https://onlinemba.wsu.edu/ blog/how-the-sharing-economy-is-transforming-business.

47. Rasa Smaliukiene, Lai Chi-Shiun, and Indre Sizovaite, "Consumer Value Co-creation in Online Business: The Case of Global Travel Services," *Journal of Business Economics and Management* 16, no. 2 (2015): 325–39, http://dx.doi.org/10 .3846/16111699.2014.985251.

48. Juliet Schor, After the Gig: How the Sharing Economy Got Hijacked and How to Win it Back (Berkeley: University of California Press, 2020).

49. Daniel Guttentag, "Airbnb: Disruptive Innovation and the Rise of an Informal Tourism Accommodation Sector," *Current Issues in Tourism* 19, no. 12 (2015): 1192–217.

50. Guttentag, "Airbnb."

51. Lily M. Hoffman and Barbara Schmitter Heisler, *Airbnb, Short-Term Rentals, and the Future of Housing* (New York: Routledge, 2021).

52 . Karen Sternheimer, "The Sharing Economy Paradox," *Everyday Sociology Blog*, December 3, 2015, https://www.everydaysociologyblog.com/2015/12/the-sharing-economy-paradox.html.

53. Waqar Nadeem et al., "Consumers' Value Co-creation in Sharing Economy: The Role of Social Support, Consumers' Ethical Perceptions and Relationship Quality," Technological Forecasting and Social Change 151 (2020): 1013, https://doi.org/10.1016/j.techfore.2019.119786.

54. US Government Accountability Office, "The Affordable Housing Crisis Grows While Efforts to Increase Supply Fall Short," October 12, 2023, https://www.gao.gov/blog/affordable-housing-crisis-grows-while-efforts-increase-supply-fall-short.

55. Washington State University Carson College of Business, "How the Sharing Economy Is Transforming Business."

56. Amina Niasse, "U.S. Second Home Sales Slide in Pandemic-Era Vacation Hot Spots," Reuters, October 30, 2023, https://www.reuters.com/markets/us/second-home-sales-slide-pandemic-era-vacation-hot-spots-2023-10-30/.

57. Kim Velsey, "Upstate Buyers Are Too Rich for Airbnb Now," *Curbed* (blog), October 30, 2023, https://www.curbed.com/2023/10/upstate-new-york-rich-buyers-airbnb.html.

58. Washington State University Carson College of Business, "How the Sharing Economy Is Transforming Business."

59. Jeffrey E. Green, "Two Meanings of Disenchantment: Sociological Condition vs. Philosophical Act—Reassessing Max Weber's Thesis of the Disenchantment of the World," *Philosophy and Theology* 17, no. 1/2 (2005): 51–84, https://doi.org/10.5840/philtheol2005171/24.

60. Max Weber, *The Protestant Ethic and the Spirit of Capitalism: The Complete Text-Inclusive of Notes*, trans. Talcott Parsons (N.p.: Pantianos Classics, 1905).

61. George Ritzer, *Enchanting a Disenchanted World: Continuity and Change in the Cathedrals of Consumption*, 3rd ed. (Los Angeles: Pine Forge Press/SAGE, 2009), 55.

62. Weber, *The Protestant Ethic and the Spirit of Capitalism*; Mario Marotta, "A Disenchanted World: Max Weber on Magic and Modernity," *Journal of Classical Sociology* (2023), https: //doi.org/10.1177/1468795X231160716.

63. Ritzer, *Enchanting a Disenchanted World*, 59.

64. Eva Illouz, *Consuming the Romantic Utopia: Love and the Cultural Contradictions of Capitalism* (Berkeley: University of California Press, 1997), 143.

65. Eva Illouz, *Why Love Hurts: A Sociological Explanation* (Cambridge: Polity Press, 2013), 159.

66. Eva Illouz, *Cold Intimacies: The Making of Emotional Capitalism* (Cambridge: Polity Press, 2007).

67. Illouz, *Consuming the Romantic Utopia.*

68. Viviana A. Zelizer, *The Purchase of Intimacy* (Princeton, NJ: Princeton University Press, 2005).

69. Zelizer, *The Purchase of Intimacy.*

70. Jennifer Senior, *All Joy and No Fun: The Paradox of Modern Parenthood* (New York: Ecco, 2014).

71. Arlie Hochschild, *The Commercialization of Intimate Life: Notes from Home and Work* (Berkeley: California University Press, 2003).

72. Hochshild, *The Commercialization of Intimate Life*, 31.

73. Elizabeth Aries, "Task and Expressive Roles in Groups." In *Men and Women in Interaction: Reconsidering the Differences* (Oxford: Oxford University Press, 1996), 24–44.

74. Christopher Lasch, *Haven in a Heartless World: The Family Besieged*, rev. ed. (New York: Norton, 1995).

75. Arlie Hochschild, "The Time Bind," *WorkingUSA*, 1, no. 2 (1997): 21–29, https://doi.org/10.1163/17434580-00102006.

76. Maria Gayatri and Mardiana Dwi Puspitasari, "The Impact of COVID-19 Pandemic on Family Well-Being: A Literature Review," *Family Journal* 31, no. 4 (2022): 606–13, https://doi.org/10.1177%2F10664807221131006.

77. Brandi Snowden and Nadia Evangelou, "Racial Disparities in Homeowner Groups," National Association of Realtors, March 3, 2022, https://www.nar.realtor/blogs/economists-outlook/racial-disparities-in-homeownership-rates.

78. Hochschild, "Commodity Frontier."

79. Eduardo Bericat, "The Sociology of Emotions: Four Decades of Progress," *Current Sociology* 64, no. 3 (2016): 491–513; italics in original.

80. Bericat, "The Sociology of Emotions," 492.

81. Michelle Y. Janning, *Love Letters: Saving Romance in the Digital Age* (New York: Routledge, 2018).

82. Michelle Janning and Helen Scalise, "Gender and Generation in the Home Curation of Family Photography," *Journal of Family Issues* 36, no. 12 (2013): 1702–25, https://doi.org/10.1177/0192513X13500964.

83. Janning, *Love Letters.*

84. *The New Oxford Dictionary of English* (Oxford: Oxford University Press, 1988).

85. *Psychology Today*, "Affective Forecasting," https://www.psychologytoday.com/us/basics/affective-forecasting.

86. Fred Davis, *Yearning for Yesterday: A Sociology of Nostalgia* (New York: Free Press, 1979), 12.

87. Davis, *Yearning for Yesterday*, 13.

88. Wing-Yee Cheung et al., "Anticipated Nostalgia: Looking Forward to Looking Back," *Cognition and Emotion* 34, no. 3 (2020): 511–25, https://doi.org/10.1080/02699931.2019.1649247.

89. K. I. Batcho and S. Shikh, "Anticipatory Nostalgia: Missing the Present Before It's Gone," *Personality and Individual Differences* 98 (2016): 75–84, https://doi.org/10.1016/j.paid.2016.03.088.

90. Batcho and Shikh, "Anticipatory Nostalgia," 75.

91. Batcho and Shikh, "Anticipatory Nostalgia," 76.

92. Daniel Miller, *Stuff* (Cambridge: Polity Press 2010).

93. Miller, *Stuff*, 151.

94. John Gillis, "Gathering Together: Remembering Memory Through Ritual," in *We Are What We Celebrate: Understanding Holidays and Rituals*, ed. Amitai Etzioni and Jared Bloom (New York: New York University Press 2004), 89–103.

95. Gillis, "Gathering Together," 95–96.

96. Gillis, "Gathering Together," 97.

97. Eviatar Zerubavel, "Lumping and Splitting: Notes on Social Classification," *Sociological Forum* 11, no. 3 (1996): 421–33, https://www.jstor.org/stable/684894.

98. Nippert-Eng, *Home and Work*.

99. Zerubavel.

Chapter 2

Role and Life Realm Boundaries

Leisure, Labor, and the Family Vacation Home Self

I interviewed Ole and Angela on the back patio of their primary residence on a warm sunny day, Angela popping in and out of the interview to take a couple of phone calls and replenish my lemonade. I asked them about chores they did in their Northwest Woods house, where they have spent a lot of weekends since retiring. Ole responded, "I do more dishes up there . . . I might help cook a little more."

Curious about the last thing he mentioned, I asked, "Why do you think that is?"

"I don't know. That's a good point," he pondered.

Then Angela jumped in: "I think a lot of that started after you [referring to Ole] started going up hunting with that big group and you realized how much work it is to do all of the cooking and the dishes. . . . You had a lot of guys that came up and did nothing that you did everything for."

"It was a chore," added Ole.

Angela chimed in, "He can cook. He just doesn't do a lot at home."

Ole's vacation home hunting trips were decidedly leisure focused, but of course, any trip carries with it various types and amounts of labor. Angela's comments serve as a helpful reminder that any household labor, whether at a vacation home or not, whether paid or not, is work—but it may be hard to see it as work if someone else does it for you.

As sociologist Karen Stein notes, people think of themselves differently, and act differently, when on vacation.[1] Ole continued talking about his chores in the woods: "There's lots of trees I've got to cut down and take brush down and pile up and get ready to burn." Interestingly, when discussing how much outdoor work was required at their vacation home, Ole noted that it "doesn't feel like work out there." Then he gestured to the large lawn we could see from the patio at his primary residence, and said, "This, I'm tired of." Ole loved using chainsaws at his vacation home and loathed mowing the lawn at his primary residence. He framed the labor of "cutting things down" differently in the two places: one as work, the other as leisure. Whether it's work reframed as leisure, work conducted in leisure settings, or unpaid domestic work, one truth is clear: what is work at home isn't necessarily seen as work on vacation, suggesting that there may be such a thing as a separable "family vacation home self." Angela's comments hint at another truth: division of labor at home makes a difference in whether someone feels as if chores on vacation are a downer or not.

While work and spending money are requirements for producing a family vacation setting for oneself or others, these very real aspects of vacation home ownership are not always a primary topic of conversation. So what exactly is a *family vacation home self*, and what labor and financial expenditures make the creation of this self possible, while also downplaying the effort of creating that self? And does it matter if the "self" who gets a vacation is the same "self" who performs the labor to create the experience?

WHAT IS A FAMILY VACATION HOME SELF?

When I interviewed homeowners, I asked them the following questions:

> Do you feel like you dress, look, speak, or behave differently at your second property compared to when you are home?
> Do you dress, look, speak, or behave differently when interacting with people staying in your second property?
> Are you the same person/self at both your properties?

For the most part, people did not see themselves as different people in different properties (or in different spaces on the same property, in the case of people who rented out parts of their primary residence). They defined the self as a unified thing. Why would they be two different selves, after all? But as I continued to ask them questions about the kinds of tasks they did, the things that stressed them out, and the ways their experiences changed over time, it became clear that people had shifting definitions of self, depending on interactions, group memberships, and location. In other words, family vacation home owners, like all people, "juggle an array of identities that have varying intensity and different relationships to self and social context."[2]

DEFINING SELF AND LIFE REALMS

Ole thought of himself as a vacationer at the home in the woods and as a non-vacationer in his primary residence, even with similar types of chores taking up his time. The self can change depending on context and activities. In sociology, we think about the *self* in a few ways. Usually, it consists of behaviors and actions (often referred to as *roles*), alongside how we think about who we are (often referred to as *identities*). This multipart definition serves as the foundation for twentieth-century theorist George Herbert Mead's conception of the *social self*, which consists of an actor going about their day (the "I"), a reflective self who thinks about the implications of their actions (the "me"), and an imagined audience that shapes both actions and reflections (the "generalized other").[3] According to Mead, when we think about who we are—our identities—we have to consider how the world's response to us may shape how we think about ourselves. Or, as famed sociologist Charles Horton Cooley offered when he coined the term *looking-glass self*, we define our self in terms of how we think the people in our social world see us,[4] which in turn becomes a mirror of how we see ourselves. The family vacation home self might be defined as a social self; it may also be defined as a *"territory of the self,"* as sociologist Christena Nippert-Eng writes,[5] in that, while it is situated in an actual geographic setting, an abstract version of the self comes to be defined in relation to the boundaries between family, work, and vacation.

An important contextual element in defining any version of the self is physical, which can include a place a person considers to be "home" and its material ingredients. The landscape, the furniture, the clothes—these can all serve as props for the enactment and creation of the self. Sociologists who study homes and housing have spelled out a clear connection between domestic spaces, material objects, and our conceptions of self: who we are is wrapped up in where we live and how we use our living spaces,[6] and a home is a piece of "identity equipment"[7] and a stage wherein our identities can be enacted. A home and its objects are key actors in the production of a "materialization of identity"[8] because the spaces and objects in our lives take on meaning that helps us understand who we are.

Further, identities are not static or settled; they are life projects that allow for adaptability in response to changing social or physical circumstances.[9] Our own conceptions of self can "develop and evolve in relation to a dynamic interplay of personal, family, social, cultural, and transcultural" realms,[10] including social institutions such as the family, education, government, religion, and our political and economic systems. Sociological theorist Pierre Bourdieu discusses how institutional building blocks of society connect to *fields*, which are the social and spatial arenas where people enact their roles, feel out the rules and values of the setting, and develop a *habitus* or disposition of character.[11] Fields such as family, work, and education are arenas in which people develop habits and skills that allow them greater or lesser success and life chances.

In this research, I use the term *life realm* as a way to combine the meaning of social institution and field: a physical and experiential location wherein roles are enacted, statuses are defined, and conceptions of self become constructed based on interactional, social, and personal identities associated with that location. The conceptions of self may intersect life realms, such as when one performs paid labor while on vacation, or they may be defined as contained within one of them, such as when one refuses to perform paid work at home. The most salient life realms in my research are paid work, family, and vacations. These all have patterns, meet people's needs, have withstood the test of time; require the development of roles, habits, and skills; and include discrete physical settings that may overlap, be kept separate, or both. I provide this term and definition here because it is in and between the life realms of family, work, and vacations where the definition of family vacation home self emerges.

DEFINING THE FAMILY VACATION HOME SELF AS A FUN, INTIMATE, TEMPORARY, RESPONSIBILITY-FREE, MAGICAL GETAWAY FROM "REAL" LIFE

What exactly is a family vacation home self? I'll begin with its definition as an *ideal type*, a term coined by classical social theorist Max Weber. An ideal type is not a perfect example of a given phenomenon; instead, it is a sort of abstract ruler against which actual cases of a phenomenon can be measured to see if they fit into a category.[12] Along these lines, the ideal type of family vacation home self is a version of the self that is experienced in a location away from a primary residence (or portion thereof) that is meant to be separated from everyday paid work and family. It is meant to include fun, family connection, and a distancing from mundane responsibilities associated with daily life. It should be distinct from a nonvacation self; a boundary between the life realms of labor and leisure is central to the concept. It is possible to have a family vacation home self by comparing oneself to other versions of a past or present self. For example, people may define themselves as "not at work" while on vacation or at home, delineating that they are not the same self as they are/were while at the office. One can have a family vacation home self by staying in one's own vacation home, and one can create a setting in which a family vacation home self may be nurtured for other people.

All of us have multiple identities that shape and are shaped by people and places that cross our paths. Vacations are moments when everyday life and responsibilities are meant to be paused, allowing us to escape and shut off our normal responsibilities and/or envision a future self.[13] One of my interviewees referred her family vacation home as a "cocoon." Presumably, these protected pauses and the capacity to escape are made possible because time constraints are fewer on vacation, and because exposure to different places, activities, and people can make envisioning other versions of the self easier. But traveling with family or having digital access to paid work can make it harder to achieve a family vacation home self, whether because of kids' food preferences, sibling rivalry, partner conflict, or a stress-inducing work email. If we travel with our family, the same kinds of choice constraints that operate at home may accompany us. When we travel with family *and* have access to our paid work tasks, a vacation self may be even harder to achieve and we may realize that, even in a cocoon, we cannot escape some of life's stresses— a point made vividly by Bonnie Honig in her analogy of home as womb: "The traditional configuration of the womb as a site free of difference, conflict, and struggle"[14] is a fabrication. In fact, places that have come to be defined as somehow safe and comfortable may also contain stress, pain, and struggle.

Thus, we start to see how the unpaid labor of everyday life is blurred with leisure and how the conception of home is contested. We start to see the porousness and shiftability of life realm boundaries and of our conceptions of self. And we start to see how family vacation homes may be framed as escapes from everyday stresses, even though they may in reality include their own stresses.

If it is rented out, a vacation home is never fully in the realm of family and never fully in the realm of work—it is always a little of both—meaning that the family vacation home self for the homeowner is never allowed a complete pause in the labor associated with family or work. But despite the porousness between vacation and nonvacation selves and spaces, the ideal type of vacation self (with accompanying spaces) carries a different kind of expectation relative to selves found in other life realms: family experiences and spaces are fun, intimate, temporary, responsibility-free, magical getaways from "real" life; family vacation homes are enchanted; and family vacation home selves are supposed to be enacted in magical cocoons.

What does this look like? Or, more accurately, what is this supposed to look like? At the vacation rental conference, I took notes as I learned from a host of experts that there are good and bad ways to decorate a family vacation home if you want to rent it to others. I learned that queen beds instill romance more than king beds, and that lamps on both sides of a bed prevent couples from fighting. Family vacation home selves are supposed to be paired with behaviors that offer fun, family connection, and a distancing from the mundanity

of the primary residence. These behaviors can come in more obvious vacation forms—games, parties, holiday dinners, puzzles, and outdoor activities
such as hiking or beachcombing—or in moments of partner intimacy. The
goal of all these activities is to avoid the stress and conflict that comes with
everyday responsibilities. This was also evident in my HGTV vacation real
estate program analysis, which showed that a getaway from "regular life" was
part of every home shopper's personal goals, since they would all be using the
properties for themselves at least some of the time. For those whose primary
goal was to rent a property to others, their plan was to also create a space that
allowed for such a getaway.

In addition to being centered on stress-free family fun, the family vacation
home self is also removed from usual temporal constraints, both in terms of
actual activities that take time and of the awareness and salience of time in a
more abstract sense. At the vacation rental conference, a lot of the messaging
surrounded the fact that vacationers rent homes in order to get away from
their everyday schedules. This included advice to place clocks only in rooms
where keeping track of time is needed. I also listened to participants talk
about "vacation diets" and guests taking a break to have a drink outside—
shockingly—without their phones.

The main goal for family vacation homeowners across all three property
groups is to create moments where the everyday stresses of life disappear, to
foster the creation of a family vacation home self. This means that, whether
it is rented to others or used by homeowners for a family getaway, the family
vacation home is defined as an oasis, refuge, and place for healing: in fact, a
cocoon. But who gets to use it?

INEQUALITY AND ACCESS: WHO GETS TO
HAVE A FAMILY VACATION HOME SELF?

The ways that the self shifted for my interviewees depended on how their
family vacation homes were framed. How people defined their "self" (or,
more accurately, selves) was different across property groups, within property
groups, and even for individual people over time. Importantly, these definitions of self also shifted depending on people's access to family vacation
homes in the first place. The people I interviewed would agree with the ideal
type of family vacation home self I defined above. However, the real versions
of the family vacation home self, uncovered in interviews and other parts of
my research, were much more varied, complex, and even contradictory. In
this sense, the ideal type of family vacation home self—all fun, family connectedness, and distance from mundane responsibility—may not be what a
real one looks like. This is impacted by a whole host of factors, including

other statuses that may enhance or limit access to this version of self. For example, across the webinars and conferences I observed, there were countless mentions of the need to ensure safety and accessibility in terms of pools, gates, wheelchair access, handrails, and clear technology operation instructions. Accessibility matters if you want an inclusive family vacation rental, especially if it is rented to others. If guests cannot operate a remote control, let alone read the tiny font in the operation instructions, they will not feel included in the population of potential guests.

The family vacation home self is a desirable version of the self that is played out via desirable behaviors, and not everyone can achieve it equally or in the same way. As one vacation rental webinar expert noted, "Your open doors are not just to your home, but also to the experience and the culture that everyone who comes through the doors is bringing with them at any point in time."[15] The capacity to experience the ideal type of family vacation self varies based on a number of experiential and cultural starting points for the vacationers beyond bodily ability and age, including level of care work responsibility, gender, social class, and race.

Care Work, Family Roles, and Gender

Responsibility for the care of other family members, whether children or aging parents, affects family vacations in any number of ways—a point made clear whenever a vacation is cut short or rerouted to an urgent care clinic because of a sick child. But the everyday care of children and aging parents or other family members, even without illness or emergency, impacts people's capacity to fully embody their family vacation home selves. The Vrbo Virtual Partner Summit webinars I examined connected family vacations with labor, referencing, for example, a "sweep" that parents do in a vacation rental home to check for safety hazards for kids or ensure the kitchen has the right cooking tools.[16] One webinar host even argued that families traveling for vacation are a culture in and of themselves, so, for her, creating a vacation home that is family friendly is as important as creating a comfortable setting for LGBTQIA+ individuals or racial/ethnic-minority families. Making a vacation family friendly, she advised, includes providing toys and pool safety fences, and highlighting features that frame the home as a villa or place where families can travel in "pods" to connect with extended family after COVID-19. The framing of family friendliness as a measure of inclusivity is a prerequisite for allowing guests to fully embody their family vacation selves. If a vacationer is spending all their time cleaning, cooking, and caring for kids, and not spending time reconnecting with loved ones, it feels more like everyday life and less like a vacation.[17]

For several interviewees, one of the main goals of second home ownership was to serve as a retreat from care work associated with an aging parent or family member who required special care. Bonnie, for example, had bought her mother a townhouse with the intention of moving in with her. But disappointment with the condo association rules and the realization that it would be too much work to live with her mother led Bonnie to keep her primary residence. Bonnie's vacation home, just fifteen minutes away from the town in Northern Lake Country where she and her mother live, continued to serve as her "place to go to get away from home": a retreat from the stresses of family care work responsibilities.

A vacation from domestic responsibilities, including child and elder care, may be a common goal for people who host other families in their vacation homes or for people vacationing in their own vacation homes, but it is not evenly experienced. Gender, in particular, matters. Stein notes that it is harder for women than men to "separate being home and away on vacation,"[18] because the unequal expectation that women are primarily responsible for housework and child-rearing does not go away when they're on vacation. In Stein's research on staycations, she notes that staying at home while taking vacation time makes it harder to create a boundary between labor and leisure, even if departure and return are simpler; in a family vacation home, the labor and leisure boundary is blurred, but the labor of departure and return is paired with the labor of housework and child-rearing in the vacation home setting, which is disproportionately done by women.

The beginning of this chapter featured a story from Ole (Personal Property group), who demonstrated a reframing of his vacation home yard work as leisure, rather than its usual description as household labor. Ole rendered this kind of labor invisible by focusing on it as part of the magic, enchantment, and fun of a vacation, even though he defined similar tasks as work when done in his primary residence yard. So while chores are not usually defined as fun, it is possible to reframe them if they're separated from the mundane parts of everyday life.

This reframing can be interpreted in two ways when it comes to gender and household labor. A critical interpretation would suggest that labeling household labor as leisure doesn't lessen inequality—it masks it. Women outperform men in domestic labor and responsibilities in primary residences. This also happens on vacations, because women's leisure is still more likely to be connected to "family time" than men's: "Even during holidays or periods of relaxation, women have been found to experience more stress than men in fulfilling domestic responsibilities."[19] Women also perceive that they relax or recover less than expected after a leisure activity.[20] On top of this, women also take less vacation leave than men[21] and spend less time in leisure activities.[22] That women perform household labor more than men, including at a family vacation home, indicates a form of engendered leisure that masquerades as pleasure but actually demonstrates inequality. Angela's ability to "see" why Ole suddenly saw dishwashing as work demonstrates this.

A less critical approach may suggest that gender roles—especially for Personal Property group homeowners—are reframed in contrast to everyday responsibilities that may be mundane, if not unfair. Vacations can offer playfulness in identity shifts, including identity elements centering on labor.[23] Business scholar Davina Chaplan finds that men and women who use rural vacation homes in Europe as escapes from everyday responsibilities redefine their unpaid labor as leisure, with men in particular treating vacation time as a retreat to a metaphorical cave, relishing in solitary DIY tasks that allow them to feel as if they're "getting back to basics," and role-playing what they imagine may come with a simple life.[24] Ole cutting down trees fits into this framing. Women, in contrast, fall into roles that include creative homemaking, shopping and socializing, and caring for family members. As Chaplan notes, "both genders are freed from the constraints of their normal working lives, but the ambivalent nature of the context which is both home and holiday is one in which work is present, in the form of do-it-yourself or doing the domestic,"[25] while simultaneously providing a chance to be playful with those roles. These experiences take place in "'liminal zones,' in which normal roles may be not so much inverted as perhaps played at or with."[26] This kind of role-playing was present among many of the homeowners I interviewed. Even those for whom creating a family vacation spot was a business, hospitality duties were sometimes framed as leisure-like and pleasant. Importantly, though, it was primarily women who framed this work hosting other families as a hobby, suggesting that gender patterns may differ in terms of labor associated with family vacation homes.

Class and Race

Access to a family vacation home necessarily requires money. As such, social class inequality prevents a large segment of the population from being able to afford to purchase even a modest vacation home. Homeowners in my research varied in terms of income, property values, and likelihood to rely on passive income related to vacation homes for financial stability. For example, Red's vacation rental in Eastern Woods, Auggie's in Eastern Oceanside, and Dusty's in Western City were all crucial for their capacity to afford their mortgages. Jean's Wine Country vacation rental cottage on their property, on the other hand, was less critical for her family's financial well-being. Nonetheless, all these people are homeowners, with most owning more than one home and some owning three or four. And yet my interviewees did not often bring up social class and wealth unprompted. The salience of social class was not very explicit in my data, with the exception of some interviewees' and vacation rental conference discussion about strategically pricing rentals higher so they were perceived as more desirable (price it higher and people will pay because it seems nicer), and some homeowners who grew up with little money who saw their vacation home as an achievement their parents would be proud of. Where social class was most salient, however, was in the visible ways that the neighborhoods I visited were filled with homes that could sell for hundreds of thousands of dollars. The neighborhoods I visited, for the most part, had plentiful streetlights, well-maintained homes, and expensive cars.

Access to vacations and the destinations where vacations take place differs not just by financial capacity, but also by race. This has deep historical roots, with explicit segregated and discriminatory practices such as inflated fees, de jure segregation, intimidation, violence, and hard-to-access sites that have made travel difficult for people of color, and African Americans in particular, well into the twentieth century.[27] Today, the travel industry shows remnants of these racist historical roots, with continued racialized redlining in the real estate industry and vacation rental companies such as Airbnb and Vrbo continuing to revise policies and practices in response to experiences of discrimination by travelers of color.[28] In light of this, resources have emerged to offer homeowners best practices that are meant to create inclusive vacation experiences while boosting their bookings. Among these resources, the webinars I examined highlighted several tips: don't use a Confederate flag, use "ethnically neutral" decor, offer varied ethnic hair care products, audit your online property listing to ensure it is not colonialist, advertise inclusive local businesses, and make sure guests of color feel safe. To the last point, the speaker noted:

> Safety looks like a lot of different things for us as travelers of color. It can look like the host needing to get to know your neighbors so that they call you instead of the cops if there is an issue. We know and have seen how the travel industry has been brought to the task after the death of George Floyd. How do we deal with neighbors who aren't open to diverse cultures? It really starts with a direct conversation. Make sure your guests of color are in fact staying safe in your property. And that includes your neighbors.[29]

This expert told viewers that they are "at the intersection of culture and commerce." Increasingly, guests are looking for explicit markers of inclusive policies in short-term rental listings, so creating family vacation homes that allow for any family to picture themselves there is important.

Owning a family vacation home, whether rented to others or reserved for personal use, affords owners a privileged status. Property can be bought and sold, and the assets of the people involved in this research are better situated to pass along generational wealth than people who live paycheck to paycheck or are riddled with debt. The capacity to migrate voluntarily and entirely for leisure is itself a privilege, and vacations are not cheap. The family vacation home self, therefore, is a status that few can achieve, even as those who possess it span a wide range of socioeconomic and other social locations, and even as home purchasing rates have recently risen across all racial groups.[30] And for those whose second, third, or fourth home are rented to provide others access to a family vacation home self, which may include laborious efforts, this high status is secured by virtue of their having greater real estate assets than most of the population. Structural inequalities associated with the family vacation home marketplace in terms of race and class are discussed further in chapter 5.

VACATION HOMES ARE REMOVED FROM WORK AND THE MARKETPLACE, EXCEPT THEY'RE NOT: THE ARTIFICIAL SEPARATION OF LABOR AND LEISURE

"This is so nice and quiet. It kind of envelops me. It's a cocoon."

—Faye, owner of a home in Northern Lake Country

"I don't disappear back in the bedroom. I say I'm happy to be social. If you want to share dinner, let me know. I let people kind of drive that."

—Giselle, owner of a multiplex in Wine Country with a short-term vacation rental apartment in a basement ADU

We all wear varied hats in our lives, each of which signifies a role we play in a particular life realm, from paid work or family to school, community groups, or volunteer work. Usually, these roles are not demarcated by actual hats, although when I worked at Dairy Queen as a teenager, I couldn't wait to remove my grease-covered hat when I got home from a long shift flipping burgers.

At times, the boundary between the roles we play in different life realms is thick. We may even think of ourselves as two different people or, as Faye said, find ourselves in a "cocoon" that "envelops us." At other times, the boundary is porous, and we traverse between realms without changing much, in the manner that Giselle enjoys. When we find ourselves blending people, activities, time, space, and objects from multiple life realms, or acting and feeling the same in these realms, the boundary between them is porous and we can usually switch back and forth easily—at least in terms of ways we can control. Sometimes, though, we are faced with constraints in one life realm or another that require us to make the boundaries more or less porous. This lens—having to do *boundary work* in order to deal with forces that push us to either integrate our life realms or segment them—is the foundation for Nippert-Eng's research on home and work boundaries.[31] Boundary work refers to the energy we have to employ to traverse boundaries when we'd rather keep them thick, or to place boundaries when we'd rather keep them porous.

Whether related to objects found in our living spaces or ways that we think about various versions of self, the separation between labor and leisure is socially constructed. At times, it seems easy to see the boundary between these, especially since getting paid for someone to use your home for their vacation is a different transaction than staying at a grandparent's vacation home for free. But the clear distinction between worker and vacationer becomes less clear as soon as larger cultural values about family come into play—and as soon as we look more closely at people who experience both roles in the same property: the Mixed Property group. The following sections detail the complex ways that boundaries between home, work, and vacation selves, as well as between family and the marketplace, are experienced by family vacation home owners, demonstrating both differences and similarities across property groups. I begin with an overview of a topic that homeowners across property groups used to delineate work, family, and vacation selves: money.

Life Stage Transitions as Opportune Moments to Talk about Money

Talking about money in relation to a family vacation home blurs life realms and "disenchants" the idealized vacation home, which is meant to be symbolically removed from the realities of the marketplace. So people across all three property groups didn't talk much about money, especially if it revealed their social class (a topic I return to in chapter 5). If they did talk about money, it took a few different forms. Some homeowners were not shy about talking about the monetary value of their homes beyond the quiet reporting of it on the surveys. At times, this took the form of the interviewees across income groups expressing their frustration over the impact of high property tax rates and their dissatisfaction with the government. At other times, this occurred among people who were already immersed in careers directly related to finance, such as Sunny (Investment Property group), who bought a beachside multiplex at Northwest Oceanside to rent out to vacationers. Sunny spent her career as a high-level executive in corporate business cultures, often as the only woman, and she had no trouble talking about either her own or others' financial status and property values during her interview. Unsolicited mention of property values was also present among people who didn't grow up with a lot of money, either as a way to illustrate a sense of accomplishment since their humble beginnings or because they felt guilty for having achieved a very conspicuous marker of wealth. As these examples show, explicit discussion of money was a way of providing context for topics related to property value that were unrelated to property group.

Family life stage transitions became the most common opportune moments to think about and explicitly discuss finances (and accompanying labor) related to the family vacation home. At the vacation rental conference, giant screens at the front of the ballroom played an interview with a homeowner who rents her home to other families. In it, she explained that she got into the vacation rental business to support her own family's financial status. Whether saving for kids' college tuition, retirement, or a lavish family vacation, the message was clear—get into this kind of business to support events across the lifespan of your family; do the work now in order to reap family financial benefits later. As past research has shown, people often consider life stage transitions opportune moments to talk about money.[32]

Having children certainly compels people to consider financial circum-stances, and real estate investment can serve to help afford future expenses, such as children's college tuition. But sometimes, the motivation is more immediate or less direct. Bella (Mixed Property group), for instance, talked about her purchase of a multiplex in Eastern Oceanside as a means to help pay bills associated with her growing family during a time when she struggled to find a job. From a more abstract motivation, Jean (Investment Property group)—who rented out her ADU to vacationers seeking some rest and relaxation in Wine Country—saw the business as a way to teach her teenage children how to be hospitable, a valuable trait for their future pursuits: "I figure it's good exposure for flexibility for my kids, and to be aware of other people, and be polite and considerate. They go out and they don't exactly strike up conversation, but they know that they need to be friendly because they're our guests."

Jean told me that her short-term rental work only felt "like a job" when it was booked solid for long periods of time, so it was not as if her mention of her kids' exposure to new skills was explicitly financially driven. But it was clear that the hospitality skills her children may learn fit solidly into the category of *cultural capital*, which Bourdieu defined as symbolic and social assets that someone may possess, such as knowledge, style of dress, and demeanor (as well as objects such as diplomas and museum passes), that give that person social mobility.[33] This was not a motivation mentioned by the Personal Property group members.

While the boundary between childhood and adulthood is socially defined, a common marker of adulthood is financial independence.[34] Across all property categories and age groups, this marker mattered. For Dianne (Mixed Property group), it certainly felt like an accomplishment to be able to afford a vacation condo that would serve as her retirement home in Tropical Paradise ten or fifteen years down the road (for now, it was being rented out for others' vacations). For Red (Investment Property group), who had spent the latter half of his working life disabled and unable to find a steady job and who explicitly noted how broke he was, turning a room in his house in the Eastern Woods into a vacation rental helped him get over some financial hurdles. And for Faye (Personal Property group), who never rented out her Northern Lake Country home to others and who thought that her kids may turn it into a rental in the future, owning the home served as a way to demarcate accomplishment and financial independence after a divorce.

Divorcing or relationship dissolution was mentioned by people besides Faye, and across property categories, especially in terms of establishing financial stability. Auggie (Investment Property group), for example, started renting out parts of his multiplex (some long-term, some short-term) to help him buy out his former girlfriend's share of the home. Marion (Investment Property group) mentioned that the remodeling she and her former husband did on their short-term rental cottage was their last joint flipping project before a divorce. In these instances, it was during a time of family dissolution that money matters became more explicit, more pressing, and more likely to be part of family and relationship conversations.

Financial independence as a marker of adulthood was also a goal for Dusty (Investment Property group), who rents out a room in his Western City home to tourists. Dusty noted that the money he and his wife make from short-term rentals covers a substantial portion of the mortgage on their single-story, 1,000-square-foot home. He talked about balancing the burden of hosting travelers with its financial benefits, and situated the balance in terms of what he observed about his parents:

> We're pretty comfortable with travelers and strangers, so it was like the amount of money that we could make for the impact on our life, the benefits definitely outweigh the cons of it. . . . I've always been interested in real estate investing and seeing that as a pretty solid pathway to get solid financial ground. I've seen that my parents have entered into their sixties and have not made great financial decisions and don't have a home that's paid off, so I think seeing that play out has played into my pretty fierce desire to work towards someday living mortgage-free.

Accomplishing financial independence while also being financially responsible motivated CJ (Personal Property group), who grew up without much money. CJ spends a lot of time with her husband at their house in Northwest Oceanside, a property that they never rent out to others. She talked at length about her childhood and how financial hardship meant they had to be careful not to spend money on frivolous things. She told a story about how she imagined what her now-deceased parents would say as she deliberated about buying this second home: "I remember kind of talking to them. I needed their approval to get this. I needed them to say, 'You're not being frivolous. Good for you. You were frugal and saved up enough money to buy this. You should be proud of yourself.'"

Stories about aging parents popped up in the interviews and in sessions I observed at the vacation rental conference, always related to property use. A growing responsibility for middle-aged people, eldercare matters when families are separated by large geographic distance and when healthcare concerns and financial burdens are accumulating—issues that are only becoming more prominent as the US population ages.[35] During one conference session on how to handle government regulations on short-term rentals, the conversation centered around suggestions to invoke hypothetical family health stories to advocate for fewer regulations: offer tales of how short-term rental vacation homes are better than hotels because they allow for greater comfort for family members with health needs, like "when Grandma needs medical treatment." This session was decidedly pro–property rights, filled with critiques of vacation rental naysayers bringing unsophisticated data on housing affordability to city councils. The discussion landed on the desire to take a middle-ground approach, including reasonable taxes and fees, ensuring noise mitigation and compliance, and removing "bad actors." The suggestion to use anecdotes highlighting family health-related travel was intriguing—this was, after all, a vacation rental conference. Yet here was a case of people frustrated with bad data and hyperbolic stories about loud parties and bad apples suggesting that the best way to advocate for short-term rental deregulation was to use family life-stage-related stories that have nothing to do with vacations.

For Personal Property group homeowners, aging and eldercare stories had totally different outcomes. More typically, those homeowners were concerned that the health of aging spouses or parents might decrease their use of their family vacation home or wondered whether it was worth the money to maintain it. Thus, health and aging (and the connection between these) was invoked in relation to money among all property groups, but the use of this invocation yielded opposite results: increased visitor stays for hosts seeking profit, but decreased stays for those seeking only personal use.

Of all the topics connecting life stages and finances, retirement was the most frequently raised in all property categories. This is not surprising, given the volume of both tools and news items that promote using real estate investment to ensure financial stability that I uncovered in my perusal of vacation home and investment property guides. But how people talked about retirement varied across property groups. For people in the Investment Property group, retirement goals were more about their own cost of living. For Marion, for example, buying a house with an ADU that she could rent out to short-term vacationers in Wine Country motivated her move away from an urban center. And for attendees at the vacation rental conference, the message was loud and clear: rent out your properties and earn money that you can eventually (or currently) use to fund retirement.

Mixed Property group members' discussions were similar to those of the Investment Property group, but their partial use of the properties complicated how retirement mattered. Bella, for example, noted that her Eastern Oceanside multiplex was "a huge investment, and it's kind of my retirement plan, so I need to make sure that I can take care of it." She visits the property a lot to fix things and, sometimes, to enjoy a little rest; when not there, she rents out the unit. Rich and Marcus, who spend part of their time in Western Desert in a house they rent to others when they're not there, bought their house to "get into the market," because they knew they wanted to retire there. The Mixed Property group includes people who bought property to use now, here and there, and rent out when it's empty, with the goal of using it more often during retirement. It also includes people who currently both use their property and rent it, but are likely to sell it to fund their retirement elsewhere.

Retirement and the owner- versus renter-occupied distinction matters for the Mixed Property group, especially to neighbors who see a house sitting empty or occupied by rotating (and sometimes loud) strangers. In public hearings associated with short-term rental regulations in Walla Walla, Washington—a site that underwent revision to these regulations after an upsurge in vacation rentals and accompanying controversy—a resident who knew an owner of a local vacation rental attempted to justify the owner's decision using retirement as the reason: "They love this community, they want to invest in it, and would like to eventually retire here." He then couched the justification in terms of economic benefit for the town, in part because the home is well-maintained, and in part because the homeowner was seen as someone whose other business could bring lots of jobs to the area. For opponents of short-term rentals in residential neighborhoods, neither the economic benefit nor the owners' plans for future permanent residency was enough. As I discuss more in chapter 5, immediate—not delayed—social benefit outweighed any economic benefit.

Homeowners in the Personal Property category brought up retirement in the context of how they currently use their vacation homes, especially among older individuals who had already retired. Retirement planning related to the initial purchase decades ago was also mentioned by people across property categories, including Carla, who spends many weekends at the Northwest Woods home she owns with her husband Dayton: "We've talked about retiring at the cabin. I'd live there year-round, and we joke about global warming, because by the time we retire and move up there, we won't have to worry about the snow." Despite the occasional mention of future retirement planning, retirement came up less among the Personal Property group as compared to the other two property groups. This was true both in terms of retirement generally and in terms of its importance for financial stability.

Worker, Hobbyist, and Vacationer: Defining, Revising, and Blurring Labor and Leisure Roles

At the vacation rental conference, I participated in as many activities as I could, including social gatherings. I arrived at one such event after a long, meandering walk through other parts of the resort, crossing the gravel-laden plaza and entering to find signs for an Old West saloon. Roulette and craps tables flanked a collection of small round tables. People were eating, drinking, and networking, some wearing cowboy boots to fit with the event's theme. There were roasted veggie platters aplenty, and oodles of slider sandwiches. I walked around with a drink in hand, mouthing along to the music, which included '80s hits like "Cruel Summer," "Don't You Want Me," "Voices Carry," and at least two Duran Duran songs. At this point I realized I was in the target demographic for people involved in the vacation rental business. As I wandered around with my drink, I noticed that all the seats were filled, so I went toward a bar-height table where a single woman was standing. I set my plate down, noticing the two full glasses in front of her. I said hello and asked if I could use the table. She smiled and nodded as her husband arrived and grabbed the glass of whiskey. They told me about how they had recently retired from their respective careers and owned a second property that they turned into a vacation rental. They shared how their spousal relationship now included a business partnership; they'd had two separate careers and now share one. The challenges, they noted, included figuring out a new division of labor and meshing working styles. Like a lot of the conference attendees, this couple had turned family into business. Their roles had shifted.

People shift roles even in life realms not related to paid work. Karen Stein talks about homes as places where we can enact roles that are not quite work, but not quite play. Stein also notes that hobbies—such as woodworking or gardening—"aid in building separate mental realms of play and work in the everyday world, and they often take place in the home. If people cannot escape from their surroundings, they can at least escape the alienating activities of work life through involvement with a favored activity that reflects their personalized interests."[36] For some of the people at the vacation rental conference, having a vacation rental was a business. For others, it was a hobby that happened to pay some bills. For homeowners in the Personal Property group, domestic work associated with the vacation property was transformed into a hobby or framed as leisure.

People act differently on vacation than they do at home or at work. Or do they? Before I began my research, I had assumed that people like the couple I met at the conference, who fit into the Investment Property group, would see themselves as paid workers, that the Mixed Property group would be the hobbyists, and that the Personal Property group would be the vacationers. I didn't expect that these roles would fluctuate within groups, and I certainly didn't anticipate the ways that roles changed over time, even within individual people's lives. Worker, hobbyist, or vacationer: these roles are more complex than we might think.

People who stay in their own vacation homes—the Personal Property group—may shift between vacationer and everyday family roles that involve cooking and cleaning, or between paid worker and vacationer, or all of these. The shift may occur in transit from primary residence to vacation home, or during the stay. If homeowners stay in their vacation properties part-time and rent it the rest of the time—the Mixed Property group—roles may shift between vacationer and business owner (and as vacationers they may take on a vacation self or everyday family role). And for people who rent their homes to other family vacationers—the Investment Property group—roles may shift between homeowner and business owner or hobbyist whose primary aim is to nurture a family vacation self in other people. For people who are considering altering the use of their second property, role shifts will come along. Whatever combination, the roles that are defined as labor may be outsourced to other workers, or they may be reframed as hobbies. As this demonstrates, the roles people occupy as family vacation home owners are far from simple.

The findings from my interviews suggest several outcomes relating to how people think about their definitions of self across life realms. The "territories of the self"[37] that come with residing in or renting out a family vacation home don't always have clear boundaries, or they may shift quickly or over a long period of time. In fact, it is often in the shift between roles—the liminal zones—where we realize what boundaries between roles we may prefer. And, despite some variation, labor is frequently and strategically reframed as leisure across all property types. I unpack these outcomes below.

Time affected how people viewed their roles, with people in the Personal and Mixed Property groups who spent more time at their properties being less likely to see themselves as vacationers. This was occasionally indicated by owners naming their property a "second home" rather than a "vacation home." Al and Ina, for example, stressed that they are not tourists and their

Great Lakes Waterfront residence is not a vacation home, even if it could legally be classified as such, because they spend nearly half of their time there, often three to four days each week. They also noted that tourists and vacationers do not (and should not) have the same rights as those who spend a lot of time in a place and who pay taxes there. Tourists have superficial connections to place; residents have rights, they argued. Interestingly, they did not see their roles as the same across both homes. Their primary residence disallowed the same kind of relaxation and slow pace as their waterfront home, but they nevertheless refused to think of themselves as being "on vacation" in their second home. Importantly, though, how much time people actually spent in their vacation homes mattered less than their perception that the amount of time was sufficient to define themselves as vacationers. This subjective use of time also played a role in whether homeowners saw themselves as entitled to participate in the community's civic and political activities, a topic elaborated in chapter 4.

Labor is part of any vacation home. Buying a home, fixing it up, furnishing it, maintaining it, and producing money used to finance all of this are all centered around work. Even in cases where a property is meant to be used for leisure (now or eventually), creating desired outcomes for the property are actual labor. Molly (Personal Property group), whose husband is a contractor who has put many hours of work into fixing up their Eastern Oceanside home, noted, "We plan to have it forever. . . . Our plan would be, because of our growing family, to put a second story on, which would make it even a larger space to accommodate, like, when all of our children are married and having children, and we want to have others down at the same time."

Putting a second story on a house is a lot of work! And yet, despite stories about remodeling and upkeep, people across all property types overwhelmingly reframed labor as leisure.

How? Even among those in the Investment Property group, interviewees only occasionally talked about the heavy burden of housework or the emotional labor of managing tasks associated with the property. In other words, even though people were asked about the chores and responsibilities they had at their properties, there was little discussion of the level of stress associated with what Arlie Hochschild defines as a *second shift*, that is, unpaid domestic labor or care work performed after a first paid shift,[38] including the work of managing an associated to-do list. The HGTV vacation home real estate shows I analyzed also downplayed labor, showing only ease of access to vacation homes and ease of property acquisition and management, despite the actual work of financial planning, paperwork, and renovation that comes with a vacation home purchase. It's not surprising that the laboriousness of vacation home ownership was downplayed in these shows, though, because their goal is to tell a story that seems accessible and not too daunting (or perhaps just daunting enough to add some drama on the way to its resolution).

Vacations are not supposed to be laborious. They're supposed to be a refuge from labor. Because of this, labor gets erased, either by downplaying or reframing it, by hiding it from guests (e.g., keeping cleaning and maintenance products in a locked owner's closet), or, in the case of some homeowners, by hiring others to do it. Among Personal Property group owners, the labor associated with getting a space ready or cleaned was framed more like a hobby than a burden, as in the case of Ole's joy at performing outdoor chores. For people in the Investment Property group, the work was also often defined as a hobby, and usually as enjoyable. They sometimes framed elements of the "business" labor—or first shift—as leisure, as a means of re-creating their own pleasant travel memories for others. This was particularly interesting because several of the homeowners in the Investment Property group had former or current careers in the hospitality and real estate industries, but they talked about their careers as labor more than they talked about the rental business as labor. Homeowners who rented their vacation homes reframed the labor associated with hospitality as a joy. And homeowners who only used their properties for their own families did the same thing. Whether the space was a business or a personal home, the work was overwhelmingly enchanted.

Importantly, there were some instances in which labor was less likely to be framed as leisure. For people in the Investment Property group whose second properties are primarily rented to others, labor was a prerequisite of owning a family vacation home. As was the case for the couple I met at the conference social event, the vacation home was a business, and businesses require labor. More specifically, those in the Investment Property group who rented out their spaces because they were financially strained—whether their rental home provided their primary income or additional income to finance their basic needs—saw this as work, not as an enjoyable hobby. Others in this group for whom the chores were hard to manage due to frequent guest turnover or guest messes were also less likely to describe these as leisurely moments. This included the labor of managing the outsourced labor of others, such as cleaning services. Miriam (Investment Property group), who rents out her basement ADU in Western City, told a vivid story of the complications of cleaning when the time window between guests is only a few hours and when guest stays vary in length. The person she hires to clean has to be flexible in terms of which days she works each week and which hours during a given day the work can take place. People with this kind of flexibility are hard to find. This is why Miriam has been tempted to switch the ADU to a long-term rental: "We have a two-nights minimum and we've had a lot of two-night stays. We've had one couple that came for two weeks. That was really heavenly, actually."

Several Investment Property group homeowners who rent out their properties now but plan to use the property in the future for their own retirement recognized that the upkeep and maintenance was a lot of work. They could not see their second homes entirely as leisure spaces today, but they looked forward to the day when they would be. Then they will feel as if they were on vacation. Finally, those in the Investment Property group who had started their rental business with informal transactions with friends noticed their preference for putting on their formal business owner hat. When we transition between roles—especially involuntarily—it can be easier to notice what the roles are and whether we feel better about one role over another (or ought to feel this way). Role change yields role visibility, and *feeling rules*,[39] which are the norms that guide us to want to feel a certain way in our everyday lives, "become most visible when they are broken."[40]

The Mixed Property group demonstrated the most complicated feeling rules via their navigation of worker, hobbyist, and vacationer roles, primarily because they switched roles most often. The process of shifting between roles crystallized role preferences and made labor more visible. Rich and Marcus, who rent out their Western Desert home to others using online booking platforms, told me that when they stay there, they block out those times on the booking platforms and even pay a cleaning fee. The separation of roles from vacationer to business owner was visible for other Mixed Property group homeowners' experiences, but for people who relied on the property for financial stability, it looked a bit different. People who don't get to experience the ideal type of family vacation feel like vacation is work. For people in this category, like Bella, frequently traversing the boundary between worker and vacationer meant never really feeling as if she was on vacation in her own home:

> When I come home, people say, "Did you have a nice vacation?" And I'm like, "No, because it's not a vacation." The one time I went with [my kids and their friends], that was probably the most vacation thing I've ever had, and even that was a lot of work because I had volunteered just as being kind of like the fellow chaperone that I would cook two meals a day for them. So I was cooking a lot, but still, that was the most relaxing time I've ever had. I wasn't tearing down a fence or putting in a stove or something like that.

The most angst about upkeep was felt by the Mixed Property group, because they experienced more moments of boundary traversal, more moments when feeling rules were broken, and more stress related to preparing the property for paying guests during their own vacations, especially if they had to spend a lot of time and money on property upkeep.

For the Personal Property group especially, when labor was involved it was framed as difficult or something that stood in the way of leisure. When there was work to be done that was not part of their vacation to-do list, they resented it. This was also true for the Mixed Property group, who switched from using their home themselves to renting it out, often needing time to adjust to their new role, as well as for Investment Property group homeowners during busy seasons with fast visitor turnover. In these instances, it felt more like work than a hobby because the labor was overwhelming or more visible. And so there were occasional times when labor was recognized as such.

Labor is part of every vacation home owner's experience, whether they rent their property, use it themselves, or both. The Investment Property group was most comfortable calling their experiences work—which is how it was framed among participants at both conference sites and in the webinars I analyzed. But even this group talked about the labor associated with hosting other families as enjoyable, a hobby, or even easy. Why? They saw the business as a way to connect with others. At the same time as people may bring work stress into their home lives, the desire for human connection at work remains strong. Sociologist Allison Pugh, in *The Last Human Job: The Work of Connecting in a Disconnected World*, describes the desire for connection and empathy at work as "connective labor."[41] As artificial intelligence and automation replace people in the workplace, we see a thirst for more nonstandardized ways of being human. Business requires metrics and profit; connection requires feelings. It is no wonder that home-sharing companies appeal to emotional connection as a way to boost business—it meets a human need in the marketplace.

In all these findings, including televised renditions of vacation home acquisition for one's own family, for others' families, or both, rendering labor invisible adds to the enchantment of family vacation homes as places of magic, relaxation, and fun. This erasure of labor by both homeowners and those who offer advice to them at conferences and in webinars demonstrates the degree to which family vacation homes are enchanted and artificially removed from the commodity frontier.[42] Only when the work was too time-consuming, too pressing to allow for personal vacation time, or necessary for the economic well-being of the homeowner was labor discussed more explicitly. The realities of insufficient time and economic resources made these challenges more visible, while the privilege of reframing this work as leisure was accessible only to those who had plenty of time and money.

First rule of family vacation homes: don't talk about the labor that goes into family vacation homes. It ruins the magic! It disenchants! But only if you can afford to ignore it.

Flexcations, Telecommuting, and Retirement: Simultaneous, Alternating, and Eventual Leisure and Labor

In the spring and summer of 2020, around fifty million Americans began working from home, due in large part to lockdowns related to the COVID-19 pandemic,[43] leaving big office buildings sitting half-empty.[44] Which "homes" people worked from varied significantly: some worked from their primary residence, while others—including some clusters of relatively afflu-ent college students—moved into vacation rentals. For tens of millions of people, the boundaries between home spaces and workspaces became blurred.

While people switch roles from paid worker to family laborer to vacationer over time, the time scale for this role switching varies. Switching between family laborer and relaxed vacationer can occur moment-by-moment, as when a poolside nap is interrupted by a crying child, then reinstated after realizing the child has soothed herself back to sleep. These transitions can also occur less frequently and take more time, for instance, for people who take a handful of weeklong vacations each year during which they leave all their work behind and "turn off" the world. Importantly, this role switching may be yet to happen, but be planned—retirement, for instance—making the element of time more about an imagined future than an experienced past or present. Temporal shifts between roles related to family vacation homes appeared across three experiential moments, uniformly discussed across the three property groups: flexcations, telecommuting, and retirement.

Flexcations and telecommuting were referenced in the pre-, during-, and post-COVID conference sessions and webinars I analyzed. Flexcations are stays in vacation rentals that may be a bit longer than a traditional vacation and are a fluid way to combine work and play to accommodate shifting pat-terns of work, school, and family life.[45] Work, in this case, usually referred to paid work, but it also incorporated schoolwork. Homeschooling, taking work Zoom calls, fielding emails, and studying or writing are tasks that are hard to do while skiing or kayaking, to be sure, but the Vrbo Virtual Partner Summit webinars highlighted the importance of providing good Wi-Fi, writing and computer desks, and nooks for work tasks as a way of adapting to contempo-rary family vacationers' needs. These amenities were framed not as business travel needs but rather as "work-from-home" needs that would allow nearly simultaneous moments of labor and leisure, albeit taking place in separate vacation home nooks—especially important since the pandemic.

My content analysis of COVID-19-related news articles from amenity-rich locales showed that second home owners and short-term renters spent lon-ger periods of time (including in the offseason) telecommuting to work or school in these places. Since the COVID-19 lockdowns ended, the world of telecommuting has undergone a shift, with people recognizing the ease and convenience of working from home and organizations scrambling to figure out the best combination of virtual and in-person work.[46] But the increased visibility of doing paid work in varied home settings has highlighted vacation homes as a desirable site for enacting the role switch between paid work, family chores, and vacationing.

Role shifting across time is not just about what people are experiencing now; it is also salient to how they imagine their future roles. As discussed earlier, retirement was discussed frequently, usually in terms of people using second home properties to secure their financial future during retirement or as a time when the family vacation home would be used more. Family vacation homes were thus seen as sites for eventual leisure, but not until the labor is done.

CONCLUSION: ENCHANTMENT ACROSS ROLE AND LIFE REALM BOUNDARIES

According to sociologist Viviana Zelizer, we live in a culture in which people are supposed to act out of love in the home, but judge people on professional grounds, not personal loyalties, in the marketplace.[47] The home is all about expressive relationships, while the marketplace is about instrumental relationships connected to labor. This set of ideals is strategically useful for people who want to retain an enchanted vision of family. And yet these idealized boundaries are rarely realized this neatly. To this point, Hochschild shares the words of a married mother of three whom she interviewed about her care work responsibilities:

> I had my husband's parents and aunt and uncle for a week at our summer cabin. It's rather small, and it rained most of the week except for Saturday and Sunday. And my mother-in-law offered to help me make the meals and helped me clear the dishes. But you know the real work is in figuring out what to eat and shopping. And the nearest store was at some distance. And [I] began to resent their visit so much I could hardly stand it. You know I don't run a bed and breakfast![48]

This story about the labor associated with a family vacation home captures my findings well: whether a version of self and its accompanying roles is defined as laborer, hobbyist, or vacationer depends on what it is compared to. The family vacation home self is a relatively defined concept, at times including elements that look a lot like labor but are framed as leisure, and at other, more stressful or resentful times highlighting ways that labor is getting in the way of leisure.

The findings in this chapter reveal three ways that the family vacation home is strategically framed as enchanted by homeowners in terms of conceptions of self and life realm boundaries: through having a family vacation home self, through untangling who has access to the family vacation home self, and through the artificial separation of labor and leisure. Below I summarize these findings and how they connect to the overarching goal of enchanting the family vacation home.

Family Vacation Home Self

Regardless of the property group they were in, the people I interviewed had the same goal: to enact the roles associated with a family vacation home self that demonstrated escape from everyday work and family responsibilities. The Investment and Mixed Property groups necessarily worked to create that escape for others but sometimes considered their own current or future family vacation home self as motivation. Personal Property group homeowners aimed to create the possibility of a family vacation home self for their own families while simultaneously having to think explicitly about the labor attached to managing a property. As Bonnie's story about retreating to her cabin to de-stress after dealing with eldercare responsibilities suggests, the vacation home is supposed to be a respite not just from paid work but also from everyday family stresses. Families seem to understand that it isn't just paid work that creates stress; family life in the primary residence can do this, too. This all supports the goal of another place for eventual escape: the family vacation home.

To see the family vacation home as an escape—a cocoon that can protect someone from these everyday stresses—is the definition of enchantment. By achieving or aspiring to have a family vacation home self, homeowners can embody the ideals associated with a getaway. Enchantment is what happens when harsh realities are covered up with magic and fun, and even though people increasingly realize that a home is not necessarily a haven from the "real world," the idealized family vacation home is a proposed alternate haven. And yet this home is also filled with the realities associated with the life realms of work and family.

Unequal Access to the Family Vacation Home Self

Accessibility and inclusivity have become important ideals in the family vacation home industry, whether these pertain to demographics such as race, class, and gender, or to family roles and responsibilities that may require a site to be *family friendly*, meaning that people with children and multiple generations would feel comfortable staying in the home. This was true regardless

of property group. For people whose family vacation homes were only for
personal use, their attention was centered on the space serving as a retreat
from care work responsibilities or a site for self-care. For those who rented
their properties to others, efforts to make the home more accessible or inclusive related, at least in part, to making money. Recognition of inequalities and
the ways in which life's challenges connect to social categories such as class,
race, and gender were present in the interviews, but only when interviewees
who fell into disenfranchised categories deliberated about the purpose of
their family vacation homes. In other words, having privileged status allowed
homeowners to frame that very privilege as invisible, especially in terms of
social class.

Enchantment of the family vacation home means not having to worry about
the hardships of everyday life, whether those are physical, sociodemographic,
or political. Further, the invisibility of class, race, and unequal division of
household labor by gender serves to remove the family vacation home from
the political realities of structural inequality. The enchanted family vacation
home self is not universally accessible, but pointing this out would disenchant. Strategic removal by the homeowner from being implicated from these
realities is elaborated in chapter 5.

The Artificial Separation of Labor and Leisure

Across property groups, the boundary between leisure and paid work and
the marketplace was porous. But this boundary looked different depending
on property group and other factors that emerged in the interviews. Labor
associated with family vacation homes was defined as leisure in many cases,
with Personal Property group homeowners defining chores as fun, Investment
Property group homeowners defining having a vacation rental as a hobby, and
Mixed Property group homeowners finding that the transition between business owner and vacationer was angst-filled. For the Mixed Property group,
the implications of the boundary between labor and leisure were more visible,
since role transitions are opportune moments to understand both roles at the
same time; for this group, labor got in the way of leisure during such transitions. Time and financial status mattered, too, with homeowners less likely to
see themselves as "vacationers" in their homes if they spent more time there,
and with financially strained homeowners seeing their labor as more work
than hobby.

Life realm boundaries in the family vacation home setting are porous, shifting depending on the use of the home, time spent there, or financial stability.
And yet the family vacation home is idealized as a place of leisure separated by a thick boundary from the paid labor market and other marketplace

transactions—it should be a stress-free place, removed from the harsh realities of everyday work and family life (even as it sometimes contains those realities).

* * *

I recently asked some of my family members if they felt like chores felt different when they were at their vacation homes. The resounding answer was yes. The choreography of domestic labor—doing the dishes, making the bed, sweeping the patio—somehow gets framed as fun when it's not in your primary residence. While doing dishes is not the same as skiing or reading next to a firepit, it's fun because it's in a place removed from everyday life. But not everyone gets to have the luxury of framing it this way, especially if they're used to noticing that they do more of this labor than others.

The pleasures of travel are often manifest in how we manage unfamiliar settings, relationships, and scripts.[49] However, family vacation homes are not so far removed from travelers' everyday experiences—after all, staying in an Airbnb is not quite as exotic an activity as extreme rock climbing. Stein writes that vacation spots become desirable when they strike a good balance between the familiar and the exotic, between "wanting to do or be something different and having the reassurance that the comfort of stability and familiarity remain."[50] But she also notes that experts recommend making a vacation spot familiar, to make travelers feel comfortable.

The findings from my research suggest that family vacation homes blur leisure and labor because they are already "home" to both people who reside there and people who rent to others, especially those who also live there part-time, used to live there, or plan to live there in the future. This pattern often goes unstated in studies that focus on vacation home owners as landlords whose roles are fixed in a static moment in time. Family vacation homes are the stable, homelike retreat from the adventures one may have on vacation, while also being an adventure themselves that is removed from the stability of a primary residence. A ski vacation at a destination that is new to a family can offer freedom and risk, but knowing that a return home will come after a temporary adventure is comforting. And if this vacation home is at the base of the ski hill, familiarity and adventure are conflated and the home becomes simultaneously part of the adventure and part of the stability. The family vacation home self is, then, an in-between identity in an in-between space.

Leisure has historically been defined as separate from, and subordinate to, the world of paid work; leisure is playful and labor is purposeful.[51] But since the late twentieth century, this distinction has begun to erode in advanced industrial societies, made particularly evident in the "interpenetration of work-leisure activities, especially among the professional and affluent middle class groups."[52] As technological innovation enables remote work in more and more labor sectors, the leisure-labor boundary gets blurrier and blurrier.

At the beginning of this chapter, I noted that the family vacation self is defined not only in terms of how we think others may see us, but also in terms of the roles we perform in the family vacation home. From chainsaws to clothing, the material dimensions of the family vacation home are meaningful locations for the sociological study of roles as well as serving as props and settings for the enactment of boundaries between people included and excluded in a family. The story of the material and social enactment of boundaries around family continues in chapter 3.

NOTES

1. Karen Stein, *Getting Away from It All: Vacations and Identity* (Philadelphia: Temple University Press, 2019).

2. Stein, *Getting Away from It All*, 10.

3. George Herbert Mead, *Mind, Self, and Society from the Standpoint of a Social Behaviorist* (Chicago: University of Chicago Press, 1967).

4. Charles H. Cooley, *Human Nature and the Social Order* (New York: Scribner's, 1902).

5. Christena E. Nippert-Eng, *Home and Work: Negotiating Boundaries through Everyday Life* (Chicago: University of Chicago Press, 1996).

6. Rowland Atkinson and Keith Jacobs, *House, Home and Society* (London: Red Grove Press, 2016).

7. Susie Scott, *Making Sense of Everyday Life* (Cambridge: Polity Press, 2009), 57.

8. Iris Marion Young, *Intersecting Voices: Dilemmas of Gender, Political Philosophy, and Policy* (Princeton, NJ: Princeton University Press, 1997).

9. Anthony Giddens, *Modernity and Self Identity: Self and Society in the Late Modern Age* (Cambridge: Polity Press, 1991).

10. James Tuedio, "Ambiguities in the Locus of Home: Exilic Life and the Space of Belonging," in *Homes in Transformation: Dwelling, Moving, Belonging*, ed. Hanna Johansson and Kirsi Saarikangas (Helsinki: Finnish Literature Society, 2009), 284–310.

11. Pierre Bourdieu, *The Field of Cultural Production* (Cambridge: Polity Press, 1993).

12. Max Weber, *Max Weber on the Methodology of the Social Sciences*, trans. Edward A. Shils and Henry A. Finch (Glencoe, IL: Free Press, 1949).

13. Stein, *Getting Away from It All*.

14. Bonnie Honig, "Difference, Dilemmas, and the Politics of Home," *Social Research* 61, no. 3 (1994): 584, https://www.jstor.org/stable/40971048.

15. Evita Robinson, "Increase Earnings through Inclusivity," Vrbo Virtual Partner Summit, https://host.expediagroup.com/vrbo/en-us/articles/vrbo-partner-summit/inclusivity.

16. Kelly Barton, "Leading the Way with Safety," Vrbo Virtual Partner Summit, https://host.expediagroup.com/vrbo/en-us/articles/vrbo-partner-summit/safety.

17. Sophie Donelson, "Designing for Families," Vrbo Virtual Partner Summit, https://host.expediagroup.com/vrbo/en-us/articles/vrbo-partner-summit/design-with -purpose.

18. Stein, *Getting Away from It All*, 97.

19. Rosemary Deem, "Women, the City and Holidays," *Leisure Studies* 15, no. 2 (1996): 105–19.

20. People ACCIONA, "Does Gender Inequality Persist Also in Our Leisure Time?" July 28, 2022, https://people.acciona.com/diversity-and-inclusion/gender -inequality-leisure/.

21. Claire Zillman, "Women Are Worse than Men at Using Their Vacation Time," *Fortune*, May 23, 2017, https://fortune.com/2017/05/23/vacation-time-women-take -less/.

22. Bruce Drake, "Another Gender Gap: Men Spend More Time in Leisure Activities," Pew Research Center, June 10, 2013, https://www.pewresearch.org/short-reads /2013/06/10/another-gender-gap-men-spend-more-time-in-leisure-activities/.

23. Stein, *Getting Away from It All*.

24. Davina Chaplin, "Back to the Cave or Playing Away? Gender Roles in Home-from-Home Environments," *Journal of Consumer Studies and Home Economics* 23, no. 3 (1999): 181–89, https://doi.org/10.1046/j.1365-2737.1999.00109.x.

25. Chaplin, "Back to the Cave or Playing Away?" 181.

26. Chaplin, "Back to the Cave or Playing Away?" 185.

27. Stein, *Getting Away from It All*.

28. Sara Clemence, "Black Travelers Say Home-Share Hosts Discriminate, and a New Airbnb Report Agrees," *New York Times*, December 13, 2022, https://www .nytimes.com/2022/12/13/travel/vacation-rentals-racism.html.

29. Robinson, "Increase Earnings through Inclusivity."

30. Robert R. Callis, "Rate of Homeownership Higher than before Pandemic in All Regions," US Census Bureau, July 25, 2023, https://www.census.gov/library/stories /2023/07/younger-householders-drove-rebound-in-homeownership.html.

31. Nippert-Eng, *Home and Work*.

32. Roberta A. Davilla Robbins and A. Frank Thompson, *Communicating Finances in the Family: Talking and Taking Action* (Solana Beach, CA: Cognella Academic Publishing, 2020).

33. Pierre Bourdieu, "The Forms of Capital," in *Handbook of Theory of Research for the Sociology of Education*, ed. John Richardson (Westport, CT: Greenwood, 1986), 46–58.

34. Michelle Janning et al., "Coming Home to College: Living Arrangements and Perceptions of Adulthood for U.S. College Students during COVID-19," *Cogent Social Sciences* 8, no. 1 (2021): 1–20, https://doi.org/10.1080/23311886.2022 .2045453.

35. Jessica Grose, "The Sandwich Generation Is Getting Squished," *New York Times*, November 2, 2022, https://www.nytimes.com/2022/11/02/opinion/sandwich -generation.html; Daniel de Visé, "What Is the 'Sandwich Generation'? Many Adults

Struggle with Caregiving, Bills and Work," *USA Today*, November 17, 2023, https: //www.usatoday.com/story/money/2023/11/17/sandwich-generation-helping-parents -children/71590330007/.

36. Stein, *Getting Away from It All*, 100.

37. Nippert-Eng, *Home and Work*.

38. Arlie Hochschild and Anne Machung, *The Second Shift: Working Families and the Revolution at Home* (New York: Penguin, 2012).

39. Arlie Hochschild, "Emotion Work, Feeling Rules, and Social Structure," *American Journal of Sociology* 85, no. 3 (1979): 551–75, https://www.jstor.org/stable /2778583.

40. Sarah Rudrum et al., "When Work Came Home: Formation of Feeling Rules in the Context of a Pandemic," *Emotion, Space, and Society* 42 (2022): 1–9, https://doi .org/10.1016/j.emospa.2021.100861.

41. Allison Pugh, *The Last Human Job: The Work of Connecting in a Disconnected World* (Princeton, NJ: Princeton University Press, 2024).

42. Arlie Hochschild, *The Commercialization of Intimate Life: Notes from Home and Work* (Berkeley: University of California Press, 2003).

43. Emma Goldberg, "Here's What We Do and Don't Know about the Effects of Remote Work," *New York Times*, October 10, 2023, https://www.nytimes.com/2023 /10/10/business/remote-work-effects.html.

44. Ben Wigert, Jim Harter, and Sangeeta Agrawal, "The Future of the Office Has Arrived: It's Hybrid," Gallup, October 9, 2023, https://www.gallup.com/workplace /511994/future-office-arrived-hybrid.aspx.

45. Vrbo, "According to Vrbo Data, Taking a 'Flexcation' Is the Latest Family Travel Trend," https://www.vrbo.com/vacation-ideas/explore-vrbo/travel-trends/ according-to-vrbo-data-taking-a-flexcation-is-the-latest-family-travel-trend.

46. Janning et al., "Coming Home to College."

47. Vivana Zelizer, *The Purchase of Intimacy* (Princeton, NJ: Princeton University Press, 2005).

48. Hochschild, *The Commercialization of Intimate Life*.

49. Cathy Stein Greenblat and John H. Gagnon, "Temporary Strangers: Travel and Tourism from a Sociological Perspective," *Sociological Perspectives* 26, no. 1 (1983): 89–110, https: //www.jstor.org/stable/1389161.

50. Stein, *Getting Away from It All*, 145.

51. Greenblat and Gagnon, "Temporary Strangers."

52. Greenblat and Gagnon, "Temporary Strangers," 94.

Chapter 3

Family and Nonfamily Boundaries

Inclusion and Exclusion via Hospitality and Decor

I asked Reede and Minnie, both now retired, whether they had ever thought about renting out their Wine Country home to others using vacation rental sites such as Airbnb or Vrbo. "No," Minnie replied quickly, then explained, "Well, once we fixed it all up and we had it the way we like it; I just don't want to rent it out to somebody we don't have a connection with somehow." They currently allow family members and friends of their kids to stay there for a small fee, making sure to lock the wine cellar during these stays.

Gloria, a single fifty-something woman, talked at length about the condo she shares with her mother and grandmother in Tropical Paradise. I asked her if the condo ever gets rented out to other families. Gloria responded, "My mom and grandma don't like to do that. They never do. They will loan it; they might loan it to somebody. . . . There are people who work for our family on our farms, and sometimes they've loaned the [property] to people who worked for us that they consider family."

"And not charged them rent or anything?" I asked.

"Not charged them rent or anything."

Ten years ago, I stayed in a family member's vacation home for free for a weekend getaway. I noticed a picture of my son displayed atop the bookshelves, along with photos of other kids in the extended family. During that visit, I learned that my relatives also rented out the place to "friends of friends" for a fee, though they never listed the property on a formal vacation rental platform. In fact, this was prohibited by their homeowners association (HOA). I also learned that my relatives did not take any photos down when they rented their home, meaning that "friends of friends" (which sometimes included strangers) were seeing our family photographs. Even though this didn't particularly bother me, the moment I noticed my child's picture in a space that may be used by people who were not family became the inspiration for this entire project. At this moment, I started to ponder how much privacy and personalization mattered in people's deliberations about who might stay in their vacation homes, and whether it made a difference if homeowners charged formal or informal fees to close or distant relatives.

Fast forward to winter 2023, when I had the privilege of writing a portion of this book over a weekend in a quaint vacation rental house in the southwestern United States. I talked with the host as I arrived, because I was having trouble with the door's passcode. It turned out that the battery in the keypad had worn out. After replacing it, she told me she had to scurry off to visit her mom in a nearby assisted living community. My own mom had just moved into a senior community a few weeks earlier, so we bonded over this experience and agreed that it is hard for those of us with work and family responsibilities to care for an aging parent. Knowing the high price tag of senior living expenses, I wondered if my host relied on financial support from her rental. I looked around the place, noticing that some of the artwork, inspired by the nearby desert landscape, had price tags. This particular rental was part of someone's home, albeit a separate wing that had been set aside for visitors. As she walked through doorway marked LAUNDRY and asked me to lock it behind her so that I could have privacy, I wondered whether the artwork was part of a business portfolio to help pay for her mom's expenses or if it was her way of supporting local artists. Either way, unlike my relatives' vacation home, this homeowner had no pictures of people in her place.

I learned a little about this vacation rental homeowner, including the parts of her life that involved family care work, because of the economic transaction of the rental space (and its troublesome keypad), even if I did not see any pictures of her mom or other family members. The people who stayed in my relatives' vacation spot could see pictures of my child but never interacted with him. I wondered whether either or both of these homeowners were strategically adding or removing decor objects to signify the spaces as usable for strangers. Did they view interactions with people renting their spaces for a fee differently than interactions with family visitors? In both cases, visitors could connect with owners, either via interaction with objects signifying the family that owns the home or with the family members themselves. But did the level of personalization affect that connection?

These two experiences a decade apart show the way a family vacation home is staged using material objects and the way a homeowner may relate to visitors based on personal connection, economic transaction, or both. Across the property groups I studied, decor (via material staging) and hospitality (via material transactions) are intertwined in complex ways, showing that family vacation homes are ideal places to witness the strategic and sometimes subtle enactment of the boundary between family and not-family.

In this chapter, I elaborate on the spatial and material elements—in the form of both physical objects and economic exchanges—that are associated with family vacation homes, with the goal of describing what it looks like (and what it means) when a family stages and prices their vacation home for personal use, rental, or both. I uncover how boundaries between family and not-family are revealed via homeowners' strategic use of material objects in the family vacation home "stage" and via their navigation of economic and social transactions for use of the stage itself. In doing so, I describe the use of imagined future kinship nostalgia across property groups to create future memories for people today, as well as the ways that privacy and the enactment of idealized family life serve to complicate rigid definitions of family while simultaneously reinforcing boundaries around family.

STAGING AND "FAMILY VACATION" DECOR: HOSPITALITY AND FAMILY MEMORY MAKING

The degree to which a space meant for family vacations is personalized depends on several factors: how closely connected visitors are with homeowners, whether the owners pay attention to personalization, what activities are desired in the space, and how much the homeowners use the space themselves. In this section, I discuss these factors, along with homeowners' understanding and use of hospitality and staging.

Hospitality is defined by Merriam-Webster in two ways, as either "hospitable treatment, reception, or disposition" or "the activity or business of providing services to guests in hotels, restaurants, bars, etc. usually used before another noun."[1] Both definitions apply to family vacation homes, whether owners rent them to others or not. How? First, one can be hospitable to one's own family members or guests in a primary residence, as the first definition suggests. And second, the words "activity" and "etc." in the second definition suggest that hospitality need not be part of a formal business or take place at a specific site. In the family vacation home context, hospitality can therefore take the form of a welcoming disposition or a set of actions meant to provide services commonly found in hospitality settings. It can also come in the form of vacation homes being rented to others via vacation rental platforms, which situates homeowners within the hospitality industry, even if they operate their businesses differently from hotel owners and managers. So hospitality, while commonly attached to the hospitality industry, can be attached to settings that are not always associated with that industry or that vary in terms of how formal they are and how much they are regulated.

Staging—or more specifically, the use of stages—is a topic that is not new to sociological inquiry, though stages usually refer to places where social roles are enacted. Erving Goffman's *dramaturgical* approach to understanding society[2] focuses not only on the shape-shifting roles that people play, but also on how setting or site may impact those roles (or people's capacity to imagine performing them). Our social lives, says Goffman, comprise *front and back stages*. On the front stage, we perform roles in front of an audience, at times putting on a face that may not reflect how we're feeling inside. Hospitality industry professionals, who are told to smile and make sure customers feel at home, play a front stage role, not unlike many in people-facing roles, as Arlie Hochschild's classic study of airline flight attendants' *emotion management* demonstrates.[3] After their shift welcoming guests, hospitality workers may retreat to a private back stage, such as a nearby office with a door or even their own home, to decompress and express the emotions they're really feeling. For anyone performing roles on these front and back stages, the former can feel performative and the latter more authentic. For people who rent their family vacation homes to others, the interactions they have with visitors are front stage performances—using welcoming language in written exchanges, smiling if they meet guests, and hiding negative emotions they may feel about the guests to ensure a good review. (Of course, people hosting family members in a vacation home may also perform these kinds of front stage versions of the self.) Importantly, the use of props via staging is part of their front stage work, creating a space designed to be welcoming, comfortable, and amenable to family memory-making activities. Materially staging the front stage of the vacation home is part of the front stage presentation of self for these homeowners, as is their emotion management when interacting with customers. For homeowners who do not rent their homes to others, there are not really customers, so the material and interactional delineation between front and back stages matters differently. But there indeed remain front and back stages in the staging process, a theme I return to later in this chapter.

In addition to being defined as the setting or location (or sometimes set design) for social interactions, staging is a practice explicitly connected to hospitality. Real estate professionals, including home staging companies, use staging to make a house look more attractive to potential buyers.[4] According to home stagers, without furniture, wall art, or other furnishings that evoke what everyday life could look like, interested buyers will be less able to imagine it as their own home. How would people know a space could be used as a media room without seeing a comfy couch and large TV in it? Importantly, staging must be generic enough to allow potential buyers to see themselves there, yet specific enough to suggest certain activities—hence, the hypothetical homeowner's family photos are removed from the media room, but the giant TV remains.

While my project is not about real estate transactions per se, home staging is something that may be used in a wide variety of hospitality-related economic transactions, including those related to renting out family vacation homes. When I attended a design conference for hospitality professionals in the hotel, spa, cruise ship, and restaurant industries, I noticed that a lot of the messaging along the aisles of furniture and design objects pointed to comfort, luxury, and family togetherness (and sometimes romance). If you want to make your guests enjoy their time in your vacation spot, you need to provide them with the comforts of home, but notched up to make it feel more luxurious, fun, or easy. And if you want to sell your products to people in hospitality industries, you need to display them in such a way that it's easy for people to imagine such products in their own spaces. But unlike a real estate agent staging a home so a family can imagine watching TV in a media room, hospitality professionals stage spaces so a family can imagine an experience removed from everyday life, especially the parts that involve work or family stress.

Guest Books and Hand-Me-Downs: Family Vacation Home Decor, Memory, and Imagined Future Kinship Nostalgia

Homes are symbolic objects, both signifying and shaping our conception of self. The roles that people play in family vacation homes are enacted in spaces using material props, such as the work nooks and clear instructions for the TV remote that were mentioned in chapter 2. This enactment carries with it *symbolic meaning*, as would be the case of displaying family photographs that convey the inclusion (or exclusion) of certain people in a definition of family. To be symbolic means to carry meaning that goes beyond a literal reading of an object or space. This meaning can also come from our relationships with objects, as anthropologist Daniel Miller has articulated,[5] whereby a home and its objects ebb and flow based on our interaction with and use of them. These interactions affect how we see ourselves and each other, and they even give homes and objects biographies. We have stories, but so does the hand-me-down couch at the cabin. As Karen Stein notes in her book about vacation identities, material objects such as clothing, furniture, and other possessions "influence the way people see us and the ways we are able to show ourselves to others. They mold the socially created self by offering both opportunities and limitations to the presentation of self."[6]

As political scientist Iris Marion Young posited, items found in a family vacation home, and the home itself, thus serve as the "materialization of identity"[7] and "material mirrors"[8] of who we are or want to be. Memory is particularly salient in the interplay between spatial/material elements of a family vacation home and conceptions of the self. Not only do we arrange things in our homes, we preserve them in order to give a stable and settled anchor for shifting versions of identity over time and across spaces. At times, we also use objects to signify these shifts. Put another way, homeowners signify and shape their identities via "creative acts of preservation"[9]—displayed family photos, memorabilia, souvenirs, and cherished pieces of well-worn furniture—that connect past to present and that serve to create imagined future visions of an idealized family life now. The objects in a family vacation home serve to bolster the creation of imagined future kinship nostalgia: creating family stories now that participants will look upon nostalgically in the future. This means the family vacation home is not just a place where a family vacation home self may be nurtured, it is where the definition of family itself is reinforced.

The symbolism of objects and spaces has been a part of sociological theorizing since the discipline's early years, including their significance in microsociological interactionist framings of social life[10] and in sociological frames that focus on macrosociological collective agreement about larger social and cultural values. With regard to the latter framing, the difference between *sacred* and *profane* has been discussed by early consensus framework theorists such as Émile Durkheim, who differentiated aspects of our social life that transcend everyday life and are made magical or special through symbolic actions (sacred) from those that are parts of our everyday lives, such as laborious family roles and work (profane).[11] For Durkheim, religion was a key social institution in which seemingly everyday objects and actions become defined as sacred through ritual and shared meaning. A wine chalice in a home is profane, but when it's imbued with religious meaning as a communion chalice in a Christian church, it becomes sacred. Even a faith-based space can be deconsecrated—made less sacred via ritual—as a church switches locations and its previous building is put to secular use. But sacred doesn't have to mean religious. It can refer to something that has been made magical or imbued with special significance and that is meant to be held separate from mundane things: so a family heirloom or sports trophy can be sacred, as can a flag or war memorial.

The use of certain types of objects to stage a family vacation home renders it a more sacred place, whether the home is rented to others or reserved for personal use. Setting the home apart from the mundane makes it enchanted, as Hochschild notes,[12] by artificially removing it from everyday burdens and the economic marketplace and turning it into a place where magic happens. This occurs via the use of memory objects, which are meant to inspire imagined future kinship nostalgia and often reinforce boundaries between family and not-family.

What does this look like? I begin with findings from the vacation rental conference I attended, where I observed that interior design is recommended to create good memories for guests. One strategy I witnessed was to ask us to close our eyes and think about home—whether a vacation home, childhood home, or a friend's home. The discussion turned to memories from home experiences: using a particular shampoo as a scent memory, hearing the pea gravel being crushed when someone arrived in the driveway as an auditory memory, imagining stroking the fur of a pet as a tactile memory. The theme across several sessions was that memory and sensory experiences were woven together, especially in terms of how a place makes us feel.

Even though many vendors at the conference were marketing new products such as noise monitors, security systems, and beds, antiques were highly valued. Vintage decor connotes priceless things—time and family bonding. More than once I overheard people advising, "If you're doing it right, never let the oldest thing in the room be you." Several sessions included tips that vacation homes, rented or not, have the potential to invoke memory by including old objects that people would otherwise not use or appreciate in their primary homes, including squeaky floors. In fact, unused, inherited items many people have in their storage closets are the same things that upscale designers may be incorporating into their chic designs. My takeaway was that even if I never liked my grandmother's china, I shouldn't throw it away. I should use it in a family vacation home. This message immediately called to mind the last vacation rental I stayed in, where I used a fancy goblet filled with water to take my daily medications. In these sessions focused on memory and decor, then, the message to homeowners was to "create moments" and that "every room needs a nod to the past."

After COVID-19 forced in-person conferences to be replaced by online webinars and virtual gatherings, the messages remained the same. The speaker in one Vrbo Virtual Partner Summit webinar in 2021 asked, "How do you take mundane moments and make them into sublimely happy moments for people?" The answer: include memory-making toys for families, so the children have something fun to do that could also serve as a way to reminisce about the trip, but also feature items that remind the adults of their own childhoods, like swings, hammocks, and firepits. I learned that adults who usually sleep with a partner sometimes enjoy sleeping in a twin bed while on vacation, something they'd never do at home but that reminds them of their childhood. Memory making equals money making.[13]

But even for those people who never rent their vacation homes out, childhood memories matter, as my interviews showed. Adrienne (Personal Property group), who vacationed at a cabin in Northwest Woods with her husband and daughter, reflected on how the property made her feel: "I felt, like, just like relaxed. Like, oh wow, here I am. This reminds me of my childhood. It's really a simple little place." Ren (Personal Property group), who spent most weekends with her husband Les camping across the western United States in their truck-top tent, made a clear connection between her current family vacation choices and her childhood: "It's a throwback. We grew up every weekend setting up a popup camper . . . so, to some inner part of me, it takes me back to my camping beginning." Memories about grown children's childhoods came up, too. Grace (Personal Property group), who has owned multiple houses in Western Mountain, reflected on memories of her now-grown children's past experiences: "That is the mountain that all of our kids know the most. That's where they learned to ski. So we have all of that history and memories. Then we had to work to create some new memories in this house."

It seems that time matters much in terms of how family vacation spaces end up mattering. Old objects, childhood memories for adult vacationers, and decor meant to inspire imagined future memories for the kids: all of these are powerful meaning-making tools made manifest in the objects populating a family vacation space. The next paragraphs detail how family vacation homes call to mind nostalgia, and how this nostalgia may or may not differ among those who use their properties for personal use or rent them out.

If nostalgia plays a role in creating the perfect family vacation home, this raises some questions. First, nostalgia about what, where, when, and whom? Second, does personal use versus use for financial gain impact the ways nostalgia is invoked? Surprisingly, I found that the strategies marketing experts at the vacation rental conference suggested to people renting their homes to others for vacations were also mentioned throughout this project by homeowners who reserved their vacation homes for their own families. Where these groups differed, however, was in how they used memory objects as a strategy for a good family vacation, with some employing them to tie their vacation to a place or locale and others using them for family personalization. In other words, while the invocation of memory objects was present, homeowners' intended outcomes varied.

Dianne (Mixed Property group) looks forward to the time when she can more frequently visit the condo she purchased in Tropical Paradise, a property she currently rents out using a local property management company and that she plans to move to full-time when she retires in a few years. As a person deeply invested in a socio-historical understanding of settler colonialism in amenity-rich locales and power differentials between wealthy landowners and local workers, Dianne reflected on how she sees the positive role of nostalgia attached to her property: "History and the present have such a great interaction with each other, so there is kind of a nostalgia. . . . Look at the artwork and see how the cultures were coming together. . . . I think as a person who is visiting, you sort of become part of that nostalgia. You can feel yourself being carried along in it."

For Dianne, the nostalgia is not about her own personal experiences or childhood memories of a family vacation. Rather, it is about the place itself, and the collective story that has emerged in the setting's history of cultures "coming together"—a phrase that demonstrates her framing of nostalgia as a positive collective outcome.

For other homeowners in the Investment and Mixed Property categories, the story of nostalgia was frequently a story about place and people outside their own family, even if the idea of family emerged in their description. People who rented out their spaces to others for family vacations sometimes invoked place history by telling a family story—not their own, but that of people who used to live there. Marion (Investment Property group), who rents out a cottage in her backyard in Wine Country and who worked with her then-husband on remodeling it for short-term rental use, detailed an encounter with a woman whose own family story played out there:

> So I look out the window, and there's . . . an elderly woman standing at the gate, and just kind of looking at the house, and so I went out and I said, "Can I help you?" And she said, "Yes, well, I just was admiring your house. I grew up in this home," and she said, "I drive by here every Memorial Day. . . . I come to take care of my parents' graves on Memorial Day weekend, and I always drive by this house." She said, "For years, I would drive by and each year it looked worse and more run down and more run down, and now every year I come and it has looked nicer and nicer." She was in her nineties, and I asked her if she would like to come in, and she came into the house, and I got a lot of stories about the house.

Marion then asked the visitor if a local plumber's story about the cottage being a summer kitchen where the family canned food to prevent heating up the main house was true. She noted,

> The woman said, "Oh, no, no, no. That was built for my grandmother to live in, and I have pictures of the grandmother standing on the porch of the house. It was built in the '30s, and they moved her into the back yard." . . . This woman's mother inherited $900 and bought that house, and then eventually built the cottage for her elderly mother to live in.

This conversation inspired Marion so much that she kept a book of the woman's story and accompanying pictures in the cottage for renters to peruse. For her, the nostalgia was about the site itself, and she knew renters would find this powerful family story and history captivating. She found it captivating, too, perhaps reminding her of her own real estate pathway. It was also a way to honor the significance of family stories more generally as symbolic markers of "home."

For people in the Personal Property group, nostalgia was also associated with the site's history, usually in the context of what made the property desirable for their family. These place-based histories included stories about the architectural history of the neighborhood, past news items about the community's social atmosphere, or environmental regulations that made certain outdoor activities more accessible. These site-specific histories revealed homeowners' personal aesthetic taste, community connections, and amenities.

Although Personal Property group homeowners raised memories about the community or location, their memory making and reminiscing were more often about the experiences their own family had had at their property: holiday dinners; kids and grandkids bringing friends to ski, hike, or hunt; and plenty of puzzles. Memory making was not reserved for the past, though. Strategies for creating future memories for guests to look back on fondly—that is, imagined future kinship nostalgia—were plentiful. Ole and Angela, a retired couple who spend weekends at their Northwest Woods home near a river, keep a logbook for visiting friends and family to note down their activities. They keep this diary to "think back to who was there and when" because, as Ole added, "you forget so much." Carla, whose reflections on building and keeping memories in her family's Northwest Woods home were included in chapter 1, embodied the goal of imagined future kinship nostalgia: create a family vacation home that not only preserves the past but also includes an explicit set of intentions meant to preserve the present, so that children can look fondly back at today from the future.

Who is the intended audience for imagined future kinship nostalgia? For the homeowners sharing ideas at the vacation rental conference, the audience for any given vacation home was clearly other people's families. This audience was abstract insofar as it constituted hypothetical future customers. For people who used their vacation homes for personal family use, the audience was simple: their own family.

Memory objects play a significant role in the creation and reinforcement of imagined future kinship nostalgia associated with a family vacation home. Recall the recommendation from the vacation rental conference to use antiques to give a place a sense of the past, and to give visitors a chance to create their own family memories in a special location to be remembered in the future. This practice was in place across property groups, with many of my interviewees using old furniture, quilts, dishes, and decorations to signify family vacation home spaces as special spots set apart from everyday primary residences. Even if the household items were hand-me-downs or from a thrift store, these objects not only called forth past stories, they were also meant to stage a place where new memories would be made.

Despite the vacation rental conference push for homeowners to invoke memory to make their guests feel at home, the people I interviewed in the Investment Property group did not necessarily do this. Or if they did, it was tied more to instrumental or economic goals than to expressive goals that evoked their own family memories. Dusty, for example, decorated his Western City vacation rental room with photos from his past travels, in part because he wanted them to be hung somewhere on his property, but primarily so that guests would be reminded of the pleasures of travel and remember his space with fondness. The decor choice, then, was ultimately about creating a vacation space that guests would be willing to pay for and within which they could experience site-based imagined future kinship nostalgia.

For homeowners in the Personal Property group, decor and household objects were referenced primarily as ways to connect to their own families, past or present. Willa's story about her Northwest Oceanside vacation home illustrates this well, including how her intentionally curated home decor objects represent or anthropomorphize certain family members:

> It has a lot of the family treasures in it, and family memories, and that sort of thing. There's just something about going back and seeing those old familiar things. We—both my sister and I—say walking into the cabin is like walking into a hug from mom. . . . My granny, who was my dad's mom, she had a covered dish that she used to put her cigarettes in. Well, we moved that into the bathroom and that holds the Q-tips. Every time we're in the bathroom, we use the Q-tips, there's Granny. My dad had a seaman's cap that he used to wear when he was at the beach, so it hangs over the threshold. My great-aunt had a bamboo shelf in her little house when we were little, and that's in the cabin.

Willa proceeded to talk about her mom's ashes, currently in an urn atop the bamboo shelf, and the arrangements she had made with her children to spread the ashes in the water near the vacation home after Willa died, because she didn't want "strange hands handling my mom."

Stories about objects inherited from parents or grandparents filled the conversations I had with people in the Personal Property group. Morgan talked about "the rocking chair that I nursed my children in" and puzzles from her childhood vacation home, both now located at her vacation home in Northwest Oceanside. Grace talked about two family heirloom tables now situated in her Western Mountain vacation home:

> I loved [my parents'] long wooden table in their kitchen dining area, and they had a round game table that I was obsessed by. I loved those two pieces because a lot of fun things happen around them and a lot of not so fun. A lot of this stuff has a lot of—there's been tears, laughter, all of it. A lot happens around those tables. I inherited those but I really loved those two parts of the house so much.

Sometimes, ancestral mementos were mixed with personal childhood objects now used only in the family vacation home. Peder, for instance, has his father-in-law's obituary mounted on a wall in his family's Eastern Oceanside vacation home:

> When he passed away, someone had sent us, it was like the obituary with a nice photo of him. It's not laminated per se, but it's, like, mounted on a mounted glossy copy of it on, like, a wood—it's not a frame per se, it's like a plaque. I don't remember who sent that to us. That's there. And also, we had an eightieth birthday party for him a couple of years before he passed, where we had a big framed picture and everybody signed it. That's hanging on the wall there too. . . . And my old stereo from when I was, like, thirteen years old is down there too.

At times, home decor objects imbued with ancestral connections made their way between primary residences and vacation homes. For Francis (Personal Property group), this came in the form of rustic wooden spoons and other old wooden tools that populate the walls of both her Great Lakes Waterfront vacation home and her primary residence a couple hours' drive away. I asked her to tell me about their significance, and she replied,

> I have a collection of darning needles or darning eggs, the old-fashioned wooden darning eggs. . . . When we moved in [to the vacation home], I went to some antique stores around and junk stores and whatever and I found a couple of these. I loved the shape of them and I bought them and then I hung them on the wall, and I thought, okay, maybe there will be others that I'll run across. So over a period of about five or six years I had maybe ten or twelve of them. It's so funny, because it's just an idiosyncrasy of mine that I like. I love the wooden spoons, which we got in the same way actually. . . . The other piece of the story is that my parents, my ancestors, come from a farm. . . . My parents inherited that farm and the farmhouse, and we spent a lot of time, my brother and sister and I, at that farm. So that is sort of influenced by that rural kind of sensibility, I guess.

Some homeowners in the Personal Property group used mementos of the recent past. Estelle, for instance, displayed a collection of photo albums depicting friends' visits over the years to her Western Desert vacation home. For the Personal Property group, then, decor was unsurprisingly less about being hospitable to others in instrumental ways and more about hospitality via staging a home so that today's family members could create memories while honoring family members of the past.

This contrasts with the goals of those in the Investment Property group, as evidenced by Carla's (Personal Property group) deliberation about the potential for her Northwest Woods vacation home to be used as a rental in the future:

We've talked about renting it out. Hunting season for a week, or snowmobiling, if people wanted to go up for a week or something like that. I'd have to [depersonalize it]. I'd have to pull all my clothes out. I'd have to pull my quilts out. We'd probably pull some of the mounts. We have some beautiful mounts up there that I just wouldn't want to have to worry about anything happening to.

Property groups differed in how they used home decor and household objects to create sacred family vacation spaces. For the Investment Property group, hospitality came in the form of decorations and furnishings that met the instrumental needs of guests, even as they may at one time have been personally meaningful. For the Personal Property group, hospitality was entirely focused inward on family activities and memory making, often via the use of ancestral objects that honored now-deceased family members. And for the Mixed Property group, hospitality shifted between using their own memory objects for their stays but hiding them away when guests rented their homes.

Despite these differences, all three groups shared a purpose: the material reinforcement of the boundary between family and not-family, between the idealized, sacred family vacation home and the everyday labor associated with paid work and family roles.

De- and Repersonalizing Stuff: Heating and Cooling Vacation Home Objects to Define Family Boundaries

People in the Investment and Mixed Property groups talked at length about the places they stored their personal items when paying guests stayed. I got to see many of these hidey holes as homeowners showed me around. Most often, this took the form of *owner's closets*: locked cupboards or rooms where owners kept meaningful objects as well as toiletries and clothing. If these owners ever stayed in their vacation rentals, they'd retrieve their things and repopulate their closets, cupboards, and tabletops, making their home more personalized. In this way, owner's closets served as a way to keep their personal stuff sacred. While they decorated their homes to create an enchanting family vacation setting for other people, this enchantment only went so far—just personalized enough, but not so personalized that strangers would break their cherished things. These homeowners deepened the enchantment for their personal use when they took their possessions out of hiding.

The movement of possessions that people use more or less frequently has been the subject of intriguing consumer studies research on how people place objects closer or farther away from their conception of self. Consumer studies scholars Amber Epp and Linda Price discuss the notion of *heating and cooling objects*, thus making them closer or more distant from the domain of the possessor's identity.[14] An object is heated if it is placed in a location that is accessible, meaningful, and findable to its owner—making it more connected to their identity. It is cooled if it is placed in a location that is harder to access, less meaningful, and at times hard to find. In general, closets serve to cool objects: they are hidden and less accessible behind a closed door. When people are not ready to get rid of an object—whether it's a childhood memento or a piece of furniture—they may cool the object in a less accessible place, like a basement or storage unit. This allows the owner to define the object as one degree removed from their sense of identity, from the domain of "me."

What happens when household objects and furniture in a primary home are moved into a family vacation home? This common practice occurred across all property groups, but how heated or cooled the objects became varied by group.

For the Investment Property group, cooled objects such as old couches, unused wall art, or hand-me-down dishes were likely to populate their vacation rental homes. Locked spaces were reserved primarily for housekeeping supplies and equipment or for business receipts associated with the property. Occasionally a homeowner in the Investment Property group would have an owner's closet filled with personal items, such as photo albums, clothing, and childhood mementos, but only if they had decisive plans to use the vacation home for personal use in the future.

For the Mixed Property group, the movement of personal items in and out of locked closets and cupboards served to heat and cool objects multiple times. Heated objects need to be protected so that they retain their usability and meaning. Rich talked about this process when he described his and Marcus's owner's closets in their Western Desert vacation home, which they rent out about half the time and use for themselves the other half, saying, "Some of the things that we have in our owner's closet that we bring out that are for us, they make this more home versus a rental home." I asked him to elaborate on the types of things he was talking about, including the holiday decorations he had set out for their winter use of the home:

> It's more like the things that make it easy for us to live here, like we have different bedding for us. And we have two owner's closets in the kitchen so that I bring out spices that I only put out for me. Because I like to cook and entertain. Cocktails or wine or spices, cooking things. Certain tools or implements for cooking. We realized that since it is a vacation rental, certain things we have to be okay with breaking. Or things not necessarily being the highest quality, but being nice enough. Because renters do stupid things.

While most of the objects that were moved from storage to visible display were portable (nobody talked about storing a couch or large table), the threat of damage motivated Mixed Property group homeowners to cool their objects when renting out their homes and "reheat" them when they stayed there themselves. Sometimes, these homeowners strategically moved something into the closet to protect it from damage. An owner's closet is like a box of old love letters hidden under a bed: it seems as if it is less meaningful because it is not as accessible as it would be if stored on a nightstand, but it is rendered more meaningful because it is protected.[15] Being physically hidden makes an object more precious, more sacred, more enchanted, because it's really being hidden from people who are not part of the family. And, interestingly, objects that are not hidden are cooled for the homeowner, yet warm enough to make the home meaningful enough for families renting it out.

For the Mixed Property group, the dilemma of how much to heat or cool an object was sometimes part of a deliberation about furnishing a vacation rental home with objects that they may not want in their primary home (thus cooling them) but that retained enough "heat" (or personal meaning) that they did not want to donate or throw them out. This is exemplified in Bella's purchase of her now-deceased mother's desk an auction—a desk that is in the vacation home she uses and rents to others in Eastern Oceanside. She talked about the furniture in the home as she walked around:

> My brother and I just went through my parents' house after they passed away, and what we found was really cute. And her desk is small, and I'm just like, I just wouldn't use it . . . I always need more space than that, so I'm, like, just let that go to auction. I'm at the auction, and somebody was talking to me on the steps. They're like, "Oh my gosh, that's probably where your mom got her degree, isn't it?" I'm like, "Yeah." . . . And then I'm like, "Oh my gosh, I need that desk." So, I'm at the auction, bidding on my mom's desk. It's my own auction, but someone is bidding against me, and finally someone was like it's her daughter. So I got her desk back.

Bella cooled the object by placing it in a vacation home that others would rent, but she heated it by retaining it, then placing it in the vacation home for her own use since it evoked memories of her mother. One desk can thus be rendered distant or close to its owner's conception of self, depending on who is using it and when.

For people in the Personal Property group, vacation homes simultaneously heated and cooled home objects and furniture. How? Many people placed furnishings from their primary residence in their vacation homes, such as old dining room sets, beds, and couches. This cooled the objects by removing them from their primary residence, while simultaneously heating them by placing them in a family vacation home, where they would continue to be used and inspire memories of their past and imagined future use. A family vacation home is not a storage unit. It is a place for possessions to be retained within the boundaries of a family. The space is decorated so it's familiar, with hand-me-down furniture, dishes, and decorations, but the fact that the decor originates from (and is only used by) the family itself makes it not just about family, but about "my family." That meaningfulness is what makes an old dining room table more heated than if it were stored away or used in a vacation home rented to others. Family vacation homes thus become repositories for objects that shift in definition of heated and cooled, closer and farther from the owner's conception of self.

The Uncanny Family on Vacation: Staging My Home for the _____ Family

I talked with a contractor in Northwest Oceanside who helps vacation home owners remodel their spaces to accommodate growing families, update decor preferences, and upgrade roofs or fences after storm damage. In our conversation about personalizing vacation homes for guests, she talked about how someone she knew loved staying in vacation rentals that were filled with the owner's things. It gave the place a sense of story and, she added, might even add to the "vacation-ness" of the visit, since other people's things can seem almost exotic. Although a lot of people who rented their spaces mentioned personalizing the decor a bit, this kind of story was unusual. More common for Investment and Mixed Property groups was depersonalizing things just enough so that other families could experience their own family vacation home selves.

To say something has an uncanny resemblance is to say it is eerily similar to the real thing, as if the genuine article has been replaced with a simulation. More than a century ago, Sigmund Freud wrote about the phenomenon of things looking sort of—but not quite—like the original. The German term he used was *Das Unheimliche*, which has as its root the word *Heim*, meaning home. Freud's term translates, interestingly, to "unhomely" or "unhomelike." For Freud, doppelgängers and other uncanny resemblances are "familiar and old-established in the mind" and yet are "alienated from it."[16] While Freud discussed this in terms of repressed childhood beliefs suddenly becoming real when uncanny things are witnessed, what's helpful to point out here is his use of homeliness (or homelikeness) as a way to signify familiarity. Something as familiar as a childhood memory from home can appear as an uncanny representation to an adult, as when a rocking horse in a vacation home reminds someone of the one they had as a child (but not quite). It calls to mind the actual childhood memory, but it's distorted. So how does the uncanny—or perhaps, more accurately, the "uncanny idealized family"—work in the context of family vacation homes? This ideal seems to be distorted differently for each property group, while simultaneously reinforcing the same broad cultural values about families in general.

For the Investment and Mixed Property groups, who have people rent their vacation homes, the home must be staged generically enough for anyone to picture themselves there, yet specifically enough to foster family connectedness and fun. At the vacation rental conference, several sessions conveyed the notion that staging a family vacation home is really about the performance of a way of living that would inspire any family to desire it for themselves. A vacation home can even be personalized for the owner without guests ever knowing about it. For example, if a homeowner has fond memories of a purple bathroom from childhood, they can paint a bathroom in their vacation home purple. To guests, it just looks like a purple bathroom. To the homeowner, its hidden message is that it's a childhood memory. Renting a vacation home to other families requires owners to keep their personal family story out of the decor, at least explicitly. At the same time, the property has to say, "This is a family place," or "This has an uncanny resemblance to your family memory-making place."

It may seem unsurprising that people renting their vacation homes or spaces to others strategically stage the spaces with "just enough" personalization to be personalized while symbolizing (rendering uncanny, perhaps) a generic family vacation setting. Real estate staging has similar goals: decorate a space so any family can picture themselves in it by removing personal family images while retaining items that suggest family activities or demarcate spaces as child friendly.[17] Importantly, this "just personalized enough" staging has been found by numerous researchers to reproduce class and race inequalities,[18] since images of families of color or items that connote lower socioeconomic class are shown to dissuade white, affluent potential home buyers and yield lower home appraisals.[19] A family vacation home that is rented to others should say, "This is a family space," but not "This is the _____ Family's space." But depersonalizing doesn't only erase specific family stories; by portraying a generic story, it can also subtly define that generic family on vacation as an intact, wealthy white family with children.

Despite not needing to stage their spaces for other families, people whose vacation homes are meant solely for personal use still follow market-driven cultural values that adhere to an ideal image of the "perfect family vacation" that any family would or should want. The decor is also specific and generic at the same time. While the deer head above the fireplace in Ole's Northwest Woods home came from his hunting expedition with family and friends, the item told a more generic story of hunting in a woodsy area. They hunted at their vacation home, not their primary residence, so the decor should reflect this, just as it would in any vacation setting where deer hunting was an expected or common activity. Similarly, while a generic family picture in a frame at a gift shop is not someone's actual family, someone who buys that frame may use it for a family photo featuring the same type of poses or outfits. This actual family photo may be specific to a household, but it is also generic if it adheres to cultural expectations about what a family photo is supposed to look like, from frame design or composition to aesthetic or size. It should say, "This has an uncanny resemblance to my family," as it could resemble *any* family.

Family stories are used for profit in the vacation rental business, as evidenced by the numerous conference sessions offering advice on how to market a rental home. Evoking hypothetical family stories in order to support the economic stability of family vacation home owners is an attempt at enchanting market transactions. It also serves to reinforce an idealized family, perhaps an uncanny one. The hypothetical family referenced in the vacation rental conference may as well be the stock-photo family from the frame you bought at the store: not real, but hearkening to a perceived reality that family life is enchanted and removed from depersonalized transactions. Likely the people in the stock photo are smiling, after all.

The uncanny family isn't just about making a space absent of specific family images and objects; it is also about making a space that has specific family images and objects that adhere to collective norms about what constitutes a family and what constitutes family vacation home decor. In either case, the objects are tools of hospitality that convey the message: Your brain is not playing tricks on you. You are indeed reminded of your own family vacation memories. This is the stage for happy family memory making. Here are the props you may need. And here are the people who get to be included.

FRIENDS AND FAMILY DISCOUNTS AND INVISIBLE MONEY: TRANSACTION FORMALITY AND NON- OR LOW-CASH CURRENCIES

Though it may seem obvious, when considering how "priceless" a property or experience may be, it is crucial to unpack what exactly constitutes a "price." Certainly, price comes in the form of dollars paid explicitly for the purchase or use of a property, but it can sometimes be a bit less straightforward. Anna (Investment Property group), for example, who rents out an apartment in a commercially zoned building in Wine Country, told a story about the stress of renting to family and friends for their vacations. Her husband's best friend's wife's parents were going to stay at the apartment, and she disagreed with his decision to split the cleaning fee with them. This meant, according to Anna, that not only were they going to lose out on upwards of $1,500 of rental income, they also were essentially "paying $75 for them to stay there." Anna equated the cost of family-of-friends staying rent-free with dollars lost—and the informality of this exchange made her uncomfortable.

Jean (Investment Property group) also talked about comfort related to pricing. She had allowed people to use their Wine Country cottage for short-term rentals a year before formally listing it on vacation rental sites. These guests were connected to a local nonprofit she supported. These visits were made less comfortable for her because they never negotiated a clear price for the stay. Now that Jean rents out the cottage formally on sites that list a clear price, she is more relaxed:

> It's a formal arrangement, but it doesn't feel more formal. In fact, it kind of—I think in some respects, because everything is laid out—the expectations are pretty clear. For the most part, you know what you're getting into. I think it actually lets people relax a little bit more. . . . Whereas the [guests connected to the non-profit] don't know what our expectations are, and I'm shy about telling them because it feels awkward.

So, while formality of pricing can come across as seemingly less personal, it also serves to lessen social awkwardness and botched expectations. Formal pricing can feel quite comfortable.

Is a bottle of wine a fee? People in the Personal Property group varied in terms of how explicitly they talked about prices associated with people using their homes. Some accepted gifts, such as wine, food, or household supplies. Others charged a cleaning fee to everyone, whether they were family or not. And some asked for payment in the form of labor, usually through cleaning surfaces, doing laundry, or ensuring electricity or the water heater were turned off. Nobody talked about people taking advantage of staying there for no or low fees or gifts, because to do so would lessen the focus on family and friend connections and would call too much attention to the stay as an economic exchange. In other words, it seems to be taboo to talk about charging family members or people who may be considered family to stay in a family home.

In chapter 2, I discussed how renting out a vacation home to other families is work, and—as part of a business—explicitly paid work. Just a few paragraphs ago, I shared Anna's story of her frustration with her husband allowing friends and family to stay for free and only pay half of the cleaning fee. But might financial exchange also be part of family vacation homes where only one's own family stays?

Hospitality can occur regardless of whether it has a price tag, as discussed at the beginning of this chapter. Certainly, paying for a hotel room or a restaurant meal makes sense, but offering money to an aunt for the use of her guest room or for a home-cooked dinner would be unusual. Or would it? What if your aunt sometimes rents out that room to strangers using online booking platforms and asks you to help her clean the room after your visit? What if you bring a gift to thank her for her hospitality? The exchange of money (or things that cost money, or things that are worth money, such as labor) when someone stays at another person's vacation home can occur in formal and informal ways.

The US government's formal classification of a property as a vacation home requires it to be rented to non–family members for fewer than fifteen days per year, even though the amount charged does not have a cap. There are formal taxation and labor rules for classifying a property for investment or personal use, but what people actually do makes these classifications fuzzy. How economic transactions occur in relation to the use of a family vacation home can also complicate people's sense of their roles and relationship boundaries. Nonmoney currency, in the form of gifts or labor in exchange for the use of a home, is not new, nor is paying to rent a room either short- or long-term. Fees, labor, or gifts can be used as compensation for homeowners renting a space. But these exchanges are not just reserved for people who formally rent their homes to others, and these forms of compensation vary along a spectrum from formal to informal exchange. This variation points to ways that the boundary between family and nonfamily (or, at times, between friends and customers) is reinforced across property groups, elaborated below.

Fees

Jean said that renting her Wine Country vacation home using formal booking platforms made her life easier, noting that informal fee negotiations had, in the past, made things confusing and awkward. Despite the fact that hosting vacationers was work for her, she found the formal fee structure to be "relaxing." She and others in the Investment Property group also noted that pricing the property high worked, since steeper fees suggest luxury and value. Many of the people in the Investment and Mixed Property groups talked about the need to charge a hefty cleaning fee, since strangers may not take care of the property the way homeowners would. Incidentally, it was in these moments that interviewees shared horrific stories of fecal messes and broken plumbing that required expensive cleanup measures. Even though price is not supposed to be discussed, it definitely came up when disaster struck.

Fees were not just reserved for Investment and Mixed Property homeowners, and not all fees in those two groups were formalized. In some cases, these homeowners rented their homes to regular or repeat customers outside of formal booking platforms and at a discount. Further, homeowners in the Personal Property group accepted money if it was offered, even if they did not explicitly charge fees. Maggie, for example, lets her family stay in her

Western Mountain vacation home for free, but occasionally charges friends a small fee.

Woody, who does not charge any fees to people in his social network to stay at his Northwest Oceanside home, argued that trust plays a big role in his decision to allow others to use the property for their vacations, even if he is not there. Woody is in the Personal Property group because he never formally charges people to stay, and he only allows people he knows to stay. He considers these people to be his family, even if they are not related, making them *fictive kin* or *chosen family*—people who are not legally recognized as family by the government but who are classified as kin, even if they do not have the same family-designated rights and responsibilities, such as inheritance. Woody said that there is more trust between homeowner and guest when no money is exchanged, noting, "If people are renting from you, they kind of believe that they own things a little bit, and when they know they're there truly as your guest, they want to come back as your guest; they know they do things right." For Woody, charging a fee would violate his assumptions about trust and friendship. For people across all three groups, the formal request for fees reinforced the boundary between family (don't have to pay) and not-family (have to pay).

Upkeep of the property was connected to fees and expenses for every homeowner. It was also connected to money when these expenses were substantial enough to warrant tax deductions (for example, with a kitchen remodel). Every homeowner talked about expenses related to the property's maintenance, from mousetraps to replacement appliances. For the Personal Property group, upkeep was needed to keep a home looking nice for personal use or for its eventual sale. For homeowners in the Mixed Property group and those in the Investment Property group who planned to eventually retire in their vacation home, renting it to others with an accompanying cleaning ritual meant the property would be well-maintained in their absence. Lincoln and Hana, for example, noted that they'd love to reserve their Great Lakes Waterfront house for their personal use all the time, but financially it works better to rent it out. This also helps with upkeep: "We also want to make sure it's a place that we want to go to, and we feel good about walking into it and it's enjoyable for us."

In addition to property upkeep, fees can be related to marketing; in an economic transaction, buyers want to understand what they're getting for their money. It seems bizarre to suggest that people should market their vacation homes to their own family, but those who wish their family would make better or more frequent use of an empty vacation home have certainly felt the need to do some convincing. While this desire to have others use a home is not about profit, it may be framed in people's minds as getting a better return on investment. Why buy or keep a vacation home if nobody uses it? Numerous

Personal Property group homeowners said they wished they or their family members would use them more. Francis, for example, lamented the decreased use of her Great Lakes Waterfront home because of her husband's declining health. Similarly, Valencia talked about her daughter's busy high school schedule as a barrier to her and her husband using their Eastern Woods home, adding that they would do so more when their daughter starts college.

Formal marketing was reserved for those seeking rental income from their properties. Unsurprisingly, these homeowners demonstrated a keener understanding of the family vacation marketplace. Several people I interviewed in the Investment and Mixed Property groups had actually spent time working in the hospitality or real estate industry and made comments that showed they paid attention to market research and larger vacationing and property trends. Many of these homeowners explicitly named their homes as businesses. Several in the Investment Property group strategically priced their rentals to align with the market—Olivia, for example, said, "I feel like the more it costs, the more people want to stay" in her Wine Country home, while Auggie experimented with price only to discover that "jacking up" the price yielded faster bookings for his Eastern Oceanside rental. Attendees at the vacation rental conference found themselves inundated with vendors explicitly talking about pricing for noise monitors and security cameras and implicitly talking about the "price of neighborliness" required to ensure a successful short-term rental business.

Pricing also related to ratings for the Investment Property group. "You live and die by these ratings," Rita noted about her short-term rental business, which consisted of a second bedroom in her house in Western City. A lot of the vacation rental conference's sessions were really about marketing and ratings: how to create "total Instagram moments," "find the right match," or use the "priceless goldmine" of user data to target new potential renters. Ultimately, these marketing tips were presented as a pathway to get good ratings and stand out in a sea of similar products.

Most of these messages didn't connect marketing to a homeowner's own family, but sometimes these lines were blurred. For example, according to James Boykin's guidebook *Investing in a Vacation Home for Pleasure and Profit*,[20] the best thing homeowners can do to know if their homes will serve as a retreat from the mundanity of everyday life is to stay there themselves. And as I learned from some Investment Property group interviewees and in one conference session, having friends or family stay, provide feedback on what needs to be improved, and write a five-star review is a good idea, too. People who rent out their homes to other families strive to have their guests leave rave reviews and make comments such as "I want to live in a house like this," but making this market- and fee-driven goal a reality often requires involving friends and family.

Labor

In chapter 2, I discussed how the boundary between labor and leisure was presented as porous for many homeowners regardless of property group, and as clear at times when labor seemed to get in the way of leisure or when renting a family vacation home to others was needed for financial stability. From cooking and washing dishes to laundry and tidying up, the use of a family vacation home requires labor, regardless of who is using it. Across all three property groups, many homeowners noted that they provide a list of arrival and departure tasks for those staying there, especially if the homeowners are not staying with them. This labor—a form of noncash currency—was expected in addition to a fee for Investment and Mixed Property homeowners and in place of a fee for many in the Personal Property group. And it was noted clearly, thus serving as symbolic recognition that leisure requires labor. However, for those in the Personal Property group who stayed in their own vacation homes with their family, their (and their family members') labor associated with cleaning up was sometimes reclassified as leisure, as in the case of Ole's tree clearing chores described in chapter 2. And it was unlikely to be written down. The boundary between family and not-family was reinforced in labor exchanges, since those in a family were less expected to perform the labor explicitly as labor.

Gifts

Gift giving can symbolically signal appreciation for something that seems, in the eyes of the gift giver, to need to be acknowledged. But is it the same as a monetary exchange? Gifts can symbolize honor, intimacy, and acceptance of a social bond, as Marcel Mauss hypothesized in his essay *The Gift*.[21] Mauss acknowledged that the received wisdom at the time writing (in 1925) suggested that gifts looked a lot like utilitarian economic transactions, yet are supposed to be motivated by goodness. Gifts are supposed to be about care, not market exchange. Citing numerous examples from cultures around the world, Mauss corrected this by noting that trades involving economic currencies are actually about maintaining tradition, strengthening friendships, solidifying alliances, and open-ended ways to make personal connections. In fact, Mauss argued, emotional connection and self-interest were quite compatible. This essay from a hundred years ago dispels the belief in the bifurcation of formal economic transactions and informal gift exchanges with empirical examples that show that economic transactions can be quite personal, while informal exchanges can actually be about money. Yet the belief that gifts do not signify economic exchange persists in the gift exchanges that accompany family vacation home use.[22] Personal relationships are not supposed to be thought of as transactions, so giving a gift for a stay in a family vacation home is less about naming it as an economic transaction and more about naming it as a symbol of personal affection and gratitude. Or, in the rare case that guests give gifts to a vacation rental owner, the monetary transaction is separate from this above-and-beyond gesture. In other words, the notion that the transaction has anything to do with money is hidden. This exchange, while removed from the formal marketplace, can nonetheless signal that whatever is received could be exchanged if the transaction were more formal.

Nobody in any property group said they required people who stayed with them to bring gifts, but of course gifts were often part of a noncurrency exchange for use of a family vacation home that did not come with a fee. It was unusual for Investment and Mixed Property group homeowners to share stories of gifts that guests had given them, although they did talk about items left behind that they got to keep. It was in the Personal Property group where gift giving was most discussed, but the gift givers were usually people in homeowners' personal networks who had stayed for free. Nobody shared a story about refusing a gift. Gift giving as a noncash currency form of exchange was primarily reserved for family and close friends, and often because no fees were charged. In this way, the boundary between family (and sometimes friends) and strangers was reinforced, as was the artificial boundary between formal monetary exchange and informal gift exchange.

ADJUSTING HOSPITALITY: PRIVACY AND FAMILY BOUNDARIES

In his book *Investing in a Vacation Home for Pleasure and Profit*, Boykin suggests that people who opt to rent out their vacation homes to others should leave a one-page note (in an upright picture frame) with a narrative wishing them a pleasant visit and an invitation for them to return, to "[c]reate a friendly and welcome atmosphere for the renters and make them aware that they are your family's guests."[23] This, of course, humanizes the connection between owner and renter, because the space is defined as a family space either way. But it also differentiates the roles of host and guest and sets the expectation that guests are entering a private space that has been depersonalized into a public one, or perhaps more accurately, a space that is serially private—made for lots of families, but one at a time. This section describes ways that property group shaped spatial, social, and material boundaries between family and not-family.

Balancing Privacy and Disclosure: Spatial, Social, and Material Strategies for Relationship Boundaries

How do family vacation home owners navigate privacy boundaries? Rita (Investment Property group), who loves meeting new people and puts a lot of effort into offering a personalized visit to guests who rent a space in her Western City home, articulated the significance of privacy:

> I just think it's already weird enough to be in some random stranger's home. You don't want to be surrounded by all their stuff that reminds you that you are naked in a weird person's home. . . . When I first started hosting, I used to leave my bedroom door open at night so the cat could go in and out, and that meant the guests could see into my bedroom. . . . I didn't leave it all the way open. I left it a crack open and I was like, I don't like having my bedroom door open at night. It's weird, and so I installed a cat door on my bedroom door.

For Rita, the boundary between "home" and "not-home" was made apparent when it was visually traversed by guests: she didn't want visitors to be able to see into her bedroom, so she placed a boundary that rendered her private space "off-limits." Having strangers stay in a home is itself a boundary traversal.

Rita continued talking about relationship boundaries with guests:

> I like meeting new people, and most of my guests are pretty reasonable, interesting people, so it's very infrequently I am like, oh, I wish these guys would just leave. If you were to encounter one of these people that you host on the street somewhere, you wouldn't be chatty or friendly or ask about their family or what brings them to the area. You might just glance at them, give them kind of a polite smile, and continue on your way, but the rules for interacting with strangers completely change when they cross your threshold, not only because, number one, they are in your home, but number two, you essentially sold them a service and a promise of a certain experience. So there is this weird sort of, like, they are paying me, but they are also living in my home. It's my home; it's not just a hotel. And so there's just some sort of, like, weird and sort of semiuncomfortable boundaries there.

Hidden spaces and personal items in Investment and Mixed Property group homeowners' closets and bedrooms demonstrates the importance of keeping some parts of the home private from renters. But privacy also matters for people in the Personal Property group. For example, Rhonda shared a story about a small party they hosted at their Northern Lake Country home that reminded her that privacy matters even for people who don't rent their home to others: "We discovered that the bathroom walls aren't very soundproof. Everybody just kind of awkwardly talked, tried to talk a little bit louder so we didn't hear what was going on in the bathroom." Having strangers in her vacation home meant private acts needed to remain private, so everyone did their best to reinforce this norm. All these stories suggest that non–family members in a vacation home require the placement of boundaries around private acts, spaces, and objects.

Privacy boundaries also occurred in the form of relationship closeness navigation and role disclosure tactics. These are cases when the Investment and Mixed Property group homeowners' back stage role is hidden—and thus kept private—from guests. At the vacation rental conference, one session focused on the recommendation that hosts should offer moments of "temporary closeness" to paying guests, getting to know them just enough to personalize the experience (a strategy many Investment and Mixed Property group homeowners mentioned), but not too much: they should take care of the home-related issues, but call a tow truck if a guest gets stuck in a snowdrift, rather than personally shoveling them out. Or use one homeowner's strategy for role boundaries: telling guests he's the maintenance guy if he visits the home to repair something while it's occupied. Another speaker advised putting in a lot of effort to personalize the relationship with a guest and then explicitly asking them for a five-star review in exchange for this personalized experience. Any closeness that may be part of the host-guest relationship is ultimately an exchange in the marketplace.

For people who rented their homes to other families, the staging and use of memory objects demonstrated a shift in meaning related to their personal items, which went from private to public use. At one moment during Jean's interview, for example, I thought she was going to get sentimental about her children's portable crib being used in her rental. But she noted that she brought it out of storage only to meet the needs of guests who had a baby. In this sense, even though she smiled when she talked about her now-adult children's younger days, her nostalgia about the object was substituted by an instrumental concern that guests have a worry-free stay. In other words, her personal (private) nostalgia was replaced by a desire to provide imagined future kinship nostalgia for others in material form.

Household objects can also define the boundaries between public spaces (for guests) and private spaces (for homeowners). Dusty (Investment Property group) talked about how his wife is more uncomfortable than he is when guests hang out in spaces outside the room they rent in their Western City home—a room decorated with personal travel photos: "I think it was just her tolerance for having strangers in our house. I think we just have different tolerance thresholds for that. I think she likes to leave stuff out more than I do." Dusty added that his wife struggled with having guests in certain parts of the home because it meant she had to depersonalize those parts. Her unease points to the fact that objects that are personal for homeowners are not really part of the experience for paying guests, but at the same time, memory objects that offer guests imagined future kinship nostalgia have been depersonalized by the owners, as in the case of Dusty's travel snaps. Red (Investment Property group), as another example, had a decorative curtain on a tension rod that he would place in the entry to his private living quarters in his Eastern Woods home, but only when he hosted guests who bothered him or gave him a sense that he didn't want to get to know them. His private memory objects were behind that curtain. So while his job was to provide a space for others to create vacation memories, he designed the space such that only people he liked were privy to his memory objects as part of their vacation experience. When guests would enter spaces where Dusty's or Red's personal stuff resided, thus potentially traversing a privacy boundary, it became clear that the boundaries between personal and guest stuff mattered. In addition to material objects and decor reinforcing the sacredness and enchantment of the family vacation home through imagined future kinship nostalgia, they also reinforce the boundaries between family and not-family. Storing, using for instrumental purposes, and strategic hiding became the actions associated with personal possessions for the Investment Property group.

For people in the Mixed Property group, the use of objects and household decor had multiple and sometimes conflicting purposes, at times situating the objects in flux between cooled and heated, between stored and displayed, between public and private. For this group, objects and spaces that were maintenance projects served as material reminders that made it hard to feel like they were on vacation. Their vacation homes were simultaneously sacred and profane spaces—reserved for their occasional family vacation and for vacation renters, but also sites for their own work. This group was also most likely to mention the need to put personal memory objects away to protect them from getting damaged or taken by guests. Bella, who depersonalizes her vacation home in Eastern Oceanside each time she rents it out, noted, "People steal stuff. I put some rocks that I had gotten in Haiti, someone had carved them into a shape of a heart. And then I just put this little box out with some sand in it, and I put the two little hearts in the sand, so cute. They're gone."

And sometimes it was simply about the desire not to share personal items that could be rented nearby with strangers, as Margot noted about her Tropical Paradise vacation home that she sometimes rents to others: "We lock up some stuff that we don't want to share, like our scuba gear and golf clubs. I lock up my personal clothing."

Confusion over Closeness: Return Visitors

At the vacation rental conference I attended, I perked up when I heard one of the speakers articulate that the reason people wanted to rent their vacation homes to others was because "you enjoy the families that come to stay in your properties." At the hospitality conference, one session focused on the theme of empathizing with visitors, suggesting that hosts and guests should find ways to see themselves in each other. But what does it look like to empathize and "enjoy the families"? How close should people get to their visitors? For many people I interviewed who rent their homes to others, the visitors who returned year after year provided some interesting stories about the boundary between family and not-family, or at least between close personal connections and distant ones.

Lincoln and Hana (Mixed Property group) rent their Great Lakes Waterfront vacation home to other families about half the year and spend the other half there with their two young kids. They told me a story about a family that had rented their home four or five times, and whom they had begun to think of as friends. But a recent incident changed how they viewed these guests. Lincoln and Hana happened to be visiting the community where their vacation home was during their guests' stay. They drove by the property to say hi to the return guests and noticed that their golf cart was on the lawn. They had a rule against guests using the golf cart, so they were immediately upset and disappointed, and sent their guests a message.

Hana established how she viewed the relationship after the incident, oscillating between feeling close to them yet defining the relationship as distant:

> You kind of think you have a relationship with these people on some level, but we have no idea who these people are. Not a relationship, but you know, they come back, so you feel like you've built up this kind of mutual trust, and so this was so disappointing. It'd be like one of your children underage drinking and you're catching them, right? It's like they've done something naughty and we're disappointed.

Lincoln chimed in, "We're not going to rent to them again."

Hana added, "On some level, I hope they never respond, because any response they give will be unsatisfactory."

They continued with a discussion of how they were grateful to be able to afford this property, but wished they didn't need the rental income so they could just allow friends to use the place. I asked if they thought the golf cart incident would look different if it were one of their friends who was caught violating the rule. Hana said it'd be easier. Lincoln said that they would "totally call them out. We would not have any problem calling out our friends."

This Great Lakes Waterfront story is juxtaposed with a story I heard from Sunny (Investment Property group), who rents out part of her multiplex at Northwest Oceanside. Sunny also has return visitors, including a family who came each year for a decade. She had grown close to this family, as she had with many families over her lifetime. She knew that the daughter in this particular family, who had stayed between the ages of three and thirteen, loved the bedspread in the rental unit. Sunny elaborated: "When I changed the bedding in the room that she slept in, I had heard from her dad that she adored this particular quilt. So I wrapped it up and mailed it to her. Her mother told me that it's still on her bed."

Sunny also mentioned times when she lamented not knowing guests well: "Sometimes, people leave me a note and say, this is my fifth year here, and I think, 'Oh shit, I don't even know them.' So I like to send them a note. But the notes always have to be sent through the vacation rental company, because they don't want hosts to know guests' home addresses, so they can preserve the client list for the company."

The border between friends or family and clients was also blurred for homeowners who asked friends and family to help them with trial rentals in the early stages of their businesses, or who asked friends to stay and leave good ratings online. For people who never rented their properties to families they didn't know, there were still blurry moments. Valencia, for instance, allowed a family member who had trouble holding down a job to stay in her vacation home for free for several weeks.

Importantly, Sunny's guests, as well as Lincoln and Hana's, were not technically family members, but elements of their relationship connoted a closeness that is sometimes associated with fictive kin. At the very least, these guests were distinct from guests whom the homeowners never met, who stayed only once, or who did not receive gifts such as a beloved bedspread.

CONCLUSION

To what degree are family vacation homes about defining who counts as a family member? A lot, it turns out—but in somewhat surprising ways. Homeowners strategically stage a home using objects that signify family vacation activities (or family connectedness more generally). They also frame transactions to either downplay the fact that they're financial or argue that formal transactions feel more "relaxing." And the importance of privacy becomes central to any definition of who counts as a family member and who does not, regardless of whether a family vacation home is rented out or not.

The findings in this chapter reveal three ways in which the family vacation home is strategically framed as enchanted by homeowners in terms of family and nonfamily boundaries: through staging and family vacation decor, through friends and family discounts and invisible money, and through privacy and family boundaries. Below I summarize these findings and how they connect to the overarching goal of enchanting the family vacation home.

Staging and Family Vacation Decor

Staging the family vacation home to create imagined future kinship nostalgia spanned all property groups. All three types of homeowners heated and cooled their family vacation home objects, making some of them more accessible and likely to help create their family vacation home selves, and others less accessible and hidden when others used or visited the home. But the groups varied, too. For the Investment Property group, hiding personal items and turning old objects into amenities for guests was common. They worked to create imagined future kinship nostalgia for other families using decor items and hospitality exchanges. They created sacred spaces for guests while performing the profane work of setting the market-driven, generic family vacation home stage. Often, the nostalgic images were about the home or neighborhood rather than the specific family who owned the home. For the Personal Property group, the memories created to evoke imagined future kinship nostalgia were about their family specifically, even if they were interwoven with historical nods to the site. Pictures and precious heirlooms—even if slightly worn out and not suitable for use in a primary residence—connoted sentimentality, emotional connection, and distance from the marketplace, even if they aligned with market-driven cultural patterns that can seem unoriginal. The Mixed Property group moved objects into hiding to preserve them for their own imagined future kinship nostalgia, with just enough personalization in the remaining decor for guests to do the same during a temporary visit.

The family vacation home contains objects and spaces meant to encourage the enactment of activities that will be viewed in the future as priceless family memories. While the family in question may change, the goal of setting a stage to foster imagined future kinship nostalgia for an idealized—perhaps uncanny—version of family is an aim regardless of whether homeowners use the space themselves or rent it to others.

Friends and Family Discounts and Invisible Money

Formal fees were more common for the Investment Property group, represented by their use of online booking platforms, reliance on ratings, and dedication to marketing. At times, this group framed the formal exchange as relaxing, free from unclear negotiating, and less awkward when interacting socially with guests. They also formed relationships with return guests, sometimes seeing them as part of their chosen family. The Personal Property group accepted gifts and sometimes required labor in the form of cleanup duties. They charged informal fees at times, differentiating between family and friends, and refused to accept fees at other times, noting that trust is greater when people don't feel as if they "own" the space they're using. The Mixed Property group erred on the side of formal economic exchange when others rented their spaces. But they, too, wrestled with defining return guests as relationally close, at least until the guests screw up and end up repositioning themselves as paying clients.

The Investment and Mixed Property groups, while more inclined to see their homes as explicit players in an economic exchange, were also likely to enchant the home by framing formal exchange as more personally gratifying, and sometimes by defining return visitors as part of their family. The Personal Property group enchanted the family vacation home more often than not by defining any kind of exchange for the home's use as informal, relational, or outside of any kind of fee structure.

Privacy and Family Boundaries

Privacy and the reinforcement of the boundary between family and not-family mattered across all property groups. For the Investment Property group, separating their personal property and spaces served to define their guests as not-family while fostering family connectedness in their space. For the Mixed Property group, objects and spaces were strategically used to hide private things when guests stayed but make them visible when they used their homes for themselves. The Personal Property group, while not renting out the home to strangers, still created boundaries between private family spaces and more public spaces where guests visited. The thin bathroom walls were more manageable to deal with when just family members stayed in the vacation home.

All these stories suggest that non–family members in a vacation home require the placement of boundaries around private acts, spaces, and objects. Keeping distance from strangers, whether those renting a vacation home or visiting one while the owners are there, reinforces the boundary between family and not-family. This enchants the family vacation home, creating a place of emotional connection and private family moments for people who are related to each other.

* * *

My relatives' vacation home—the one where my child's picture is displayed on the bookshelves—no longer gets rented to "friends of friends." But it does get used by extended family, including a one-year stint as a remote workplace for a family member whose office was shut down during COVID-19. Nobody pays a fee to use the space for a vacation anymore. It is decidedly for family only, a place where only family members can access photos of my son.

As I was writing this book, several Vrbo ads came across my Facebook feed with this description: "A place for your together awaits! Explore whole vacation homes that are made for you and whoever you call family."[24] The message is clear: Sharing vacation spaces with strangers is not part of the presumed plan.

That this ad includes no explicit definition of who counts as "whoever you call family" is not surprising, given the increasing diversity of family forms in the United States, greater prominence of the notion of fictive kin or chosen family, and the fact that people vacation with non–family members, especially in the era of COVID-19 "bubbles." Ads are designed to boost revenue, so they must appeal to people who can map their definition of family onto the stories presented and avoid alienating anyone who feels that their version of family is excluded. The word family, though, is explicit. This vacation rental listing reminded me of a 2022 Vrbo television ad I saw with the tagline "Only Your People," in which images of families are present. The voiceover says, "No stranger at the dinner table making things awkward, or in another room taking up space. It's just you and your people. Because why would you ever share your vacation home with someone you wouldn't share your vacation with?" Commentary from Hector Muelas, senior vice president of global creative at Expedia Group (Vrbo's parent company), confirmed that this ad was about families: "Our latest creative work illuminates the reason why families choose whole homes on Vrbo."[25] The relationships in the 2022 ad depicted are private and loving, the opposite of "awkward" interactions with outsiders—in short, they read as "family." And the ad I saw more recently explicitly used that word.

The definition of family, and who counts as such, is socially constructed. What counts as family has changed over time and varies from place to place and culture to culture. Despite cultural changes that signify more diversity in family forms and greater acceptance thereof, there is a quiet stability regarding family: a hearkening to a particular version of family that is subtly present even among those eager to recognize diverse family forms, even in the midst of shifting social and cultural patterns, and even given the very real connection between families and "strangers." Family remains an institution that has the power to exclude outsiders and reframe or exclude market forces that connote an impersonal set of transactions. This belief—that there is such a thing as "your people"—seems to reinforce the notion that there are insiders and outsiders in our lives, and that we get to define the boundary between them.

In short, there is more and more variation in how we determine who counts as family, but people continue to identify and set boundaries—even blurry, artificially constructed ones—delineating family from not-family. No matter how or why people set these boundaries, the fact that we set them remains a strong cultural pattern, and family vacation homes are vibrant sites to see how these family boundaries come to be made, reinforced, or challenged, and how the enchantment of family as artificially removed from the marketplace comes to be.

One thing that complicates these boundaries are sites beyond the marketplace, such as the neighborhoods and communities that connect family vacation home owners to the rest of the world. The story of how family vacation homes connect properties to communities continues in chapter 4.

NOTES

1. "Hospitality," Merriam-Webster, https://www.merriam-webster.com/dictionary/hospitality (accessed January 20, 2024).

2. Erving Goffman, *The Presentation of Self in Everyday Life* (Scotland: Doubleday, 1959).

3. Arlie Hochschild, *The Managed Heart: Commercialization of Human Feeling*, updated with a new preface (Berkeley: University of California Press, 2012).

4. Kelcie L. Vercel, "Feels Like Home: How Home Stagers Construct Spatial Rhetorics to Persuade Homebuyers," *Consumption Markets and Culture* 24, no. 6 (2021): 545–74, https://doi.org/10.1080/10253866.2021.1891894.

5. Daniel Miller, *The Comfort of Things* (Cambridge: Polity Press, 2008).

6. Karen Stein, *Getting Away from It All: Vacations and Identity* (Philadelphia: Temple University Press, 2019), 107.

7. Iris Marion Young, *Intersecting Voices: Dilemmas of Gender, Political Philosophy, and Policy* (Princeton, NJ: Princeton University Press, 1997), 149.

8. Young, *Intersecting Voices*, 161.

9. James Tuedio, "Ambiguities in the Locus of Home: Exilic Life and the Space of Belonging," in *Homes in Transformation: Dwelling, Moving, Belonging*, ed. Hanna Johansson and Kirsi Saarikangas (Helsinki: Finnish Literature Society, 2009), 294.

10. Herbert Blumer, *Symbolic Interactionism: Perspective and Method* (Berkeley: University of California Press, 1969).

11. Émile Durkheim, *The Elementary Forms of Religious Life*, trans. Carol Cosman (Oxford: Oxford World Classics, 2008).

12. Arlic Hochschild, *The Commercialization of Intimate Life: Notes from Home and Work* (Berkeley: University of California Press, 2003).

13. Sophie Donelson, "Designing for Families," Vrbo Virtual Partner Summit, https: //host.expediagroup.com/vrbo/en-us/articles/vrbo-partner-summit/design-with-purpose.

14. Amber M. Epp and Linda L. Price, "The Storied Life of Singularized Objects: Forces of Agency and Network Transformation," *Journal of Consumer Research* 36, no. 5, (2010), 820–37, https://doi.org/10.1086/603547.

15. Michelle Y. Janning, *Love Letters: Saving Romance in the Digital Age* (New York: Routledge, 2018).

16. Sigmund Freud, "The Uncanny," in *The Complete Psychological Works*, vol. 27 (London: Hogarth Press, 1955), 241.

17. Ashley Pasquale, "Home Staging Techniques to Appeal to Families," Seattle Staged to Sell, September 15, 2021, https://www.seattlestagedtosell.com/home -staging-techniques-to-appeal-to-families/.

18. Elizabeth Korver-Glenn, "Compounding Inequalities: How Racial Stereo-types and Discrimination Accumulate across the Stages of Housing Exchange," *American Sociological Review* 83, no. 4 (2018): 627–56, https://doi.org/10.1177 /00031224187817.

19. Debra Kamin, "Home Appraised with a Black Owner: $472,000. With a White Owner: $750,000," *New York Times*, August 18, 2022, https://www.nytimes.com /2022/08/18/realestate/housing-discrimination-maryland.html.

20. James H. Boykin, *Investing in a Vacation Home for Pleasure and Profit* (Mason, OH: Thomson South-Western, 2006).

21. Marcel Mauss, *The Gift: The Form and Reason for Exchange in Archaic Societ-ies*, trans. W. D. Halls (New York: Norton, 2000).

22. Gili Kliger, "Keeping the Score," Aeon, November 10, 2022, https://aeon.co/ essays/give-and-take-how-gift-giving-forges-society-and-ourselves.

23. Boykin, *Investing in a Vacation Home for Pleasure and Profit*, 144.

24. Vrbo, "Cabin in Rockbridge," Facebook, January 23, 2024, https://www .facebook.com/100064955641000/posts/7077655112273867.

25. Vrbo, "Vrbo Releases 'Only Your People' Creative Campaign" (press release), July 25, 2022, https://www.vrbo.com/media-center/press-releases/2022/vrbo-releases -only-your-people-creative-campaign.

Chapter 4

Material and Geographic Boundaries

Site-Specific Symbols, Economic Connections, and Local-to-Global Community

Miriam and her husband rent out a basement apartment in their Western City home to vacationers. Miriam doesn't feel particularly close to her immediate neighbors, in part because she believes that the wide street where her house is situated—which she described as "almost like a big river"—makes it harder to meet neighbors in person than if she lived on a narrower and therefore more walkable street. She has decorated the rental unit generically enough to accommodate visitors from all corners of the globe, with little reference to the city itself. Now that Miriam and her husband's kids are grown, this short-term vacation rental business allows her to find valuable social connection with guests from around the world—a world Miriam perceives as one of increasing conflict: "Things are so grim, I feel like there is so much hatred, I feel like people are shit. That's how I often feel. This counterbalances that: I feel like these strangers who are coming to my house are so great. It's like, I am meeting these wonderful people from all over the world. Really great. Like, most human beings are wonderful. That's what I feel."

Auggie takes a different approach to his Eastern Oceanside vacation rental, which, like Miriam's, is a part of his home and is not necessarily decorated to call attention to its geographic surroundings. When asked about the social implications of having a short-term vacation rental, he said, "I'm not fooling myself that I'm doing a service in the community." Auggie, a single man in his thirties who loves spending time outdoors, stays with friends or goes camping when he rents out his own living space in his home.

Olivia told a story about a neighbor who lives next door to her Wine Country vacation rental home, which includes a lot of artwork that references local cuisine and viticulture. Olivia's neighbor was sharing an interaction that she had had with some guests: "She was like, 'I was yelling across the porch at these guests you had.' And I went, 'Oh shit, what's going on?' And she goes, 'Oh, I told them all about the market and this restaurant.' She is more neighborly with the guests than she honestly has been with me. She's so proud of [Wine Country] that she's the personal tour guide. It's kind of been amazing."

For Olivia, her neighbor's presumed social connection to her was supplanted by an economic role as local tourism marketer. Olivia labeled the actions as "neighborly." Later in the interview, in response to questions about how close she felt to the community in which her vacation home is situated, Olivia noted that "everything starts with your neighbors."

The ways in which Miriam, Auggie, and Olivia viewed and interacted with their guests differed based on how they thought about the concept of community. Miriam desired a connection with guests that might give her more hope about the global community, yet she didn't feel close to her neighbors. Auggie referred to community only in terms of his immediate neighborhood, acknowledging that his vacation rental business may not be a great way to be neighborly. Olivia felt close to her neighbor precisely because of that neighbor's support for her rental business, which was beneficial to businesses in the community. Property use among these three homeowners looks similar from the outside (they are all in the Investment Property group), and yet they raise different questions about how (and how big) a community is defined by those who own vacation spots: is it solely the immediate neighborhood around the vacation home, or also the world beyond? How might the local community be supported socially, economically, and symbolically?

But what is *community*? Sociologists define this term in many ways, but the definition often includes geographic and social connection. The *Oxford Bibliography of Sociology* notes that a community consists of people interacting with each other, often but not always within a particular geographic location, and often but not always in relation to a set of shared values, interests, or behaviors.[1] In this sense, we can think of community as consisting, at the very least, of people who interact with each other and who may be defined either by themselves or others as a boundaried group. But such interactions may be direct or indirect and may occur in a specific geographic location or not, the people in the community may meet or may not know each other personally, and the group may or may not have unified beliefs. While there may be as many different definitions of communities as there are social scientists, it may suffice to say that most communities come together because they share a geographic place, a set of values or interests, an identity, or all of these.

For my research, the distinction between geographically situated communities and those with connections that are based on interests, values, or identity is important. I refer to these as *geographic communities* (where members reside in the same geographic location) and *social communities* (where members share goals, values, and interests). However, there are distinctions within these types of communities that are revealed in family vacation home owners' experiences, as well as overlaps between social and geographic communities, such as when a cause one believes in manifests locally to create change.

Controversy surrounding family vacation homes, with particular emphasis on those rented out to others for short time periods, has centered on the notion of community. Daniel Guttentag notes that these types of short-term rentals are not only controversial but can, in some localities and by some landlords and HOAs, be prohibited.[2] This may be because the properties "detract from the community fabric,"[3] do not adhere to local health or safety standards, create noise or security issues, or affect local housing markets by reducing supply and upping rents. But these rentals may have benefits, too, including enhancing local tourism, generating income for homeowners, and bringing tourist dollars to neighborhoods that are not normally advertised as tourist zones. In other words, short-term vacation rentals may bring some economic benefits, but critics claim these are not nearly beneficial enough. In addition, Guttentag argues, because every community with increasing numbers of vacation homes is unique, the creation and regulation of laws and taxation issues varies widely, as does the use and popularity of these kinds of spaces. This makes their impact challenging to study, and Guttentag thus suggests that more research is needed to understand both the economic impacts of this kind of informal exchange and the factors at play in residents' positive or negative attitudes about them.[4]

This chapter delves directly into these attitudes: how site-specific connections are framed by homeowners and other stakeholders in terms of homes' physical decor, connections to local economies, and involvement in social and political activities that connect homeowners to larger causes (in some cases) or the local community (in others). When investigating all three types of connection—symbolic, economic, and sociogeographic—homeowners' material and social attachment to place and connection with community took myriad turns.

SEASHELLS, DEER MOUNTS, AND HISTORICAL NODS: HOW FAMILY VACATION HOME DECOR SYMBOLIZES PLACE ATTACHMENT

Just as the regulation of properties used for vacations varies from place to place, the neighborhoods where family vacation homes are situated in my research vary by topography, climate, location, amenities, seasonal use, spatial layout, and property value. Some are rows of modern townhouses where neighbors share walls and common areas are maintained by people hired by the HOA, while others are modest ADUs or portions of homes situated in a residential neighborhood made up of older single-family dwellings. Some neighborhoods have *covenants, conditions, and restrictions* (CC&Rs) that range from limited exterior paint colors to allowances for short-term rentals, while others are in areas where regulation of any kind is met with protest (a subject discussed in chapter 5). Some are in neighborhoods populated with opulent homes where residents live year-round, while others are clusters of small cabins that are closed up during cold seasons. And some neighborhoods where family vacation homes are situated are not permanent neighborhoods at all, as in the case of those whose vacation home is an RV, tent, or other portable home. Understanding how all these kinds of places and properties have anything in common is a real challenge. But they do, in fact, share one commonality: their definition as family vacation homes relies on a connection to particular places, and this place attachment is part of their definition as enchanted.

Place Attachment

In chapter 1, I shared Ole and Angela's emotional story about placing a photograph in their vacation home in Northwest Woods of their now-deceased son with a buck he had shot. While the definition changes across academic contexts, this photograph symbolizes *place attachment*, a term that can be understood to encompass the "emotional link formed by an individual to a physical site that has been given meaning through interaction."[5] Richard Stedman includes in his definition physical setting, human activities, and social processes,[6] while Chiara Rollero and Norma de Piccoli describe place attachment as "a multifaceted and complex phenomenon that incorporates different aspects of people-place bonding and involves the interplay of affect and emotions, knowledge and beliefs, and behaviors and actions in reference to a place."[7] All these definitions inform this analysis, with particular focus on how attachment to place matters differently based on geographic versus social community connections.

Place attachment can vary among stakeholders in amenity-rich settings where second homes are prevalent, regardless of the style of home or arrangement of homes in a neighborhood. Research focusing on place attachment in these contexts defines boundaries between insiders and outsiders, often framed respectively as "permanent" and "transient" residents.[8] According to this research, tourists, visitors, and those who do not have residential status may have an inauthentic sense of place, because their connection to the locale is based on infrequent and spectacular experiences rather than everyday life and deep social connections.[9] For vacation home owners and their families, though (and perhaps even for people who stay in vacation rental properties), a part-time residence can create high levels of authentic place attachment.[10] Temporary residence does not preclude strong attachment to place,[11] and, importantly, senses of place are not necessarily stable, "because the social processes that create them are continuously changing . . . and are not unitary since people can belong to multiple social groups with overlapping or contradicting senses of place."[12]

Permanent residents and family vacation home owners can exhibit high levels of place attachment to the settings where their homes are situated, albeit somewhat differently. Year-rounders define where they live as home, and the meaning of home comprises not just the dwelling itself but also social connections and a feeling of community. For vacation home owners, the setting is more likely to be defined as a getaway or escape, especially in terms of aesthetics and amenities, and to be framed as "not-home" and separated from everyday life,[13] even if family members who are present in primary residences are also present in these second homes. When the setting itself is packaged as a tourist destination,[14] second home owners often frame the place as an amenity-rich escape from the stresses and responsibilities (and mundane vistas, presumably) of everyday life. But year-round residents are not necessarily in opposition to this kind of meaning, since both their and visitors' framing of place grows out of a shared appreciation of amenities and aesthetics that emerge over time. To further complicate this, the influx of seasonal residents is often seen as necessary for economic stability which, in turn, is a reflection of year-round residents' definition of the locale as a desirable place. Additionally, vacation home residents form social ties with year-round resident neighbors and community members (if they make frequent or extended visits) by socializing and becoming involved with the community, or, sometimes, due to conflicts with neighbors.[15] Thus, attachment to a particular geographic place carries with it connections that may be defined as social, economic, or both.

Authenticity and Site-Specific Motifs

Symbolic objects, such as Ole and Angela's photograph, can represent connection to place. If you spend any time in the northern part of the United States dotted with thousands of small lakes, you will inevitably find local shops selling home decor depicting lake activities: fishing, swimming, canoeing, and lakeside firepits with faces aglow next to perfectly cooked marshmallows squished between graham crackers and chocolate to form delicious s'mores. Often, these decor items can be personalized with a family name, suggesting that, even with a nod to the physical landscape and local leisure activities, the vacation story is really meant to be about family. In most cases, site-specific decor can help visitors remember that their vacation spot is different from their primary residence and that vacation activities are not the same things they do in their everyday lives. In other words, site-specific decor doesn't just provide visual clues of *authenticity of place* (meaning that the home includes material and spatial elements that situate it in a real place that can be seen by just looking out the window); it does so with intentional separation of this family vacation place from a primary residence.

Sociologist Karen Stein's research on vacation sites discusses how site-specific motifs offer vacationers the right balance between the comforts of home and the adventures associated with a new locale.[16] With regard to tropical resorts in particular, Stein observes that site-specific art, furniture, fabrics, and decorations end up hearkening to place: "[S]elect elements of the exotic are brought in. The attention of visitors is distracted from elements that do not fit with the theme or may appear to be extraneous and is directed to a few key elements and images of the locale outside the grounds."[17]

The family vacation home owners in my research are not resort owners. So what happens to site-specific motifs when the vacation spot is also a home to a family, whether for the family's own use now or in the future, or for use by others (or both)? Beyond questions of building materials and house shapes that are chosen to withstand certain kinds of weather or landscape constraints, I wonder: How might the place where a family vacation home is situated inform the decor? In chapter 3, my findings revealed the salience of objects and spaces for defining a family vacation home. When defining the neighboring community as a family vacation home spot, how does the physical manifestation of place show up? How do decor and other objects serve to connect the vacation home to the geographic community, and does this connection connote only closeness to physical features, or can it also signify connection to the people who live nearby? Does decor signify place attachment just in terms of place, or also in terms of people? And does this differ by property group?

I conducted many homeowner interviews in my interviewees' vacation homes, often preceded by a walk or drive around the area and often followed by a tour of the home. During these tours, people were eager to point out decorative items that called to mind physical features and common leisure activities associated with the community in which the home resides. I saw end tables with arranged seashells in homes in coastal areas, mountain photographs in ski area homes, deer mounts in woodsy cabins, and cork-themed items in wine country. I also saw connections to the people whose stories took place in the community where the vacation home was situated, often via antiques or decades-old photographs, as well as other items that signified the story of that neighborhood's former residents. One such example was Marion's (Investment Property group) aforementioned display of a prior resident's photo book in her backyard cottage in Wine Country, which she rents out to tourists: "When I rented the space, I kept a little book about the history of it, because I think some people find that interesting, and so I had a little guest book, and it told the story of this woman who lived in the home."

While the people in the Personal Property group were more likely to intersperse family photos and personalized mementos alongside site-specific decor than those in the other two groups, it was common for homeowners to intentionally incorporate visual nods to place in their decor, regardless of property group. After all, these are vacation spots where the motifs of the location serve as material reminders of the purpose of the visit. If people-specific decor was included, such as photographs, it was more likely to be in the Personal Property group homes and to depict only the family and close friends. In contrast, the Investment Property group and to some extent the Mixed Property group included only people whose stories connected to history of the dwelling itself. Homeowners in the Personal Property group included few ties to community in a social sense, and those in the Investment Property group who included social elements of community in their decor did so as a way to market the home as part of the interesting local history.

RESTAURANT RECOMMENDATIONS AND FINANCIAL CONNECTIONS: ECONOMIC SUPPORT AS SOCIAL SUPPORT

Deciding to buy a vacation home, offering that home for rent using an online platform, and paying taxes on it all involve both social and economic exchange. The buying and selling of goods and services (and spaces) has always been of interest to sociologists—and so have the social relationships that connect with economic transactions. Since early sociological theorizing about the interplay between the economy and social relations, as discussed in chapter 1, additional thoughts have geared scholarship toward the *social* dimension of economic exchange. In particular, the conceptualization of *substantivism* by Karl Polanyi[18] and updated empirical studies using his work by scholars such as Daniel Jaffee[19] suggest that focusing only on the economic portion of an exchange between people, or on a rational calculation of the benefits and costs of the exchange in purely economic terms, misses important details about how these interactions operate as substantive social exchanges. In other words, to focus only on the financial aspect of a financial exchange between people ignores the more subjective relational, emotional, cultural, social, and political elements. On the other hand, ignoring the financial elements of a transaction while focusing only on its social aspects is equally incomplete, as Viviana Zelizer has noted in her work on the pricelessness of childhoods,[20] and other elements of personal life that we define as artificially removed from marketplace transactions.

A family vacation home is certainly about emotional and social connection—its enchantment.[21] But it also quite explicitly connects to the economic well-being of a host community, since property values are variable depending on the cost of living and the value of homes and businesses located there. Following this line of thought, buying a second home (or renting someone else's) may be a question of cost and potential return on investment. But it may also be about more social and affective elements: the home's location; its nearness to neighbors, family, or work; its imagined potential for family activities and structure (e.g., whether there's room for cousins to visit); a status associated with its grandeur; its aesthetic or size; the possibility of certain activities taking place there; or even a "gut feeling" about it. In cases where people deliberate about whether the financial cost is "worth it," they often take into consideration factors that are highly subjective, can change over time and between people, and are not easily found in any architectural plans or building codes. For example, Stedman's research using concepts surrounding people's migratory patterns found that second home owners in rural Wisconsin who spend a lot of time in their vacation home enjoy the enhanced social network they gain, while infrequent visitors tend to cite environmental quality and escape from the daily grind as benefits.[22] In this sense, then, the definition of the social meaning of second homes can include both economic factors and noneconomic factors, that is, those that go beyond financial concerns to encompass things such as subjective interpersonal relations. Focusing on the subjective meaning of second homes for owners and other stakeholders, and not just these homes' cost or their effect on local housing prices, allows the complex qualitative dimensions of the social-economic relationship of family vacation home communities to become visible.

Economic-as-Social Support

Social connection is one way a community may come to be defined. However, in the case of family vacation homes, my interviewees often framed economic connections *as* social connections. I asked homeowners what benefits and drawbacks they thought their second home may bring to the local community in terms of both social and economic factors. I asked these questions first by requesting they say where these kinds of homes fit on a scale of 1 to 5 (where 1 is not beneficial at all and 5 is very beneficial) in terms of both economic and social benefit to the local community. I then asked them to explain why they chose the two numbers they did—one for economic benefits and one for social benefits—and to elaborate on how the two may be different and/ or connected. In these conversations, the numbers were high, there was little difference between the two numbers, and the economic benefits were disproportionately framed as social benefits by all property groups. The ratings questions were hard for people to answer, because they didn't see a big distinction between the social and economic benefits of vacation homes—and these homes' residents—to their host communities. Interviewees justified the positive impact of their properties on the economic well-being of the local community by framing that impact as good for the community's social well-being, regardless of property group.

However, the ways that the economic and social impacts of second homes on amenity-rich locations were interwoven were framed differently for each property group. For homeowners in the Investment Property group, renting out their homes to others for vacations necessarily meant supporting local businesses. In fact, some saw their vacation rental work as a business, thus situating locals as peers participating in the instrumental task of profit making. The framing of business support included rhetorical nods to social connectedness and respect for local residents, even if it was ultimately to benefit the vacationers. Rita, who rents out her room in Western City, shared her sentiments: "They want it to be an authentic, local experience, so you're not just booking a place to stay. You're kind of booking that experience with your host, and I'm going to recommend them to the places that I like."

Jean shared a story about her family's local wine club membership at a nearby business in Wine Country as a way to situate herself both as a member of the community and a supporter of local business: "It's not that I have a preference for their wine. It's definitely: if this is your first time here, you should go enjoy the view."

I clarified that the winery she was referring to was less than a mile away. She responded, "Exactly, so that's sort of a neighborhoodie thing, but it's also a great experience, and what I want is for people to come here and have a great experience. In some ways, I feel like I'm a salesman for [Wine

Country]." For Jean, the reciprocal support between two geographically close business entities translated into social ties—what Jean referred to as a "neighborhoodie thing."

Rita and Jean live at the site of their vacation rentals. Olivia, whose comments about her neighbor being a sort of "tour guide" for local restaurants appeared at the beginning of this chapter, does not. Yet all three of these Investment Property group homeowners demonstrate the same thing: that social connections with local residents are economically grounded. For homeowners who live in the place being rented, the connection comes in the form of seeing businesses as neighbors. For homeowners who live elsewhere, the connection is tied to seeing their (supportive) neighbors as business marketers. But for all three, it is economics that connects them socially to neighboring entities.

Personal Property group homeowners utilized similar framing in their discussion of economic-as-social connectedness, although the impetus for their comments was not a need to market their vacation homes as businesses. For these homeowners, who did sometimes have to justify their existence to locals who were critical of wealthy outsiders, the economic-as-social connection took the form of comments about visits with locals whom they see on a regular basis in commercial spaces. For example, Francis shared her impression of the proprietors of a local store in Great Lakes Waterfront, interactions in the store, and her belief that vacation home residents are key to this store's success:

> I can't think of their last name. They've been there about twenty [years], a little longer than we have. It's just a place where you go in the morning and you buy the papers. They sell marvelous ice cream cones there in the season. They have a little bit of everything else and they sell lottery tickets . . . and they have gas pumps out in front, and that's it. People come and they're, "How have you been?" and "Where have you been?" It's a little bit of a hub, but that's about it. But I think that absolutely the summer people are vital, or if not vital, certainly helpful to that store.

Similarly, Morgan describes social connections with the people who run businesses in Northwest Oceanside: "I know individual shop owners of businesses that have been here for over a decade, and I frequent those businesses on purpose because of those people." Willa also talked about seeing the same people every time she visited local businesses in Northwest Oceanside: "Because when we go to [the hardware store], we see the same clerks there. When we go to the restaurants, there's a lot of the same people there. We feel free to engage with them. It's a little more than 'Hi,' 'Thank you,' 'You're welcome.'"

Beyond connecting socially with people in local places of business, family vacation home owners across all groups shared how their shopping habits supported the local economy. Carla, who is in the Personal Property group, expressed what she saw as a clear connection between her family's spending in the town where her Northwest Woods vacation home was and that town's well-being: "And the economy, I think that's a huge thing. Several neighbors, for the last few years, said they don't buy anything until they get to town . . . so now there's five or six people on that street that we know that don't buy anything until they get to town, and so now they buy all their groceries [there]."

Carla's husband Dayton added that the store was almost shut down, but now is succeeding because of these efforts by vacation home owners. The social interactions in places of business, especially for the Personal Property group, meant that they were supporting the local economy at the same time as developing relationships with people that went beyond merely saying "hi."

But not all homeowners in the Personal Property group articulated connections that would suggest positive economic or social benefit. CJ, who grew up without much money, felt a bit guilty about buying property at Northwest Oceanside when not many people could afford to do so. She and others like her acknowledged that the economic benefit for the community may help businesses, but that the residents who worked in those businesses could not afford to live in these communities as more affluent individuals bought properties, made improvements, and presumably raised the median home price. She was also worried in general about places being rented out, and had even considered the implications of renting out her primary residence while she and her husband were at their vacation home: "I have really mixed feelings about jumping on the bandwagon and renting our house in [hometown] that way. I also worry about if there will be people in there that will bother our neighbors, that will be noisy at night sitting on the porch, that kind of thing. They've been nice neighbors. They're nice people, and I don't want to do that."

People in the Mixed Property group framed their interactions with local business in both ways: their homes supported local businesses (since visitors would spend money in town), and they themselves connected with local business owners socially when they were there. In all groups, the framing of economic connection as social connection served to make the economic transactional nature of their existence in the host communities less explicitly about money, even with some acknowledgment that their presence supported the local economy. It was easier for homeowners to frame the benefit as social, thus humanizing the transactions. The less explicitly a family vacation home is connected to the financial bottom line of a community, the more enchanted the home becomes.

Affordable Housing

Perceptions about a lack of affordable housing in the local community was one issue that came up among all property groups when they talked about supporting the local economy, albeit differently for each group. For Investment and Mixed Property group homeowners who rented their second homes to others, a lack of affordable housing resulting from vacation rentals was likely to be framed as an exaggerated issue invoked by people who have outdated views about neighborhoods in places where tourism is central to the local economy. People in these categories shared stories of local naysayers evoking mythological images of 1950s neighborhoods that represent some kind of fictitious neighborliness. Stakeholders I interviewed who worked in tourism, hospitality, and mortgage lending offered similar critiques of people claiming that vacation rentals were making homes less affordable in any given community. In fact, they argued, this kind of neighborliness has never been ubiquitous and may actually serve to perpetuate racist and classist images of white, middle-class neighborhoods with sanitized images of tidy homes and artificially smiling faces, an argument revisited in chapter 5. Plus, as I discuss below, the data used by critics to make a causal link between vacation rentals and decreased housing affordability was not convincing to these homeowners.

For Personal Property group homeowners, such as CJ, there was a bit more guilt about the issue. This led some to offer help to the community in other ways, while others claimed ignorance about the actual impact of vacation homes on local housing affordability. Homeowners in all property groups also deflected commentary about local economic problems, including housing affordability, by focusing their personal efforts toward noneconomic issues and support for issues that unite communities beyond the town where their vacation homes are situated, a pattern that serves to perpetuate the enchantment of the family vacation home, elaborated in the next section.

GEOGRAPHIC AND SOCIAL COMMUNITY CONNECTIONS: VOLUNTEERING, CHARITABLE GIVING, AND ADVOCACY

Travel,
because traveling teaches to resist,
not to depend,
to accept others, not just for who they are
but also for what they can never be.
To know what we are capable of,

to feel part of a family
beyond borders,
beyond traditions and culture.
Traveling teaches us to be beyond.

—from "Viaggiate" by Gio Evan, translated from Italian[23]

As discussed in the previous sections, homeowners often visually referenced local characteristics in their decor and defined economic connections to their communities as social connections, mostly in terms of relationships with geographically local people and places. But recall Miriam's reflection about her Western City guests as compared to her immediate neighbors: "I am meeting these wonderful people from all over the world. Really great. Like, most human beings are wonderful." Community isn't just about being in the same geographic place, and many family vacation home owners situated their connection to community as a much broader social project, either as a way to build *expressive* (emotional) connections via shared values, interests, and beliefs, or as a way to build *instrumental* (task- or project-specific) connections via communities, such as national boards related to their housing type. Across both geographic and social communities, family vacation home owners cited how their volunteering, charitable contributions, and advocacy work connected them with others. Who and where the others were, however, paint a more complex picture.

Involvement beyond the Vacation Home Community

What did it look like for family vacation home owners "to feel part of a family beyond borders" (as the lyrics above say) even if, as discussed in chapter 3, they saw their homes as ways to create boundaries between family and not-family? Community involvement in the form of philanthropy and advocacy efforts beyond the local vacation home site were common among homeowners in all property groups. I interviewed people who had marched with Dr. Martin Luther King Jr., who are dedicated to animal rescue efforts, and who belong to national and international groups dedicated to social justice, land conservation, and many other causes. Involvement in larger causes also came in the form of activities connected both directly and indirectly to the vacation home. Some homeowners were involved in national boards relating to their type of property (e.g., homes on US Forest Service land) or participated in fundraising for environmental issues that impact the topography, climate, or amenities in their vacation home community (e.g., tsunami preparedness in coastal areas). Others got involved in advocacy directly related to their capacity to rent out their home to short-term vacationers.

Homeowners I spoke to were involved in affinity and interest groups, national political parties (though not too loudly if they rented their homes), and global advocacy groups, whether in the form of financial contributions, volunteering time, or serving on boards. The goal of these activities was to affirm their personal values by way of connecting with like-minded others spread across a large geographical area—something the interviewees did regardless of whether they were in their primary residence or a vacation home, and regardless of whether the efforts related directly to their property. This meant that family vacation homeowners, at times, framed their connection to community in a more global context rather than a local one. This issue-based social community connection was embedded in the tasks associated with their everyday lives, remaining mostly removed from the relaxed, distant-from-responsibility expressive lifestyle they envisioned for vacations.

Local Connections

When homeowners discussed issue-based or social geographic community connections, the connection to the place their vacation home was situated more often centered on timely issues or instrumental tasks, not on establishing deep expressive relationships with neighbors and other locals. This was predominantly true for people in the Personal and Mixed Property groups. For example, Morgan (Personal Property group) talked about the fact that she knew all her neighbors' names in Northwest Oceanside, but "it's not like we hang out in their backyard over a fire." Adrienne (Personal Property group) talked about getting to know friendly local logging industry workers in her Northwest Woods community as a way to better understand the environmental and economic issues facing locals. Several homeowners talked about being part of their HOA, attending meetings when they were in the area and paying attention to any issues that impacted their homes directly. In other words, across Personal and Mixed Property groups, most people saw their local community connections as instrumentally motivated; they did not see their family vacation homes as a way to turn geographically close neighbors into friends.

There were a few exceptions to this, although the definition of "neighbor" matters. Sometimes, especially for Personal Property group homeowners, vacation home neighbors felt closer than those near their primary residence. Rhonda noted that she and her husband know their Northern Lake Country neighbors better than their primary residence neighbors: "[I]n our suburb anyway, it seems that people open the garage door to drive their car in and then close the garage door and you never see them again and you don't talk to them." Al and Ina even went so far as to say their vacation home neighborhood in Great Lakes Waterfront had "kinder and gentler" people than their primary residence—an urban high-rise. They lamented, however, how much their vacation home neighborhood had started to lose its feeling of community among neighbors because fewer residents were spending as much time there. Ina noted that community parties used to be potlucks with everyone bringing something, and now these events are catered. Al shared that he started working more closely on a local newsletter and created a community website to stay connected with neighbors.

For these Personal Property group homeowners, whose vacation homes were situated in neighborhoods filled with other vacation homes, it may seem as if the chance to get to know neighbors was, to some extent, about location (nonurban meant closer ties), time (more time meant closer ties), and type of dwelling (visibility of people outside of homes meant closer ties). But as they elaborated, it became clear that it was less about these factors and more about the culture of place that these factors symbolized in the minds of the interviewees. Rhonda continued, "I actually went to a block party at the lake versus avoiding the one at home. I don't know; I think knowing my neighbors better at the lake means I would go and talk to them and ask them questions about their cabins. When I was at home, I would never do that." There was something about being in a vacation home community that allowed for easier demonstration of expressive relationships with neighbors, something Rhonda found in her cabin vicinity and something that Al and Ina lamented being lost as residents in their vacation community spent less and less time there. But importantly in both cases, the neighbors with whom an expressive relationship could be forged were other vacation homeowners, not local, year-round residents.

Those who mentioned involvement with local geographically close communities made distinctions between permanent local residents and friends who lived in the same area but were not immediate neighbors. While the likelihood of connecting with local communities was centered more on instrumental tasks and issues than on expressive connections, the definition of "local" affected any sort of closeness homeowners had with people in the geographic vicinity. At times, local social connections were not with neighbors or permanent residents, but with friends who were neither neighbors nor locals. In fact, these friends—like the other cabin owners Rhonda mentioned or former neighbors for Al and Ina—were other vacationers. Grace, also in the Personal Property group, talked about her Western Mountain neighborhood, noting that "we don't know a lot of our neighbors. We know a lot of other people that have places up there." Rich and Marcus discussed their local social community similarly. They are strong advocates for gay rights, both in the city where their primary residence is and with national groups. As members of the Mixed Property group, they rent out their Western Desert home sometimes and use it for themselves at other times. Rich elaborated that they had sought a place to vacation and eventually retire where they feel welcome, and that they are "building a chosen family of people that we want to spend time with" in their vacation home community, which currently consists primarily of other gay individuals who live in the community but not necessarily in their neighborhood. Rich said he views his immediate neighbors as distinct from his "chosen family," given that their home is sometimes rented by others whom his neighbors are unlikely to get to know:

> So if you showed up at the same time as your neighbors showed up who were vacationing, then you got to know the people who were around you that way. But when it's a different person showing up potentially every week in the wintertime, my neighbors aren't going to want to know who's here. They couldn't care less. When we show up and our neighbors see us, they're friendly to us. They may not remember our names. I may not remember theirs. But they know that we're the owners of the house versus just another set of renters in the house.

Rich then contrasted this with memories of his childhood spent at a vacation home with family in Northern Lake Country: "I think in our parents' generation, it was probably, they weren't renting it out, so the same people were showing up all the time. So I think that is a different social network. . . . Here, it's a more transient population; there it's a more permanent population of people."

Although Grace and Rich had different goals for their respective properties (Grace is in the Personal Property group; Rich is in the Mixed Property group), their local connection was the same: expressive relationships not with locals or immediate neighbors, but with other visitors who are there at the same time. Across the Personal and Mixed Property groups, in which homeowners spent at least some time in the vacation locale, a "local connection" was often actually a connection with another visitor. And for Rich, the other vacationers were defined as his "chosen family," a term that serves to maintain the boundary between family and not-family when framed as part of the family vacation home experience.

Outside social relationships with others in the vacation home locale, involvement in the local community took such forms as short-term volunteering, participation in local causes, and financial contributions. Homeowners were not likely to get involved in local political activities that centered around elections, political candidates, or controversial social issues—at least not loudly or in the form of candidate signs in their yards, especially if they wanted to rent the home to others but not have the visitors feel "put off."

The causes that people spent the most time volunteering with (and contributed the most financially to) included historic preservation, disaster preparedness and public safety, community gardens, nonprofit arts organizations, libraries, museums, and conservation efforts. Some of this involvement was based on expertise or interest, but most was connected to the homeowners' goals of preserving the local landscape and the natural and aesthetic amenities that attracted them to the site in the first place. Ole and Angela (Personal Property group), for example, have strong views about what they perceive as ineffective environmental efforts in their Northwest Woods community, leading to increased fire danger. Rather than protest these issues, though, they opt to participate in local activities adjacent to political causes, such as four-wheeler rides and potlucks where locals can gather to talk about fire concerns and strategize conservation efforts. Angela noted that "I don't feel like I'm an outsider from another state, but I'm just not a local, I guess." For Ole and Angela, their involvement in an advocacy group was somewhat indirect, and did not lead them to form friendships with local residents or deep involvement in local issues.

Across the Personal and Mixed Property groups, more direct involvement in advocacy efforts occasionally led to friendships with locals. But these connections tended to be made in contexts that related directly to the property, and most often led to friendships formed with other visitors who spend a lot of time in the vacation locale rather than long-time permanent residents. As a person who rents out his Western Desert vacation home part-time to others and uses it the rest of the time for his own vacations, Joseph, for instance, was heavily involved in local groups fighting against short-term rental regulation. Adrienne described a similar experience in relation to her Northwest Woods vacation home, which she reserves for personal use:

> My husband and I were very community-minded people. He was an educator, and so we, even though we weren't there all that much, we made it a point to meet people and to know what was going on and what the issues were, and we joined a very active cabin-owners association. There is a national organization for people who have cabins on Forest Service land, because there are issues nationally. So we had our local chapter of that, and it was really valuable for us to get to know other people. People who could be there more, and also the people who worked for the Forest Service and local folks. It was a very interesting experience.

And what about the Investment Property group, for whom connection to the local had a tie to their economic goals of renting out their vacation home? Here is an instance where two parts of my research contrast each other. Evident in advice offered in several sessions at the vacation rental conference I attended, connection to the local community beyond support offered to local businesses for these homeowners was framed as a decidedly market-driven activity. In these sessions, homeowners who rent their homes to others for vacations were encouraged to support local causes that aligned with their own values, but primarily as a way to bolster their rental business. This meant that homeowners were encouraged to get involved with historical preservation to support local stories that may be used in tourist documents to draw visitors to the area. Or they were pushed to donate time or money to local medical organizations to justify advertising their short-term vacation rental as a homelike place to stay (especially in urban areas) when a family member undergoes a medical procedure. Or they were told to volunteer with arts groups whose work could be listed among the local activities for visitors to enjoy. Or they were shown the importance of getting involved with public safety or land use groups to ensure the property is safe and likely to survive any disasters. For homeowners whose primary interest is in renting out the home to others as a business, geographic community connection was primarily instrumental and market driven: meant to support the bottom line, but not necessarily their own personal interests.

The story of local connection for Investment Property group homeowners I interviewed looked drastically different from the stories I heard at the vacation rental conference. This was because all but one of the homeowners in the Investment Property group had their primary residence in the same community as their vacation rental. Their community connections were much more likely to be expressive. In other words, if Investment Property group homeowners live in the same town where they rent out their property, their friendships and their local community involvement may be less about the vacation property and its profits and more about affective connections that people typically form in the neighborhoods and communities of their primary residence. For this reason, controversies surrounding who is entitled to rent out their residences often connect to whether homeowners live in the town dealing with the rentals, elaborated in chapter 5.

Depoliticizing Involvement

Some of the aforementioned causes and projects are both political and controversial, such as short-term rental regulation efforts and economic and environmental disputes about land use. But more often than not, homeowners in all three property groups aimed to separate themselves politically from locals, either of their own accord or because they felt pressure not to get involved. In fact, the interviewees avoided talking about politics much at all, especially their own views or voting practices. Many acknowledged the deep political divide in the country, though, situating themselves as reasonable voices in a sea of extremist views on both ends of the political spectrum.

The reasons for disengagement from local issues centered around deservedness, a desire to prevent alienating other people, and a desire to keep politics out of anything related to family vacations—sometimes in combination. These reasons spanned all three property groups.

Red (Investment Property group), who rents out a room in his Eastern Woods home, admitted that he tends to be less involved because he doesn't have kids in school and he isn't physically capable of helping with groups like the rescue squad or fire department. Faye (Personal Property group) also felt removed from local politics in her Northern Lake Country vacation home community, in part because she didn't feel qualified to join: "I'm not part of the way that little town is run. I don't have any idea who is in charge of anything. I step away from all of that at the cabin. I would never think that, because I can go up there as much as I wanted, that I would be qualified to be on the board of anything. When I go to the cabin, I can turn that part of me off."

Morgan (Personal Property group), who was very busy with her professional work life, treated her time at their Northwest Oceanside vacation home as a respite from anything resembling responsibility: "[W]hen we go up there on weekends, we're kind of hermits. We are not involved politically. We are not on committees." Like several others, she also noted that she was uninvolved in a faith community in her vacation home community, even though she was heavily involved in one back home. Valencia (Personal Property group) shared a story about attending a town council meeting in Eastern Woods, thinking she'd be interested in participating in local politics. But as soon as she witnessed a discussion about a proposed law against paganism and witchcraft because local residents feared the impacts of a local psychic who had recently moved into the downtown area, she recognized that she did not belong there. She saw herself as vastly different politically and socially from local residents—a view she used to justify her lack of involvement. If she were to get involved, she'd either alienate locals (which she wanted to avoid) or be insulted by them (which she saw as a result of their vastly different political views). To avoid these troubling outcomes, she stayed out of politics.

In contrast, Sunny (Investment Property group) was quite involved in local politics. She observed that a lot of the people involved in local politics at Northwest Oceanside are affluent retired men who are used to holding positions of authority in their paid work roles, so she felt a bit excluded. Sunny perceived herself to be deserving of a voice (especially about vacation rental issues, elaborated in chapter 5) because of her views on which kinds of voices tend to get excluded from local political discussions. Valencia distanced herself from local politics because she wanted to avoid conflict and alienation. Red, Morgan, and Faye did not see themselves as deserving of a political voice, but they had never experienced any negative impacts resulting from local property, zoning, or other regulatory deliberations that jeopardized their vacation home use (as Sunny had). And Faye defined her qualifications in terms of her family vacation home self: "I step away from all of that at the cabin."

CJ, who was mentioned earlier in regard to her guilty feelings about housing affordability in her Northwest Oceanside community, told me she doesn't vote in elections at her vacation home because she believes that until she lives there full time, she should not publicly state her opinion. For now, she's on a sports-related local steering committee.

Sociologist Brian McCabe notes that property ownership often leads to investment in community affairs, offering an "enhanced citizenship."[24] Property owners are more active than, say, long-term renters; they form deeper social bonds with neighbors and they volunteer more. Property owners are more politically engaged to protect their financial investment in homeownership. Political involvement, therefore, is driven by money, which can lead to exclusionary practices (the subject of chapter 5). McCabe focuses primarily on principal residences. What about this kind of citizenship and political involvement for family vacation homeowners? Homeowners whose properties were not part of local political deliberations could step away from local involvement (and local social connections) even as they thrust themselves into larger social and political issues that connect them with a more global community. Homeowner political views are thus hidden by people whose properties are not part of local political deliberations, which serves to enchant these homes. At the same time, people whose vacation homes are part of political deliberations, such as short-term rental regulations and land use, are more likely to make their political voices heard. This actually serves to enchant the homes, too, since being vocal about these issues supports the meaning of the family vacation home as an enchanted place for people to enjoy. How intriguing that the opposite social actions of silence and vocal expression of views can both lead to the same outcome, depending on whose voice is present and why.

CONCLUSION: ENCHANTMENT ACROSS MATERIAL AND GEOGRAPHIC BOUNDARIES

Does displaying a local photographer's art depicting a ski slope count as connecting to community at a vacation home in the mountains? What does it mean to support your community? And what does "your" mean? Being socially connected to a community can manifest in many ways. It could come in the form of driving a neighbor to the airport or joining an online advocacy group for a cause that is meant to eradicate an inequality beyond the neighborhood or community where a vacation home is located. Or it could take the form of welcoming vacationers to your neighbor's vacation rental and bragging about a local restaurant. To be a part of a community may mean you know your neighbor's voice. It may mean fighting alongside like-minded people for causes that give voice to those who go unrepresented. Homeowner attitudes about the family vacation home serve to place these ways of viewing community at odds with each other. And yet these opposing views end up serving the same purpose: enchanting the family vacation home.

The findings in this chapter reveal three ways that the family vacation home is strategically framed as enchanted by homeowners in terms of material and geographic boundaries: through the use of site-specific decor, through reference to support for local economies, and through strategic and varied framing of community as geographic/local or social/not-local. Below, I summarize these findings and connections to the overarching goal of enchanting the family vacation home.

Site-Specific Decor

Site-specific decor was used across property groups in order to establish authenticity and attachment to place. Local motifs connecting properties to leisure activities, scenery, and place history were not uncommon. The Investment Property group used these motifs primarily to offer visible evidence of the place-based authenticity, and therefore desirability, of their vacation rental property. Whether via pottery, old photographs of the town, or boogie boards, it made financial sense to supply these places with local art, decorations, and equipment that reference the amenities, activities, and histories available just outside the front door. For the Personal and Mixed Property groups, site-specific decor certainly offered a nod to place and added to the homes' place authenticity, but it wasn't necessarily to make visitors feel like they got their money's worth. For the Personal Property group, in particular, site-specific decor was usually displayed alongside items meant to signify the homeowner's family stories—memories of the authentic vacation place were part of the personal memory-making project with and for the family. And it was the Mixed Property group whose decor items were in flux: personal items hidden when others stay, site-specific motifs on display all the time.

Family stories and imagined future kinship nostalgia played out using material and spatial props that align with the designation of the home, and perhaps the geographic place itself, as enchanted. Connection to the local community was used via place authenticity to contextualize family memory making and add legitimacy to the enchantment.

Local Economies

Material connections with host communities came not just in the form of symbolic objects but also in the form of economic relationships. Across all property groups, explicit discussion of money was downplayed. But when it came to the community's well-being, mentions of economic exchanges changed shape. For all groups, economic support for the host community was framed as social support, even as its framing differed across groups. For the Investment Property group, social support for the community was defined not just as economic but explicitly as support for local businesses. This happened to some extent in the Mixed Property group as well. For the Personal Property group, local businesses were more likely to be mentioned not as interchangeable with "social support for the community," but rather as places where social connections between visitors and locals occurred. When it came to concern about broader community economic issues, such as housing affordability, the property groups varied quite a bit: Investment and Mixed Property group members argued that the concern over the perceived decline in housing affordability for locals was exaggerated and inappropriately sprinkled with outdated images of unattainable middle-class white neighborhoods. Meanwhile, the Personal Property group talked about housing affordability either by acknowledging their own guilt or by distancing their own role from the issue while noting their concern for the community.

Downplaying questions of money was one way that homeowners kept their family vacation homes enchanted, removing them symbolically from economic references to the local geographic community. This happened via reframing economic relationships with local businesses as social support or as places where social relationships may be fostered. The harsh realities of housing affordability in the local community were kept distant from the salience of the family vacation home, either by downplaying the seriousness of the issue or by distancing a personal role in it.

Geographic and Social Community

The interplay between feeling connected to local (geographic) and nonlocal (social) communities showed up in complex ways. For the most part, the interviewees were politically engaged people, especially in their home communities and also in their vacation home communities if the issues were directly related to their properties. But most often, they distanced themselves from partisan political involvement in vacation home communities, sticking with arts and conservation groups that organize social events or low-effort volunteer or financial philanthropic opportunities. They reserved their political activism for their hometowns or for communities beyond the vacation home locale, at times noting that the people they meet while either vacation-ing at the home or renting it to others represent a more globally diverse group of people. When it came to reflecting on the state of relationships between different political groups, it was clear that the deep political divide in the United States led homeowners to lament the chasms at the same time they avoided trying to bridge these chasms in their vacation home communities. This would nevertheless have been difficult to do, since they saw them-selves as quite different from permanent local residents, unless they were Investment Property group homeowners who lived in the towns where they rented out their vacation homes to others. The expressive social ties Personal and Mixed Property group homeowners made in vacation home communi-ties were most often with other visitors or property owners whose primary residence was elsewhere—often yielding even closer ties than those at their primary residences. Deep friendships with host community residents were likely only among people whose vacation home (usually a rental) was in the same place as their primary residence.

Homeowners generally distanced themselves from controversy and politi-cal engagement in local communities as a means of keeping their vacation homes enchanted, except when the capacity of their vacation home to enchant was threatened. For people whose vacation homes were not in the same town as their primary residences, close social ties were unlikely to occur with local permanent residents but instead be with other vacationers, thus perpetuating the full social (and occasionally political) experience in the community as unequivocally tied to the enchantment of the family vacation home.

* * *

I end this chapter with a timely news story that highlights many of my research findings, and that takes place in an area similar to many of my research sites: Washington State's Puget Sound.

The Puget Sound shoreline in Washington State spans hundreds of miles, with one end point situated in the southeast corner of the Olympic Peninsula at Oakland Bay, near the town of Shelton. Not known as a tourist destination despite being geographically close to resorts and multimillion-dollar homes along Hood Canal and any number of islands and beaches near Seattle, Tacoma, and Olympia, Shelton has a population of about ten thousand. Oakland Bay is a quiet place where the view across the water is interrupted only by the occasional kayak or family of seals poking their heads above the surface. Known for its logging and seafood industries, Shelton is not a wealthy town: the median household income is just under $60,000, which situates it at about 75 percent of the US median household income.[25] But just south of the city center lie several large homes along Oakland Bay, some of which have recently sold for upwards of a million dollars.

A recent controversy has shaken the homeowners living in these homes. Taylor Shellfish, a company headquartered in Shelton, is attempting to place a fifty-acre oyster farm in the bay, disrupting the view of calm water, lush trees, and clean shorelines. In a news story in the *Olympian* reporting on the homeowners' formation of a nonprofit organization called Friends of Oakland Bay—which consists of people who spend vacation time along Oakland Bay as well as those who have purchased homes there for retirement—homeowners were interviewed about their group's aims to stop the oyster farm. As of the time of this writing, there are around a dozen vacation rental listings on the bay with Airbnb and Vrbo, suggesting that while some of the disgruntled homeowners are permanent residents, many may be those who fit into the property categories in my research. This makes this location's story a helpful place to scrutinize the processes that I have uncovered in my interviews and other data sources.

One homeowner interviewed for the news story noted that the bay has been logged by sawmills for eighty years, resulting in a high level of toxins in the water that she fears may end up in the oysters. To situate a giant oyster farm here, she argued, would be a public health problem because some of the toxins have been found to cause cancer and birth defects. Another person offered additional motivation for the cause:

> We've been put on the forefront of this because we're lucky enough after years of hard work to be able to own a property out here. . . . A private corporation wants to come in with a DNR [Department of Natural Resources] lease, . . . take over this bay, block access, ruin it aesthetically not just for the people that live on the bay, but for all of the citizens of the state of Washington and anybody else that might like to come out here to visit. This access is going to be blocked, the bay is going to be ruined. Tourism is massive in the state of Washington, actually far larger than the seafood industry, so to take over this bay by a private company at the expense of everybody else is just not right. . . . We kind of feel like we're stewards of this bay now that we live here, but not just for ourselves but for the public at large.[26]

These comments demonstrate the important ways that owners' involvement in a vacation home community is likely to become political when there may be a threat to the value or meaning of the property. To lose both the view of and access to a clear vista of water not only means the homes may be devalued; it also means the imagined retirement and/or family vacation activities that are to take place at the home are hampered. Of course, these are intimately related. Add to this a visual reminder of a corporate powerhouse made successful by wielding local political power, and the family vacation home becomes disenchanted. In this instance, support for a local business— Taylor Shellfish—is not defined as socially good, but rather as socially detrimental. While these homeowners support local businesses by shopping in town, and while they may define this as social support, they do not support the one business that threatens their vacation properties.

Importantly, homeowners framing this issue as problematic for their family alone—especially wealthy, white homeowners—can both alienate a town's local residents and come across as self-serving, elitist, and entitled. Because of this, the rhetorical strategy used here framed the problem as one of legitimate collective and public concerns: toxins in oysters and ruined views and activities for residents of the entire state (not to mention the state's tourism revenue). Powerful and emotion-inducing threats to food safety, public health, and widely accessible tourism amenities are evoked in order to preserve an enchanted investment. Here, referencing broader social communities rather than local geographic ones is strategic. Or, perhaps more accurately, referencing broader social communities and semilocal (within the state, but not within the town) geographic ones is strategic.

That homeowners and residents here could afford to form a group to battle the oyster company, and that they could arrange news coverage of this story in coherent and persuasive ways, speaks to their privilege: a privilege that allows for strategic framing of community that intends to frame the homeowners as morally right and that ultimately meets their need to enchant the vacation home. The story of how privilege, inequality, and conceptions of right and wrong matter in the enchantment of family vacation homes continues in chapter 5.

NOTES

1. Zachary P. Neal, "Community," *Oxford Bibliography of Sociology*, https://www.oxfordbibliographies.com/display/document/obo-9780199756384/obo-9780199756384-0080.xml.

2. Daniel Guttentag, "Airbnb: Disruptive Innovation and the Rise of an Informal Tourism Accommodation Sector," *Current Issues in Tourism* 19, no. 12 (2015): 1192–217, https://doi.org/10.1080/13683500.2013.827159.

3. Guttentag, "Airbnb," 1200.

4. Multidisciplinary empirical and theoretical scholarship conducted outside the United States provides an important backdrop for a sociological understanding of the community-level impact and varying definitions of vacation homes in general, though most focus on economic factors and are located in publications geared toward housing, geography, economics, and tourism and hospitality. For example, researchers have studied the following important topics:

• the negative environmental impact and colonialist elite second homeowners' impact on fragile poor rural economies in the United Kingdom and other parts of Europe (John Terence Coppock, ed., *Second Homes: Curse or Blessing?* [Oxford: Pergamon, 1977]);

• an increase in second home ownership in rural areas as a means toward enhanced economic development and a challenge to the dichotomized views of second homes as either positive or negative in rural South Africa and locations in the Global South (Gijsbert Hoogendoorn and Gustav Visser, "Focusing on the 'Blessing' and Not the 'Curse' of Second Homes: Notes from South Africa," *Area* 47, no. 2 [2015]: 179–84, https://www.jstor.org/stable/24811767);

• economic gain but also loss of community due to housing market disruptions, gentrification, and economic woes during off-seasons when homes are not occupied in the United Kingdom (Nick Gallent, *Second Homes: European Perspectives and UK Policies* [Ashgate, UK: Routledge, 2014]);

• the unique effects of socialist housing policies and state institutions on the increase in urban second home ownership and housing prices in China (Youqin Huang and Chengdong Yi, "Second Home Ownership in Transitional Urban China," *Housing Studies* 26, no. 3 [2011]: 423–47, https://doi.org/10.1080/02673037.2011.542100);

• the prominence of second home ownership in Nordic countries, yielding a fuller empirical investigation of everyday practices, attitudes, and level of community connectedness associated with different second home neighborhoods (e.g., Sari Janhunen, Maija Hujala and Satu Pätäri, "Owners of Second Homes, Locals and Their Attitudes towards Future Rural Wind Farm," *Energy Policy* 73 [2014]: 450–60, https://doi.org/10.1016/j.enpol.2014.05.050; Thor Flognfeldt and Even Tjørve, "The Shift from Hotels and Lodges to Second-Home Villages in Mountain-Resort Accommodation," *Scandinavian Journal of Hospitality and Tourism* 13, no. 4 [2013]: 332–52, https://doi.org/10.1080/15022250.2013.862440);

• the importance of compensation and typologies of second home owners in Germany, the Netherlands, and Ireland based on whether they desire to escape from their (sometimes) dissatisfying primary residence (Martin Dijst et al., "Second Homes in Germany and the Netherlands: Ownership and Travel Impact Explained," *Tijdschrift voor Economische en Sociale Geografie* 96, no. 2 [2005]: 139–52, https://doi.org/10.1111/j.1467-9663.2005.00446.x; Michelle Norris and Nessa Winston, "Second-Home Owners: Escaping, Investing or Retiring?" *Tourism Geographies* 12, no. 4 [2010]: 546–67, https://doi.org/10.1080/14616688.2010.516401);

• and the impact of second homes on local taxes in Spain (Emilio Torres and J. Santos Domínguez-Menchero, "The Impact of Second Homes on Local Taxes," *Fiscal Studies* 27, no. 2 [2006]: 231–50, https://www.jstor.org/stable/24439994).

5. Melinda J. Milligan, "Interactional Past and Potential: The Social Construction of Place Attachment," *Symbolic Interaction* 21, no. 1 (1998): 1–33, https://doi.org/10.1525/si.1998.21.1.1.

6. Richard C. Stedman, "Understanding Place Attachment among Second Home Owners," *American Behavioral Scientist* 50, no. 2 (2006): 187–205, https://doi.org/10.1177/0002764206290633.

7. Chiara Rollero and Norma de Piccoli, "Place Attachment, Identification and Environment Perception: An Empirical Study," *Journal of Environmental Psychology* 30, no. 2 (2010): 198, https://doi.org/10.1016/j.jenvp.2009.12.003.

8. Stedman, "Understanding Place Attachment among Second Home Owners."

9. Yi-Fu Tuan, *Space and Place: The Perspective of Experience* (Minneapolis: University of Minnesota Press, 1977).

10. Stedman, "Understanding Place Attachment among Second Home Owners."

11. Lee Cuba and David M. Hummon, "A Place to Call Home: Identification with Dwelling, Community, and Region," *Sociological Quarterly* 34, no. 1 (1993): 111–31, https://www.jstor.org/stable/4121561.

12. Susan R. Van Patten and Daniel R. Williams, "Problems in Place: Using Discursive Social Psychology to Investigate the Meanings of Seasonal Homes," *Leisure Sciences* 30 (2008): 452, https://doi.org/10.1080/01490400802353190.

13. Stedman, "Understanding Place Attachment among Second Home Owners."

14. John Urry, *Sociology beyond Societies* (London: Routledge, 2000).

15. Stedman, "Understanding Place Attachment among Second Home Owners."

16. Karen Stein, *Getting Away from It All: Vacations and Identity* (Philadelphia: Temple University Press, 2019).

17. Stein, *Getting Away from It All*, 149.

18. Karl Polanyi, *The Great Transformation: The Political and Economic Origins of Our Time*, 2nd ed. (Boston: Beacon Press, 2001).

19. Daniel Jaffee, *Brewing Justice: Fair Trade Coffee, Sustainability, and Survival*, updated ed. (Berkeley: University of California Press, 2014).

20. Viviana Zelizer, *The Purchase of Intimacy* (Princeton, NJ: Princeton University Press, 2005).

21. Arlie Hochschild, *The Commercialization of Intimate Life: Notes from Home and Work* (Berkeley: University of California Press, 2003).

22. Stedman, "Understanding Place Attachment among Second Home Owners."

23. Gio Evan, "Viaggiate," track 18 on *Mareducato* (Polydor, Universal Music Italia, 2021).

24. Brian J. McCabe, *No Place Like Home: Wealth, Community, and the Politics of Homeownership* (New York: Oxford University Press, 2016), 7.

25. US Census Bureau, "QuickFacts: Shelton city, Washington," https://www.census.gov/quickfacts/fact/table/sheltoncitywashington/PST045222.

26. Shauna Sowersby, "Shelton Residents Push Back against Proposed Taylor Shellfish Oyster Farm in Oakland Bay," *Olympian*, November 12, 2023, https://www.theolympian.com/news/politics-government/article281260723.html.

Chapter 5

Legal and Moral Boundaries

Citizenship and Conflict in Host Communities

If a tree falls at a vacation home one acre away from the next, does the neighbor hear it fall? And if they do, will they complain about it to a local regulatory body? Jean, who rents out her ADU on the edge of town in Wine Country, explained why she believes her vacation rental has not been on the radar of local critics who want more regulation to protect their vision of a "good" neighborhood: "We're far enough away from our neighbors that it is really not a noticeable thing. We don't allow parties. There are a lot of things that could be a problem that we just won't tolerate, so that doesn't impact them, as far as I can tell. In town, I think it could, and I know a lot of the controversy has to do with parking and stuff, which is not an issue out here."

Despite Jean's claim, neither housing density nor the proximity of houses in a vacation home's neighborhood seems to affect homeowners' social closeness to the local community, a topic introduced in chapter 4. Even those who cited spatial distance as a reason not to get to know their neighbors said that other factors mattered more, particularly their desire to retreat from everyday life and escape the perceived need to get involved with local people socially or politically—which also meant avoiding conflict whenever possible.

What factors shape someone's feeling of being included or excluded in a community? What happens when there is conflict between community members that points to moral claims about family vacation homes, and how and how much should this conflict be prevented, managed, or regulated? Sometimes, debates between vacationing neighbors relate to noise, cutting down trees on a property line, or too many parked cars in driveways. But beyond the idiosyncratic squabbles that often relate to local regulations and landscapes, larger group differences and structural inequalities play a role in how family vacation homes are defined, legitimated, and experienced. And they make up the key elements in the political story of family vacation homes, especially when community may be defined differently depending on a person's approach to interpersonal relationships, social position, views about the function of a property, or political or moral beliefs.

The subsequent sections examine classed and racialized practices and views associated with family vacation homes—both those that are used privately and those that are rented to (deserving or undeserving) others. In chapter 3, I discussed who counts as an insider or outsider to a family. Chapter 4 described ways that homeowners do and do not connect to the local community in material and social ways. This chapter discusses insiders and outsiders more broadly, as well as the systematic exclusion, discrimination, and differential experiences of different race and class groups in the family vacation home marketplace. My research makes it clear that there is no monolithic experience of privilege for family vacation home owners, nor is there a singular way privilege is experienced or demonstrated; however, the existence of privilege itself is ubiquitous. This chapter reveals the varied ways that privilege manifests for people who own family vacation homes, especially in terms of how community is framed in ways that may contextualize that privilege.

NEIGHBORLINESS AND ENTITLED CITIZENSHIP: VOTING, TAXES, ZONING, AND TIME

To vote or not to vote: that was CJ's dilemma. In the previous chapter, I noted that despite being generally politically engaged in their hometowns or with national or global issues, homeowners were not likely to get heavily involved in local politics in their vacation home communities unless the issues centered on their property. At times, this hesitance also related to homeowners not wanting to get involved in conflicts or feeling that they did not deserve a political voice. The civic and community engagement connections they did make, however, were meant to legitimize themselves in the eyes of local residents, especially if they were in town infrequently and/or rented their home to others.

Sunny (Investment Property group), for example, pointed out that her role as a permanent local resident in Northwest Oceanside was at times ignored when other locals critiqued her vacation rental business. Being heard in public forums was her way to clarify that she was, indeed, a local, as evidenced by her frequent local volunteer work. Whether the consideration is voting, time spent in a community, or apparent dedication to that community, who deserves to have a voice in local goings-on is a big part of any discussion of family vacation homes and their surrounding communities.

What does it mean to be a good neighbor? More poignantly, what does it mean to feel connected, and are neighbors part of the picture? More than two decades ago, sociologist Robert Putnam put forth an argument in his book *Bowling Alone* that our *social capital*—the network of people that gives us access to valuable resources, such as social support, jobs, and information—has been declining in contemporary society.[1] Gone are the days of bowling leagues, neighborhood potlucks, and faith-based small groups, replaced by disconnection, individualism, and declining civic engagement (and sometimes social ties fostered primarily in the paid workplace). Putnam's critiques have faced their fair share of countercritiques, ranging from causality and definitional ambiguity[2] to lack of connection of social capital to the reproduction of inequality.[3] But in spite of these critiques, movements that seek to boost neighborhood social connection are strong, including those that continue to cite Putnam's work as inspiration.[4]

Strong Towns is an organization dedicated to collaborating with local governments to develop cities that are financially stable and "safe, livable, and inviting."[5] It produces articles, research, and workshops intended to build up the social and economic fabric of a communities, albeit with a greater emphasis on economic development. In one article that focuses more on interpersonal relations, Tiffany Owens Reed defines neighborliness as "taking time to invest in building loose ties with the people who live near us." Reed notes that this means being friendly, willing to help if neighbors need someone to grab their mail, or at the very least saying hello in passing. But that's not enough, says Reed, who advocates for "more extra-mile gestures of inclusion, like inviting neighbors over for meals, hosting block parties, or launching interest groups."[6] Reed frames an ideal version of neighborliness as different from what we currently expect, noting that radical hospitality—while not expected in any kind of dutiful moral relationship code—is highly desirable. Reed suggests that neighbors have "loose ties," but advocates for strengthening them so that they move beyond casual greetings to closer and more expressive relationships.

How best to define closeness among neighbors is contested. Olivia (Investment Property group), who is temporarily renting out her home in Wine Country to vacationers while she and her son live elsewhere, recounted a story about a neighbor who criticized allowing short-term rentals in their residentially zoned neighborhood. She had heard that he wished for closer ties between neighbors, something that wasn't possible with transient visitors: "He said, 'I feel like if I go outside and, like, I tripped in the winter and I fall, there'll be nobody around to help me.' And I went, 'Huh, okay. Got it.' He thinks vacation renters wouldn't see a fallen person and ask them if they needed help."

Despite the claim in the Strong Towns article that neighborliness, alas, does not typically carry a moral obligation to offer "extra-mile gestures," it remains a moral issue in any form. The story goes: "Good people help neighbors; bad people don't"—sentiments embedded in Olivia's neighbor's comments, even if Olivia stressed that of course a vacationer would help someone who had tripped. Being a good (or bad) person doesn't automatically get assigned to someone based on the length of their stay in a neighborhood or knowing someone's name. So while neighborliness is a moral issue, the likelihood that a temporary or permanent neighbor is seen as "neighborly" depends on one's assessment of those people's deservedness to be called a neighbor. It also depends on how closely matched people's current neighborhoods are with their visions of what they wanted them to be when they moved there.

The delineation of deservedness for "good" and "bad" people is highly salient to discussions of family vacation homes, since deservedness is intimately commingled with property and voting rights in public debates, legal property classifications, and even interpersonal conflict between neighbors. Indeed, while the legal and formal classifications of investment properties and vacation homes are evoked in debates about their use and impacts on neighborhoods and communities, it is the more qualitative dimensions of actual use, perceptions, and interactions that tell the full story of moral considerations of vacation homes. And, perhaps surprisingly, the use of a vacation home for personal family vacations or to rent to others doesn't seem to matter as much as larger cultural values about citizenship and moral considerations of neighborliness. These values, importantly, carry with them both visible and hidden structural inequalities along class and race lines.

Trick-or-Treating, Taxes, and Time

Kal and his partner rent out their vacation home—which was their primary residence until they moved a few years ago—in a residential neighborhood in Wine Country. Kal is well aware of the critiques of short-term rentals in the community, and disputes them: "The most common complaints are, 'The kids don't trick-or-treat on our street anymore.' If you get an entire block of Vrbos or Airbnbs or short-term rentals, what is the harm? These homes are well maintained. They're well kept. They pay their taxes. They pay their property taxes. What is the harm?"

When I began this project, I had no idea that trick-or-treating would be raised frequently as a symbolic manifestation of people's idealized citizenship categories and neighborhoods. How interesting that a once-a-year event could become such a powerful symbol in the debate over deservedness to visit or live in a neighborhood.

Incidentally, trick-or-treating is changing, both in terms of its overall decline and the form it takes, as more kids are being taken outside of their neighborhoods or to city- or organization-sponsored "trunk-or-treat" events to get the goodies.[7] According to some stakeholders I observed at the Walla Walla City Council short-term rental regulation public meetings, this lamentable decline is a result of the influx of short-term vacation homes in a neighborhood that was once filled with permanent residents—an influx that means we are losing those traditions that go beyond "loose ties" and that support neighborhood families with rituals that are fun and safe for children. Critics of this argument counter that trick-or-treating started to decline when it moved to more centralized community locations and that parents are just taking their kids to neighborhoods that are further away instead of sending them out the front door alone. Pair all of this with demographic trends that show young families moving away from city centers with small homes and yards and toward suburbs and outskirts with more room,[8] and trick-or-treating ends up symbolizing much larger trends about family, neighborhood, and place. Short-term rental critics use a nostalgic view of trick-or-treating to create a powerful image of good times, good people, and good places—idealized neighborliness. Along with compelling evidence of homes sitting vacant from Monday to Thursday in their neighborhoods, they might argue that these good elements have been replaced by bad times, bad people, and bad places—troubling substitutes for a powerful nostalgic version of neighborhood.

Much of the debate about deservedness surrounding vacation homes depends on how people frame their opinions about who is eligible to make decisions about these properties. Eligibility, for some, is defined by voting rights, which are based on time spent in residence but not necessarily on property ownership. In contrast, others may view eligibility as based on ownership via property taxes, but not necessarily voting or time spent in residence. Someone may own a vacation home and not spend much time there. They pay property taxes but don't get to vote in local elections. Another person may rent a home for a year as their primary residence and be allowed to vote in local elections, even though they don't own or pay taxes on the property.

The link between deservedness and voting was made evident by CJ (Personal Property group), who felt that she needed to have lived in her vacation home longer (or more than part-time) before she would be entitled to participate in local elections. Establishing residency in a home requires a certain amount of time spent living there, as outlined in discussions of IRS classifications in the appendix. Voting is something that gives people a voice to shape local deliberations. And when local deliberations are filled with controversy surrounding property owners' or renters' deservedness to do what they want with their properties, voting counts even more. Rich (Mixed Property group) noted that his Western Desert community was swimming in short-term rental conflict. He and his husband felt pressure within their friendship group, and especially from others with vacation homes, to switch their residency status so they could vote against excessive short-term rental regulations in their vacation community: "A lot of our friends or people we've met have said one of us should change this to be our primary residence so one of us can vote here." At the vacation rental conference, a similar message echoed throughout the sessions: if your community is starting to overregulate vacation rentals, be sure to share emotional stories about how your property does a lot of social good with locals who can vote to deregulate. Importantly, other interviewees who live in Western Desert talked about ensuring votes for property owners and for those whose livelihood depended on those vacation homeowners. But, as Estelle (Personal Property group) noted about that community, people like gardeners and house cleaners cannot afford to live there, so they would not be eligible to vote anyway.

Voting rights are directly tied to property rights. But this connection is complicated, because long-term rental tenants can vote, whereas homeowners who don't spend a certain amount of time at their second property may not be considered local citizens and are therefore ineligible. The key arguments surrounding deservedness for vacation home owners, whether they rent their homes or not, contrast the power of voting with the power of property owner-ship, including how property taxes operate. Al talked about how he and his wife Ina may move into a different second home in a neighboring state along Great Lakes Waterfront in order to pay lower property taxes, and live there just a bit more often so that they can vote in local elections. How that would affect their voting rights in their primary residence went undiscussed.

Woody's housing situation also highlights how taxes operate in the minds of homeowners: he lists his vacation home in Northwest Oceanside as an investment property on his taxes so he can deduct the interest. He and his wife have a third home in another amenity-rich locale, which they have deemed a vacation home in the eyes of the IRS—meaning they cannot deduct property taxes—because it is worth less than their Northwest Oceanside home, where he feels a bit more like he's on vacation. In any case, his voting and other political behavior occurs primarily in the community of his first home, which works well for him because he does not feel that his Northwest Oceanside home community is pushing for overregulation of vacation properties.

For Al and Woody (both in the Personal Property group), deservedness to be in a community was connected to property ownership, but their focus was mostly on saving money. In the Walla Walla City Council meetings I attended where short-term regulations were being debated, people who owned proper-ties in town but didn't live there either expressed their disappointment that they didn't get to vote in local elections, where ballot initiatives may be found, or asked local residents who were their allies to speak on their behalf.

To them, having no voting rights meant they felt they had a lesser voice in deliberations related to their properties.

At these same meetings, several residents debated the role of *long-term rental* properties, those rented for months or years at a time. On one hand, critics of short-term rentals said that it would be better for local neighborhoods if homes were turned into long-term rentals. Short-term renters, they argued, are not invested in the long-term well-being or upkeep of a neighborhood. Also, they're noisy. Turning short-term rentals into long-term rentals, they said, would also meet some local housing shortage needs and serve to make the neighborhoods feel lived in by residents who care about the town. One stakeholder I interviewed who had been outspoken where he lived about his own town's regulation deliberations said more long-term rentals would be great because it would mean neighborhoods would be filled with people willing to drive neighbors to the airport, lend a helping hand, and keep an eye out for each other—not just the "loose ties" of a casual hello. He and his wife owned such a rental property on the other side of town. They were both frustrated with an increase in vacation rentals in their residential neighborhood.

But interestingly, other stakeholders who worked in the real estate and tourism industry, as well as vacation rental owners and public meeting attendees who supported vacation rentals in town, considered long-term renters a liability, saying that they can't afford a mortgage, don't care about the homes they're living in because they don't own them, and decrease feelings of safety and aesthetic beauty in a neighborhood. Also, they're noisy. Turning long-term rentals into short-term rentals, they said, would beautify neighborhoods, keep the community's economy vibrant, and make the neighborhoods feel supported, because visitors would go home and talk about how great the town is. Many of the outspoken attendees and several of the stakeholders I interviewed owned second properties. Unlike the stakeholder mentioned above, who owns a long-term rental, these people were far more likely either to have switched from owning long-term to short-term rentals or to own both kinds. Thus, they based their argument on comparisons they'd made about their own properties and the types of people renting them.

These arguments point to a key truth: residence in a neighborhood—not vacationing there—comes with a vote. Property ownership may or may not come with a vote. Depending on one's position on short-term vacation rentals, people with longer residencies may be seen as more responsible voters in the eyes of regulation supporters.

The framing of eligibility to be neighborly based on short-term or long-term stays in a neighborhood suggests that length of time in that locale matters. People across and within the property groups varied in terms of how much time they spent at their vacation properties. Some in the Investment Property group visited a few times a year to see how the property was holding up; others lived next door or on the same property and visited daily. Some in the Personal Property group visited four times a year, while others spent nearly half of the time there. And people in the Mixed Property group were in the middle: several times a year for personal visits, another few visits for maintenance, or visiting infrequently if the property was currently rented out and they planned to make more frequent visits after retirement.

In chapter 2 I noted that perception of the importance of time rather than actual time spent at a property affected how people viewed their family, work, and vacation roles. When considering homeowners' deservedness to partici-pate in local issues, time spent in a family vacation home, while variable, mattered not so much in terms of actual numbers of days or weeks, but rather in how both homeowners and host communities perceived the value of time. It even mattered in their overall perception of a vacation place as being filled with people who deserved to be there. Margot (Mixed Property group), who rents her Tropical Paradise condo about half the year, noted that the condo neighborhood is filled with retirees and families with young children who live there year-round. And so, she said, the place is "really their [the locals'] home." That makes her feel good about being there, and it makes her feel as if the vacation neighborhood is similar to her primary residence neighborhood, even though she sometimes rents it out to strangers. In general, deservedness was unlikely to be felt by homeowners who visited four or fewer times per year. But even this amount of time could be enough to justify someone's feel-ings of connection with the local community and, in turn, their involvement in local issues.

People in the Personal Property group exemplified this. Morgan, for instance, noted this about her Northwest Oceanside vacation home: "Even though we only come here four times a year, we've gotten to know the com-munity." (She then proceeded to describe in detail all her neighbors' quirky traits.) And Willa noted about her Northwest Oceanside vacation community that "the people who don't live there have more say than the people who do live there," given that temporary residents with vacation homes outnumbered permanent residents nearly two to one. Al and Ina refused to call their home a vacation home because they spent so much time there, which also led them to justify their involvement in local politics and goings-on.

Among all property groups, those who followed local regulations and spent "enough time" at their property felt justified in their belief that they were enti-tled to a voice in local issues—even if they were not legally entitled to vote in local politics. The fact that this sentiment was raised as often by people who spent one month a year at their vacation home as those who spent five months there suggests that it's not the amount of time per se that matters, but rather the strategic use of time to meaningfully support entitled citizenship.

Defensive Othering

Interestingly, some of the properties owned by the interviewees and by the people who attended the vacation rental conference were located in commercially zoned neighborhoods, while others were in residentially zoned spots. Though I assumed that debates would look different depending on zoning, this did not pan out as anticipated. Anna (Investment Property group), who has an apartment vacation rental in Wine Country, told a story about how she excitedly announced the opening of her new rental at her table at a local fraternal organization luncheon. Her news was met with scowls and furrowed brows. This confused Anna, since most of the people there were very supportive of initiatives that benefited the local economy. But in a time of local debate surrounding short-term rental regulations, some of her tablemates were advocates for greater regulation and fewer rentals. Their scowls softened—but only a little—when Anna explained that her property was located in a commercially zoned neighborhood. Amid a larger debate about property use in the community, how her vacation rental property location was zoned mattered less than the fact that the property was being rented at all.

Most of the ways that homeowners talked about their deservedness to have a voice in local goings-on were tied to a desire to distance themselves from labels that were deemed morally bad. If they didn't vote or feel entitled to vote, they justified this by saying they didn't spend enough time in the community or didn't know it well enough yet. But even those who did feel entitled did not use the monetary value of their property as justification. Instead, they framed themselves on the correct moral side of good versus bad people, noting that the time they spent in their vacation community legitimated their local involvement. At times, they also distanced themselves from the immoral side of issues by referencing worse people and places, pointing out the bad acts of locals, and noting others' tendency for hyperbole. Anna, for instance, by clarifying her vacation rental's status in a commercially zoned area, implied it wasn't as bad as other rentals. Ole and Angela (Personal Property group) differentiated their modest and controversy-free vacation home neighborhood from a more affluent area one hundred miles away at a lake populated with million-dollar mansions, celebrity sightings, and debates about short-term rental regulations. Woody (Personal Property group) said that locals were the noisy ones, not vacationers. Sunny (Investment Property group) complained about a local vacation rental critic in Northwest Oceanside whom she claimed irrationally worried about "rapists and murderers" renting vacation homes. Even Vera (Personal Property group), who was not involved in local politics and who loved that her Great Lakes Waterfront community had very little controversy surrounding vacation homes, distanced herself from a morally bad act: "Neighbors talk if they see people coming and going on weekends.

I've given my house to people for a week or a weekend, but I never charge them. That defeats the purpose of renting your house out, but it's not violating the ordinance if you do that."

The strategy of distancing oneself from the negative parts of a group that one is part of is called *defensive othering*.[9] It is used to manage *stigma*, or a negative label, often when people who are part of a stigmatized group or category simultaneously claim that they are not like the problematic members of that group and that they themselves are victimized or othered. When vacation home owners feel like they are seen as having a bad influence on a neighborhood or community, they work hard to assure people that they're "not like the bad people." The moral differentiation of good from bad—nonstigmatized from stigmatized—occurs in the family vacation home marketplace across a number of binaries, including short-term renters versus long-term renters, as mentioned earlier, as well as in comparisons between vacation rental owners and local residents, vacation rental visitors and homeowner visitors, responsible neighbors and irresponsible neighbors, and wealthy elites and responsible citizens.

If not mentioning labor is the first rule of family vacation homes, then not mentioning affluence is the second rule. Explicit reference to home value was hard to find in the interviews I conducted (though property values were collected in the surveys). A common pattern across all three property groups was the use of defensive othering via *status apologetics*: either avoiding the discussion of actual dollar amounts attached to property values or costs, or downplaying economic status attached to ownership of valuable vacation properties. In some cases, the goal was to abide by societal taboos related to talking about money. In others, people distanced themselves from stigmatized attributes of wealthy people, such as irresponsibility toward others, exploitation of resources or people, or undeserved access to wealth. For homeowners, it was important to come across as socially responsible, morally good people, especially during an era when conspicuous mention of wealth is stigmatized.[10] Of course, economic privilege makes it easier to avoid the topic of money, while economic precarity is more likely to place people into situations where they are required to disclose their financial story whether they want to or not.

Indeed, the status of being a vacation homeowner itself shapes how and whether people talk about money. Despite class variation and property values ranging from five to seven or even eight figures, everyone included in this research has a valuable asset that situates them in a more stable financial situation than people who don't own property. They didn't go out of their way to talk about money—they didn't need to in order to have something interesting to say about their homes.

In terms of downplaying wealth, homeowners in all property groups I interviewed sometimes reclassified their property by, for instance, referring to a detached house as a "cabin," regardless of its size or potential to be used year-round. In other cases, they defined their family vacation home as modest in relation to a lavish neighbor's home—a pattern that occurred across income groups. Francis (Personal Property group) talked about a neighbor whose home she differentiated from her own in Great Lakes Waterfront, for example: "He also bought an old house, but he essentially expanded it. They have a gorgeous swimming pool. It's a much fancier house than ours. It was sort of, how would you say, higher style in terms of decoration and stuff. Ours is just very simple and very easy and very comfortable." Francis noted on her survey that her "simple" vacation home is worth $500,000.

Housing terminology and defensive othering came together when talking to Ole (Personal Property group), too. He talked about how a newcomer built a "lodge" in the neighborhood of "cabins" where his vacation home was situated, which was seen as problematic because its aesthetic connoted a braggartly display of wealth. This wasn't just a question of aesthetic taste; it was a challenge to values of modesty, hard work, and deservedness. It also challenged the meaning of family vacation home: a place meant for family activities and fun, not to show off to others or dishonor the culture of a neighborhood. For vacation homeowners, it was strategic to admit they were in a privileged category while also distancing themselves from the irresponsible, privilege-inducing behaviors they perceived in others.

As I reflected on the interviews, I wondered if my presence as a researcher mattered. After all, it is more socially desirable to downplay wealth, especially to someone who may be perceived—correctly or incorrectly—as less wealthy, more socially minded, and less familiar than close friends or family. But there were many moments when people trusted me with private stories and sentiments. They were not trying to hide anything. Perhaps unconsciously they were trying to distance themselves from bad traits—exploitative, irresponsible, braggadocious—and avoiding mention of an asset's value is a strategy to gain moral legitimacy, even in one's own eyes, a finding consistent with sociologist Rachel Sherman's research on the conflicted feelings of progressive-minded wealthy people in an unequal society.[11]

All of this points to an ideal of a middle-class homeowner whose voice matters if they own property and if they can demonstrate social connectedness and moral responsibility. When Americans are surveyed about what social class they think they belong in, an overwhelmingly large proportion select "middle class."[12] Why? First, most people can see how they are situated economically between other groups. Second, it's comfortable and desirable to feel normal, and middle class signifies a "norm." And finally, being situated at either the top or bottom of the socioeconomic spectrum in the United

States is stigmatized: those at the bottom do not work hard enough to achieve the American dream, while those at the top reap the benefits of others' hard work while coming across as elitist and undeserving. To avoid being seen as undeserving, wealthy people may not only emphasize public and community good over and above personal benefit from a vacation home (as the Washington State homeowners opposing the oyster farm discussed at the end of chapter 4 did); they also may strategically downplay their economic status, distancing themselves from the stigmatized features of the affluent: elitism, irresponsibility, and selfishness.

CLASS AND RACE DISTINCTIONS AS MORAL PROJECTS

"Especially up here, the idea that you have two houses just feels a little bit, yeah, pretentious is a good word. This is not an area that is very pretentious at all."

—Martina, Northern Lake Country (Personal Property group)

"There are times when I'm here, I feel guilty because across the street there are rentals with families that are struggling. They're not real well-off, and I think they must look across at this house that's kept up and empty most of the time."

—Minnie, Wine Country (Personal Property group)

"[Western Mountain] has a tremendous number of retired PhDs, a tremendous number of retired lawyers. . . . For their entire work career, they were very important, very influential people that, when they spoke, people listened to them. Their brains are still functioning and they feel marginalized and they think that everybody needs to listen to them. I'm always amazed at how many people in these mountain towns feel the need to inform you of their education credentials when they're talking about something that has absolutely nothing to do with their field."

—City employee, Western Mountain

Income, education, occupational prestige, and wealth: these are often the ingredients for a robust definition of socioeconomic status. But the qualitative elements of how it feels to be at a certain status level, or what the everyday choreography of that status demonstration may look like, are important dimensions of how class actually works in society. The affective dimensions of class hinted at in the quotes above—pretentiousness, guilt, entitlement—vividly show how class is lived and perpetuated, often subtly. The same goes for race: as racism plays out at the level of social structures and collective cultural systems, it also can be seen in everyday practices, perceptions, and interactions. The emotional experience of feeling included or excluded in family vacation homes, or in vacation communities, is intimately connected to larger systems of class and race inequality.

Racial inequalities also connect to the material dimensions of family vacation homes, and to conceptions of neighborliness. One of the vacation rental webinars I analyzed focused explicitly on inclusion, with numerous mentions of race. The speaker, travel expert Evita Robinson, advised that homeowners who rent their home to other vacationers, especially if they want to be inclusive and draw more African American customers, should stock their home with a variety of ethnic hair care products, use decor that welcomes people from different backgrounds, market local businesses that are explicitly open and affirming, and audit the language in their online listings so it doesn't offend people (e.g., remove colonialist references). She noted that people are looking for more values-driven travel, seeking places with explicitly inclusive policies. She also acknowledged that guest and host experiences are not limited to a single transaction but are part of a larger historical and collective process: "Your open doors are not just to your home, but also to the experience and the culture that everyone who comes through the doors is bringing with them at any point in time."[13]

Online vacation rental companies have changed their policies in the last two years to account for discriminatory practices toward guests of color.[14] The remnants of the deep and wide historical roots of racial discrimination in both housing and vacation markets—from real estate *redlining*[15] to vacation sites segregated by *ethnic enclave*[16]—can still be seen in current family vacation home experiences. The sentiment of "not in my back yard," or *NIMBY*—with all its subtle and not-so-subtle race and class markers—is alive and well in neighborhoods and communities built upon the ideal of leisure for white middle- and upper-class families. Property and residence as markers of deservedness are woven into the fabric of the United States. As sociologist Brian McCabe notes, citizenship in the days of the drafting of our founding documents was limited to wealthy white male landowners.[17]

While racial exclusion in real estate practices is less explicit than in the past, it remains an issue across the country in the neighborhoods filled with family vacation homes, evident in the data I collected. Homeowners see it, recognize it, and lament it, but both the exclusion itself and acknowledgment of it come in the form of material and spatial subtleties, rhetorical strategies, and racial claims disguised as generalized moral claims. Class discrimination in the family vacation home marketplace includes elements similar to those that characterize racial discrimination—NIMBY, the deep and wide historical roots of differential access by income and wealth, and class-based segregation—and homeowners acknowledge these issues similarly. Still, class differences were, to some extent, easier for people to talk about.

Most of the homes included in this study are situated in amenity-rich places where second home owners are more affluent than local residents. They're also more affluent than people living in nearby towns who help maintain other people's vacation homes and—reflecting the general trends in the areas included in this research—are populated disproportionately by white people. The findings elaborated below show ways that family vacation homes serve to reinforce racial and class inequalities, including material and spatial means, strategic rhetorical turns, and complicating race and class inequality as real estate moral projects about "good" and "bad" people.

Vacationing in Poverty and Exoticism: Spatial and Material Dimensions of Inequality

As earlier chapters detail, the spatial and material dimensions of social life can be helpful indicators of identities, group differences, and connection to memories of place or people. They can also be indicators of structural inequality. Valencia, Morgan, Vera, and Marion's comments illustrate this well:

> "That's the Confederacy out there. You still see people with Confederate flags on their trucks and their houses. Mostly white . . . there are some African Americans and I think there are some Latinos, too, but they're all, I shouldn't say all, I shouldn't generalize like that—my perspective is that they tend to be on the poor side. So here [in her primary residence city] you get a lot of diversity but the socioeconomic level is high. . . . [T]hat's not true out there. There is a meth problem."
>
> —Valencia, Eastern Woods (Personal Property group)

> "A high percentage of the businesses have 'help wanted' signs up, and they cannot find staff, because people cannot live on minimum wage down here. They can't find any place to rent, and we've been joking about it. Someone needs to come down here and build a couple bunkhouses for summer help."
>
> —Morgan, Northwest Oceanside (Personal Property group)

> "This is not a wealthy community. That's why there was a beach fest last night . . . to raise funds for individual organizations and to run the town

because the tax base has not been here. . . . A lot of Jews who were escaping Europe in the '30s ended up here . . . and [people from] the Baltic countries. . . . They think of [this place] as reminiscent of where they lived in Europe."

—Vera, Great Lakes Waterfront (Personal Property group)

"There were some people that lived in the alley behind the guest house. . . . They were renting this property, and they just began to fill up the entire alley with junk. . . . People would drive up and think that they were going to the ghetto."

—Marion, Wine Country (Investment Property group)

Karen Stein discovered that amenity-rich resorts use local motifs to call to mind their locales. But these motifs exoticize and oversimplify the people living in that place, "thus, limited motifs are displayed that channel attention to a particular vision of the culture that is based on a stereotyped ethnicity or national identity."[18] So vacationing isn't just about the seashells that are brought into the vacation home as decor—it is also about who gets to live where those seashells are found, and how homeowners perceive (and may consume or display) the racialized and classed dimensions of their vacation home communities. While they can symbolically represent the surrounding location, landscape, or culture, these material objects can also be sites for social group identification and separation.

Homeowners recognize these differences and inequalities, especially if they are involved in larger social justice organizations or philanthropic efforts and if their vacation homes are in locales that are easily identified as vacation destinations. But even if they are careful not to appropriate local cultures' ways of life, some homeowners may still don clothing or use decor that signifies both their awareness of the local group of people to which they do not belong and their intent to contrast themselves with this group. Often, this is racialized, as in the case of those in Tropical Paradise wearing clothing with culturally prescribed motifs. The result, as Stein noted, can be a stereotyped representation of ethnicity or national identity. In this way, homeowners' use of material objects to either downplay differences or "fit in" may actually serve to reproduce inequalities, because visitors can leave this sartorial vacation at any time.

Many vacation home owners talked about wearing clothes that fit their vacation activities: ski boots, swimsuits, and so on. But just as common were clothing references that showed homeowners trying to blend in with locals, attempting to remove the social line that divided them, especially in terms of class. Franklin talked about his experience shopping for "ratty clothes" at a local thrift shop in the Great Lakes Waterfront community where the vacation home he owns with his wife Neva is situated. When in his hometown, Franklin wears expensive suits to work, something he is proud of because he grew up without a lot of money. The worn-out T-shirts and flannel shirts he leaves at his vacation home not only help him feel relaxed but also help him blend into the community, which is made up of people who are much less affluent than those in Franklin's current social circle. In this sense, he is "vacationing" in a lower socioeconomic class, a practice that allows affluent people to distance themselves from the stigmatized markers of affluence that may signify an inability to relate to people from varied backgrounds.[19] Of course, while it is easy for affluent people to return from vacation to their usual affluent ways, it is much harder for those with less money to symbolically traverse the class boundary upward—and this ability to move easily between class statuses perpetuates class inequality. Incidentally, Franklin told me that when they sell their vacation home, he'll donate the clothes back to the thrift store where he got them.

It isn't always the case that vacationers want to blend in, however. Material objects can signify social group belonging or be strategically used to signify difference. Clothing, for instance, served to differentiate family vacation home owners from local residents, especially when visitors' hometowns and vacation towns had similar racial demographics or a similar climate and accompanying wardrobe. Ole, for example, said that he can "pretty much pick out [local] people by their dress" and that his more expensive wardrobe showed locals in Northwest Woods (whom he referred to as "native people," by which he did not mean Native American) that he was there to spend money and support the local economy. In Ole's hometown and his vacation hometown, most residents were white people.

Clothes help construct identities insofar as they help people play a vacationer role differentiated from their everyday role, reinforcing the notion that realm-specific objects help create a "temporary identity shift,"[20] as discussed in chapter 2. They also signal this role to others, situating people as identifiable in ways they hope allow them to blend in with others and not seem like elitists or culturally insensitive outsiders—a stigmatized identity that carries with it assumptions about irresponsibility. In terms of race and class identity, then, clothing was a particularly powerful tool for homeowners who wanted to give a favorable impression of their responsible natures, whether it was used as a marker of privileged status or as a disguise.

Silence and Depersonalization: Rhetorical Dimensions of Inequality

While material and spatial symbols of group identities can serve to segregate people or allow others to "vacation" in a different social group, the way that people talk about (or don't talk about) race and class also matters. My media analysis of HGTV shows about vacation real estate reveals that television shows devoted to family vacation homes summarily exclude mention of race and class inequalities even though the people depicted in the shows are racially diverse and the property values vary. This is, in part, because racial and class inequalities are not frequently at the top of the list of themes for life-style television. These are reality shows, but the stories—like vacation homes in general—are meant to be set apart from the harsh realities of everyday life, including social inequalities. Importantly, though, this absence is also present in how family vacation home owners talk about their properties.

Rhetorical turns and silences by homeowners and experts in the family vacation home rental industry demonstrate not only a recognition of structural inequality, but also strategies to acknowledge it just enough for their own benefit. In this way, family vacation home owners—whether using their homes or renting them to others—evince the *ease of privilege* that sociologist Shamus Khan identified as a key trait of affluent individuals in contemporary society. Ease of privilege, Khan says, is the capacity for people in elite social groups to be able to feel comfortable in a variety of social settings and situations.[21] While Franklin enacted this with his clothing purchase, it can also take the form of rhetorical strategies.

What did these rhetorical strategies sound like for family vacation home owners? Usually, they took the form of explicit acknowledgement of local inequalities that relate directly to the existence of family vacation homes. But this acknowledgement was mostly framed using third-person pronouns and passive voice, as in the case of Estelle's (Personal Property group) commentary on her Western Desert vacation home, which she uses for her own family and never rents out:

> Some of the workers that live there year around probably look at the snowbirds as being spoiled rotten. . . . There is some antagonism there because they are the ones that do all of the work and stay there all summer and do all the labor in the gardens and this and that. It's a very large Hispanic area down there. I don't know anything about the illegal stuff. I don't know. I have no idea how many of them are legal.

Estelle used first-person pronouns to express her ignorance, but not when talking about the larger housing issues taking place. Sunny (Investment Property group) also did this when she talked about the Northwest Oceanside community where her vacation rental is located (and where she also lives): "There are no jobs. . . . Those urban exiles aren't going to clean houses or check them or wash windows or go fiddle with kitchen fans that don't work."

This wasn't always the case, though. Auggie (Investment Property group), for example, told a story demonstrating clear recognition of racial discrimination in his neighborhood in Eastern Oceanside: "One of my downstairs tenants is African American, and he had a bad experience around the corner on my block about three years ago. There's a VFW bar, like a veterans' bar there. . . . The bartender came out and had accused him of being in the neighborhood for no reason, and he told him he lived there. She told him that he was lying, and she didn't recognize him."

I asked Auggie about the racial composition of his neighborhood. He said, "My eight-block radius is super white. Outside of that, it gets a little more diverse. But my exact neighborhood is, I would say the average person is thirty years old, in a relationship, no kids, with a dog." Auggie, while recognizing an instance of racism, discussed the racial composition of his neighborhood in two ways: first, explicitly in terms of the proportion of white people who live there, and second, using markers that were conflating race with other traits like age, relationship and parental status, and even pet ownership. Race as marked by other characteristics serves to perpetuate expectations that a certain type of person should live in a neighborhood where people rent vacation homes.

Carla (Personal Property group) shared a compelling story showcasing socioeconomic status differences between local residents and vacation homeowners in Northwest Woods. She said that many of her vacation home neighbors—all part-time residents—pooled donations for a local person whose house burned down: "[One neighbor] donated five or ten grand, whatever it was, to help them rebuild. They're just good people. Everybody came together, everybody helped purchase the fundraiser items. Everybody donated, so traditionally . . . in that specific area, the people that own vacation homes consider themselves part of the town, part of the community, and do what they can to contribute back."

In this story, Carla distances herself from local residents by virtue of her (and her neighbors') financial stability but at the same time uses that difference to justify her inclusion as "part of the town."

Strategic discussion of social inequality also took the form of depersonalizing the issue, making it entirely about structural conditions that made an individual's efforts either futile or insignificant. Property owners often claimed, especially in conversations about how vacation homes and short-term rentals may lessen affordable housing options, that the market would correct itself. Olivia's (Investment Property group) comments illustrate this: "You just can't keep neighborhoods middle class because you want them to be what they were fifty years ago." And Dusty (Investment Property group), who rents a room in his Western City home, said, "Definitely have noticed the demographics of the neighborhood changing. I think just, like, from walking around and living in the neighborhood, it seems probably like two-thirds Latino families and one-third white families, and now it seems like we're seeing more and more Caucasian people every day. It's crazy how gentrification happens." He could see it happening but did not talk about his role in it in any direct way. Homeowners thus employed the rhetorical strategy of removing themselves personally from the collective story, even as they acknowledged local social inequalities.

Ease of privilege can also be found in how people talk about gaining access to vacation homes. The homeowner on the Puget Sound mentioned in the news story at the end of chapter 4 talked about how he was "lucky enough after years of hard work" to be able to afford a property, even if he was trying to protect it from corporate interests. Several of my interviewees talked about saving money for years to be able to afford their place, while others told me that renting out part or all of their home was necessary to be able to afford the mortgage. In other words, for people who had to worry about money, buying a family vacation home was hard—and it had nothing to do with luck. But the difficulty of buying a vacation home was downplayed among more affluent interviewees.

Difficulty was also downplayed in the HGTV television shows I analyzed about vacation home searches. The opening line of *Beachfront Bargain Hunt* goes like this: "Warm sand between your toes. An afternoon dip in the endless blue sea. Jet skis and sunbathing. And that's just in your backyard. This is beachfront living, and it's only for the rich. Or so you thought." Missing from this opener is recognition that this kind of purchase is unattainable to most people. Part of the enchantment of family vacation homes, even investment properties, is to downplay how hard it is to have one. If price is mentioned, thus tying the magic of family to the marketplace, it may be depicted as a barrier, but for the show's homeowners it ultimately doesn't stand in the way of getting the house of their dreams. This ease of access was demonstrated across all racial groups depicted in the show. And any recognition of the larger impacts of vacation homes on local communities, including issues such as housing affordability, racial segregation, or even environmental impact? Missing.

Earlier I shared findings about how vacation home owners downplayed wealth via status apologetics—for example, calling a 3,000-square-foot home a cabin. This served as a way to distance themselves from some of the negative stigmas often attributed to those with material wealth, such as a lack of social responsibility, exploiting people or resources, or not having earned their privilege. People did not want to be associated with the perceived negative elements of vacation home ownership—gentrification, declining housing affordability, environmental degradation, and not spending enough time in a community to really know the people who live there. Ease of privilege requires downplaying responsibility just enough to come across as socially responsible in general but not personally responsible for local problems. It also requires justifying disengagement, because vacations are enchanted activities that are supposed to be removed from real social inequalities.

Good and Bad People

Race and class are part of the moral considerations of access to and use of family vacation homes. Anna (Investment Property group), who worried that her vacation rental was seen as damaging even though it was situated in a commercially zoned neighborhood in Wine Country, recognized the importance of financial standing in her new enterprise. When discussing how she and her husband decided what to charge vacationers to stay in their rental, she said, "I feel like the rent is such that it's good people coming."

Earlier in this chapter, I mentioned attending Walla Walla City Council public meetings held in the time preceding a decision about short-term rental regulations. I heard people who wanted deregulation so they could rent their properties to short-term vacationers tell stories that invoked a moral tone about "good" people and "bad" people. The stories contained a clear demarcation between renters who were long-term community residents and visitors renting only for a weekend or short vacation stay. Renting to short-term visitors, these individuals claimed, meant "good people" would be in the neighborhood, whereas long-term renters were noisy and uninvested, left ugly furniture outside, were associated with groups prone to get in trouble with law enforcement, and were sometimes late with rent. In other words, they did not uphold the class- and race-based aesthetic and acoustic norms required of a "good" neighborhood. It was the short-term out-of-towners, who could afford to pay high rental fees, who were seen as responsible people. A good neighborhood is one where the properties are well maintained and residents—permanent or temporary—act in a way that does not disrupt others. They "fit in."

In comments from people who pushed for more regulation, I heard a contrasting set of claims: it is the short-term renters who are the "bad" people. People who made these claims pointed to loud bachelorette or wine weekend parties, trash left in the front yard, or absence of evidence of investment in neighbor or community well-being. By having long-term renters or homeowners who reside in a neighborhood permanently, these opponents argued, the community would return to how things were in the past: front porch lights on all week, neighbors lending a hand, and trick-or-treaters crowding the sidewalks on Halloween: helpful disruption, as it were. These residents "fit in."

While people on both sides of these debates made seemingly contrasting claims, these claims actually pointed to the same thing: that good neighbor-hoods consist of well-maintained properties that house people who can afford to live there, who are invested in the community in visible ways, and who behave well. These are racialized and classed expectations.

Interestingly, the use of the phrase "bad people" also came up in interviews where vacation home owners complained about full-time local neighbors. Some went so far as to say that they (or their renters) disliked their vacation time because of how annoying the neighbors were. The biggest complaint? That the neighbors were noisy.

Explicit mention of race was absent when reference was made to "good" or "bad" people among the people I interviewed and at the vacation rental conference, except obtusely with the use of terms like "ghettos" or "crack houses." It was more likely to be mentioned when acknowledging racial inequalities in a vacation home community, but this was not framed as connected to homeowners' acquisition or use of property. Class was more explicitly discussed when referencing the moral compass of owners, renters, and neighbors, but referenced differently depending on whether someone supported vacation homes as investment properties or as places that should be reserved for owners' use.

LAND USE, HEALTH CODES, AND VACATION NOISE: REGULATING NEIGHBORHOOD CONFLICT

In Wine Country, Marion's (Investment Property group) back-alley neighbors' pile of junk led her to file a formal complaint with the city. It got resolved when the neighbors moved out of their long-term rental. Neighbor conflict is not isolated to communities where there are vacation homes. Squabbles over fallen trees, noise, junkpiles, and parking occur everywhere.

But when concerned neighbors fret over the impact of vacation homes that are rented or used by part-time residents, the formal path to resolving these conflicts is often regulation, from noise ordinances to parking rules and land use permits, or—as occurred during COVID-19 lockdowns—health and safety policies designed to regulate local impacts. But really, the rules in place may be less powerful than the norms surrounding what it means to be a good neighbor. Earlier, I discussed how debates about regulating vacation homes connected to moral claims about "good" and "bad" people. It is in deliberations about rules and regulations that we also see important socially defined conceptions of good neighborhoods play out. But in these conceptions, there is a lot of variation in how people come to define "good," including in their use of evidence to plead their case. The result is that their definitions are based not on their position in a particular property group, nor on actual distance from neighbors or understanding of policies or statistics. Rather, their beliefs are about larger cultural values surrounding neighborliness and evidence for what counts as neighborliness.

Parking and Falling Trees: Neighbor Conflicts

I started this chapter with a quote from Jean (Investment Property group), who noted that local conflict about vacation rentals in her Wine Country community "has to do with parking and stuff, which is not an issue out here." She justified this by saying that they live far away from neighbors. There were a number of times during interviews when I thought, "I could write a whole chapter just on parking." An unsurprising topic for neighbor conflict, parking came up as a topic of dispute in some instances where homes were closer together. However, in most cases distance from one's neighbors mattered not necessarily in terms of actual distance, but rather in how people used it to selectively justify decisions about their properties.

Presumably, Jean posited, vacation homes in denser neighborhoods would lead to more conflict. This makes sense. After all, it's easier to hear a barking dog in a condo complex than it is on a farm a mile away. But that wasn't always the case: Dusty (Investment Property group), for example, had no conflicts with neighbors in his Western City home, despite their homes being barely ten feet apart. He even said some guests would hang out in the backyard smoking weed, and the neighbor would join them. And Bonnie (Personal Property group), whose Northern Lake Country home is far enough away from neighbors that she enjoys a lot of peace and quiet regardless of what they're doing, still complained about a neighbor who parked equipment on her property while he brought his dock in for the winter. Yet she didn't confront him, because her lakeside place was meant for relaxing, not dealing with the everyday headaches caused by annoying neighbors.

So neighborliness (along with confronting conflict) seems to depend not so much on how far apart people are, but on how they interpret other elements of their relationships. Some of the interpretation depended on whether a community was clearly defined as a tourist destination in the minds of locals and visitors. Rich (Mixed Property group) noted this about Western Desert: "This community was built as a second home destination for rich people . . . and so the idea that only full owners should be in homes is kind of ridiculous. I mean, we did this because we want this to be our community. But in order for us to make this our community in the long run, we need to be able to rent it out a bit. Otherwise, it becomes cost prohibitive for us to own two houses."

Rich and Marcus, who spend half their time in Western Desert and plan to retire there, could not understand why there was so much conflict and how renting out homes to vacationers somehow violated the community's purpose.

Others' interpretations of neighborliness centered on how locals were sometimes the ones causing disturbances that ought to be regulated, as Marion's alley neighbors' "pile of junk" exemplifies. Grace (Personal Property group), for example, described a conflict she had about tree sap with her year-round neighbors in Western Mountain: "They felt that it was our duty to power clean their deck because our tree got residue on their deck. You're living in the woods. Are you kidding me? We don't think this is our responsibility, but we pretty much did it in the spirit of being neighborly." Peder (Personal Property group) described what happened when his next-door neighbors in Eastern Oceanside moved away, along with their fence: "Their side we were using to fence in our yard, because they already had the fence up. They then sold off the panels from their fence. They're trying to get some kind of money out of the house before they got foreclosed on. They left all the posts up, but the fence was gone."

What about complaints from locals about people who stay in a vacation rental or who come to their community to stay in a family vacation home? Auggie (Investment Property group) told me he'd never had any complaints from neighbors about renting his home in Eastern Oceanside but added, "I haven't told them I'm doing it." He then said that the people in his building knew, and that he requested that they not smoke pot in the entryway where guests arrive. He has received a couple texts from other tenants about noise, which he has been able to remedy by messaging the guests to quiet down. Bella's (Mixed Property group) vacation rental is situated in a multiplex at Eastern Oceanside. She has rented the spaces to long-term tenants and short-term vacationers. She juxtaposed these two types of renters in a story about a neighbor calling to complain, noting that since she started renting the place to short-term vacationers, the calls had stopped. She hypothesized that the neighbor was not invested in developing long-term neighborly relationships with short-term visitors, so she didn't bother to complain about their behavior. Valencia (Personal Property group) talked about a story in a local newspaper near her vacation home in Eastern Woods that showed how disputes between local and vacationing neighbors are framed: "One of the neighbors was really mad because his neighbor would shoot deer and then let them die on his property. Then the other guy just made some comment about how these city folk come out here and try and change our way of life."

Sometimes the complaints worked in two directions: complaints about local neighbors from vacationers and about vacationers from locals. Reede and Minnie (Personal Property group) complained about their immediate neighbor in Wine Country, whose lawn was filled with dandelions that the wind would carry directly into their yard. Reede interpreted his neighbor's behavior by saying, "He has probably a different way of looking at life. He used to repair motorcycles and cars." Minnie added her two cents about neighbor relationships: "Last winter was the first time we got notified by a neighbor that we should be shoveling our sidewalk." I confirmed that there was indeed a lot of snow in her neighborhood last winter, and she continued, "Yeah, and we don't worry about that. We just assume it's okay." On the one hand, Reede and Minnie were annoyed with their neighbor, whose behaviors they suggested were somehow related to his social position (though they wished he would get rid of the dandelions), but the snow that they're supposed to shovel? It's fine to leave it.

Arguments about Evidence: Data Disputes

When debating regulations surrounding vacation homes, including those rented to others, what evidence do different stakeholders use to make their case?

As I introduced in chapter 1, a foundational concept in sociology is the sociological imagination,[22] which requires that we take into consideration both personal stories and larger sociohistorical context when considering any issue. So for a study on family vacation homes, it's important for me to share both individual stories and the patterns found among those stories, placed in a particular time and social context. In my own writing and speaking, it's safe to say that my motto is, "It's always about patterns in the data, and it's always about the stories." What data to use and how to define groups and patterns in this research proved to be challenging, mostly because the groups I uncovered defy legal and formal classificatory schemes. If I was writing a book that advocated for particular policies surrounding vacation homes and investment properties, I would need to utilize more formal and recognizable data that could be reliably analyzed to make claims about the industry as a whole. But my project is more about perceptions, everyday experiences, and symbolic uses of time and space, allowing for a more qualitatively informed classification. But the question always remains in social science research: Which kinds of data best answer a question? If the question is, "Are family vacation homes good for the neighborhood and community?" the classification of evidence used to answer the question as good or bad depends on the goals of the person using and interpreting the data. In other words, what the numbers are may matter less than a person's belief that particular numbers (or any numbers, really) tell the best story about what's going on in a neighborhood.

Rich (Mixed Property group) talked about Western Desert's vacation rental debate, noting that "it's dramatic what the studies are showing. But that doesn't sway the mayor or some of the other key members of the city council." Rich works in a financial profession, so numbers and spreadsheets are easily decipherable to him, as are outcomes framed as financial gains. I saw some of the studies Rich referenced—lots of numbers, spreadsheets, and maps. In an interview with a stakeholder elsewhere who was part of a group advocating for increased vacation rental regulation, I was given pages of maps, charts, comparative numbers from similar towns, graphs showing housing stock changes over time, and timelines, all meant to sway local officials to curb the influx of temporary vacationers. These two quantitative data fans used nearly identical types of data (and nearly identical findings, actually) to provide support for oppositional claims in two different places.

At the vacation rental conference, I noticed an interesting paradox pertaining to the use of data and stories. On one hand, when facing regulators or critics, homeowners were advised to point out flawed data (for example, claims that make a causal link between second home ownership and housing affordability) and to note that anecdotal evidence is not enough to justify policy changes. On the other hand, they were told by vacation rental experts to use compelling family- and community-centric stories to show how their vacation rentals do good in the world—for example, stories of providing housing for people traveling with a sick family member—all in support of deregulation. In these cases, the type of data (or anecdote) was less about the objective efficacy of a particular piece of evidence and more about using evidence to make the most compelling case for your side of the issue.

COVID-19 and the Infusion of Health and Safety in Enclosing "Pods" of "Your People"

COVID-19 lockdowns during spring 2020 offered a unique moment when the use and regulation of family vacation homes became intertwined with moral claims about health, safety, social inequalities, and community well-being. Vacations changed during the pandemic, due in part to social and governmental pushes for people to create "pods" or "bubbles," to travel less, and to be more attentive to health and safety in places they visited. At the same time, affluent people with second properties in amenity-rich communities utilized these properties in new ways, sometimes—and increasingly during heightened COVID-19 restrictions—telecommuting to work from places that were once used only for leisure (or renting them to others doing the same thing).

The influx of affluent professionals (and sometimes young adults using their parents' vacation homes) into amenity-rich vacation home locales during lockdown offered a new way of thinking about the purposes of these spaces and places, and not just because the stays were longer than when used as vacation spots. In my content analysis of local news articles from 2020 published in these tourist locales,[23] vacation homeowners who shifted their paid work from an office near their primary residence to telecommuting were framed as undeserving outsiders by locals quoted in the stories. People who could afford to rent other people's vacation homes were also seen this way. While visitors framed their presence as beneficial to local economies and the collective health of their (often more densely populated) primary residence communities, locals framed it as morally problematic. In these tourist areas—especially during quiet or *shoulder seasons* (the time between offseason and peak season)—the inequity of COVID-19's impacts on labor, income, and health resources were apparent, with many community members suddenly unemployed while others struggled to keep up with all the work to be done.

In terms of framing the right to reside in a particular locale based on property rights and taxes during lockdown, vacation home owners still predominantly framed their right to stay based on owning property; locals still predominantly framed their discontent around a definition of community connectedness centered on long-lasting social connections. In addition to property rights and taxes, the perception of time mattered for local residents. With the onset of the pandemic, vacation home owners spent more time in these places at an unusual time of year, yet locals did not frame this as bolstering vacation home owners' status as insiders. Instead, outsiders spending more time in these communities meant more risk for locals, hence less concern for community well-being. Pandemic-induced policy revisions and confusion over social norms made establishing a clear shared definition of connection difficult.

Vacation home owners still viewed their migration to these places as an escape from the stresses of everyday life.[24] But now, these stresses were related to health rather than long work hours or rush hour commutes. Stays were not as likely to be framed as getaways or vacations, because many visitors were not actually vacationing: they were continuing their everyday lives, including going to work and school, but from afar. Doing this was framed as morally good by vacation home owners, since they were removing themselves from densely populated areas while still fulfilling their everyday responsibilities. This wasn't about leisure; it was about making the right call to balance safety and responsibility in a time of stress. In this sense, self-interest was recast as collective good, with vacation homes playing a crucial role as nonleisure spaces.

At the same time, locals perceived visitors as spending time there *only* for leisure (even if they were telecommuting to work and school), all while buying groceries, taking up space, and adding risk by increasing population density. Locals, then, reinforced their sense of community connectedness by framing vacation home owners and renters, in explicitly moral terms, as undeserving, elite outsiders who, by vacationing during a pandemic, were depleting access to shared spaces, hospital beds, and supplies in communities where people don't have a lot of resources and maybe can't even afford to live there.

CONCLUSION: ENCHANTMENT ACROSS LEGAL AND MORAL BOUNDARIES

My childhood memories from watching *Mr. Rogers' Neighborhood*[25] take me back to a place where I learned that being a good neighbor means loving everyone, helping those in need, collaborating to solve problems, and trying to understand people in your community. When talking about family vacation homes, what does it mean to be a good neighbor? Does it depend on what the local ordinances say, or on what people decide to use as their own moral compass? And why is a moral compass a strategically useful guide when deciding how to defend the use of a family vacation home as an enchanted place?

The findings in this chapter reveal three ways that the family vacation home is strategically framed as enchanted by homeowners in terms of legal and moral boundaries: through the framing of neighborliness and entitled citizenship, through reference to race and class distinctions as moral projects, and through discussion of regulatory processes pertaining to property and neighborhood conflicts. Below, I summarize how these findings connect to the overarching goal of enchanting the family vacation home.

Neighborliness and Entitled Citizenship

Homeowners made moral distinctions between good and bad people to support the specific way they used their family vacation home. For Investment Property group homeowners, long-term renters were framed as morally problematic while short-term vacation renters were morally good, especially for neighborhood well-being. For the Personal Property group, and especially for local neighbors who were critics of the Investment Property group, it was more common to suggest that long-term renters (or even vacationers such as themselves) were better citizens because they spent more time in the neighborhood. Time spent at a vacation home mattered less than the perceived importance of time as a way of establishing deservedness, however. All property groups strategically distanced themselves from any morally bad image of homeowners via defensive othering techniques, including downplaying their own affluent status.

Their goal in doing so: to preserve the enchantment of the family vacation home. Nobody wanted to be the villain in a fairy tale meant to be an escape from conflict and stress of everyday life.

Class and Race Distinctions as Moral Projects

Homeowners across property groups—a group of relatively affluent and predominantly white people—recognized the realities of structural racism and classism in contemporary society. At the same time, they perpetuated inequalities by disguising classist and ethnocentric references to local community members as morality claims, especially if they were in a more financially stable position. They also absented the role of their family vacation home story from the story of structural inequality, often using rhetorical strategies to create distance from the issue. While property groups differed in how they did this, an idealized image of a middle-class white neighborhood was often present in rhetorical strategies used to defend the use of vacation homes, whether they used the homes themselves or rented them out.

Enchantment of the family vacation home—its framing as a magical place removed from the harsh realities of everyday responsibilities—is intimately intertwined with larger systems of class and race inequality. When vacation rental companies were investigated for discriminatory practices against vacationers of color, the problem boiled down to unequal access to good and valuable experiences: leisure, escape, and less stress than one would find in normal life. Across property groups, a nostalgic image of neighborhood was consistently evoked to justify the use of a vacation property. This nostalgic image, which has never been accessible to people without high incomes or those who belong to racial groups that have faced discrimination across the housing, tourism, and hospitality industries, serves to perpetuate inequality even as it supports a vision of the family vacation home as enchanted. Privilege allows for the capacity to absent oneself from parts of collective life that are "too real."

Regulating Neighborhood Conflict

Conflicts between neighbors and attitudes about vacation home regulations did not vary as much by property group as they did based on factors that are present in any neighborhood. Actual distance between properties mattered less than the perception of distance as salient to a disagreement, especially about noise and land use. The designation of a community as clearly meant for tourism (or not) affected how much people saw the use of a home by outsiders as appropriate, although not everybody agreed about community tourism designations. Everyone used evidence to support their desired use of a property, but whether that evidence came in the form of numbers or stories depended on a homeowner's goals. During lockdowns associated with the COVID-19 pandemic, vacation home owners and renters who temporarily moved to amenity-rich communities in offseason times were seen by permanent residents as undeserving outsiders.

Conflicts between neighbors occur across family vacation home property groups, but in all cases the management of (or sometimes desire to ignore) conflict serves to preserve the family vacation home as a place removed from everyday responsibility, negative interactions, and, well, conflict. Enchantment cannot happen if there are arguments about who pays for the removal of tree sap from a deck or if the town doesn't see itself as a magical tourist destination.

* * *

It's no fun to think about conflict and politics, or the ways that leisure may perpetuate structural inequalities, when you're on vacation. And yet this perpetuation is a big—albeit sometimes hidden—part of the story. If this wasn't the case, Anna would not have equated "good people" with a willingness to pay a higher price for her vacation rental, located in a community where furrowed-browed locals were hoping for greater regulation of such rentals. When I asked Kal about similar local vacation rental regulation deliberations in Wine Country, he also furrowed his brow and offered this response:

> We're not looking at a bunch of crack houses. So that's my first question. How do you legislate a way of life? That is creepily close to ordinances about who's allowed to move into a neighborhood. So now we're only going to allow families with kids between this age and this age who like to trick-or-treat? Now we're going to do a personality test and see how many people will be interested in a block party? Can you legislate that?

Strong Towns writer Tiffany Owens Reed, mentioned earlier in this chapter, suggests an increase in "more extra-mile gestures of inclusion, like inviting neighbors over for meals, hosting block parties, or launching interest groups."[26] This quote—which, like Kal's, references block parties—intersects inclusion, social connections, and dedication to collective causes, albeit via small group interactions. Kal's comments showcase the integration between competing (and in his mind, outdated) views of neighborliness, the role of regulation in preventing conflict and enhancing the nostalgic dreams of neighborhood, and boundaries between the types of morally good or bad people whose presence would only lead to regulation if they lived in "crack houses." The use of this visual reference, one could argue, skirts dangerously close to stereotypical images about race and class even as it is meant to connote more freedoms for any kind of homeowner. Kal hoped for less regulation so that he and his partner could continue to rent out their second home (which used to be their primary home). However, when he mentioned elsewhere in

his interview a troubling relationship with the vacation home's local neighbor, Kal's strategy for dealing with this nuisance was not to push for regulations that could curb her behavior or their relatioinship; rather, he just moved
to a different house and turned the first into a vacation rental. Kal's solution
to social conflict was not regulation, but financial maneuvering.

Incidentally, but interestingly, in addition to owning a vacation rental,
Kal works in the tourism and hospitality industry. One of his main priorities
throughout his career has been to create more accessible and socially inclusive travel options for groups otherwise excluded or marginalized from
amenity-rich locations. When it comes to property, it is not uncommon for
people to separate their story from larger systems of inequality. This inconsistency is strategically useful for the perpetuation of self-interest, especially
when it comes to private property. Add to this the claim that deregulating
private property helps to remove considerations of home from the political
realm (since property is held in the private realm), and it's easy to see how
all of this may perpetuate the enchantment of the family vacation home even
in the midst of troubling references about bad neighbors.

People I interviewed were proud to own a family vacation home, but some
felt a little guilty (and even lucky) to be so privileged in a society rife with
inequality, perhaps explaining why many supported social causes, talked
about wanting more social connection in a fractured world, and tended to
share stories that painted them as community minded. But this isn't just about
psychological processes associated with guilt, pride, or shame. It is about
strategic (and understandable) decisions that are embedded in a particular
economic system and a particular set of cultural values that are intertwined.
It is understandable to downplay the wealth associated with a family vacation
home in a society that stigmatizes wealth-based elitism and enchants anything
associated with families. It is also understandable to employ defensive othering, status apologetics, and even silence when it comes to acknowledging
one's role in a racist and classist society. To acknowledge one's place in these
structures is to take direct responsibility, a challenging feat in a setting like a
vacation home, which is meant to be removed from everyday responsibilities.
The fact that these strategies played out regardless of homeowner wealth or
race, and across all property categories, shows just how pervasive the goal of
enchanting the family vacation home is.

Although family vacation homes are meant to be set apart as priceless
places removed from the marketplace and politics, they can be politicized by
issues such as regulation-related conflicts and the level of perceived closeness or distance from inequalities on a local or global level. Enchanting—and
thus depoliticizing—family vacation homes can make strategic definitions of
community and uses of privilege harder to see. And yet, varied definitions of

community and uses of privilege become a powerful tool in the enchantment of these homes for morally deserving leisure-seekers.

The delineation of deservedness for "good" and "bad" people is highly salient to discussions of family vacation homes, since deservedness is intimately commingled with property and voting rights in public debates, legal property classifications, and even interpersonal conflict between neighbors. Indeed, while the legal and formal classifications of investment properties and vacation homes are evoked in debates about their use and impacts on neighborhoods and communities, it is the more qualitative dimensions of actual use, perceptions, and real interactions that tell the full story of moral considerations of vacation homes. And, perhaps surprisingly, the use of a vacation home for personal family vacations or to rent to others doesn't seem to matter as much as larger cultural values about citizenship and moral considerations of neighborliness. And these values, importantly, carry with them both visible and hidden structural inequalities along class and race lines.

So the strategies used by homeowners not only preserve status, they also demonstrate an adherence to powerful shared cultural values about family being somehow enchanted. The by-product of these understandable cultural actions, though, is a damaging structural one: the perpetuation of unequal access to leisure, space, wealth, safety, and rights. As long as the intimate connection between family and the marketplace is downplayed, and as long as vacation home owners distance themselves from their role in perpetuating structural inequalities, the powerful forces of privilege will remain invisible. It's only possible to take a vacation from the effects of structural inequality if you're in the category of people at the top. This, of course, has deep historical roots in systems of inequality. The story of historical and generational change in family vacation homes continues in chapter 6.

NOTES

1. Robert Putnam, *Bowling Alone* (New York: Simon and Schuster, 2000).

2. Steven N. Durlauf, *"Bowling Alone*: A Review Essay," *Journal of Economic Behavior and Organization* 47 (2002): 259–73, https://doi.org/10.1016/S0167 -2681(01)00210-4.

3. Institute for Social Capital, "Putnam on Social Capital—Democratic or Civic Perspective," https://www.socialcapitalresearch.com/putnam-on-social-capital -democratic-or-civic-perspective/.

4. Yuval Levin, "'The Upswing' Review: Bowling Alone No More?" *Wall Street Journal*, October 9, 2020.

5. Strong Towns, "About Strong Towns," https://www.strongtowns.org/about.

6. Tiffany Owens Reed, "The 'Je Ne Sais Quoi' of Neighborliness," Strong Towns, October 10, 2023, https://www.strongtowns.org/journal/2023/10/10/the-je-ne-sais-quoi-of-neighborliness.

7. Julie Beck, "Trick-or-Treating Isn't What It Used to Be," *Atlantic*, October 31, 2018.

8. Laurel Walmsley, "Young Families Continued to Leave Cities Last Year—but at a Slower Pace," NPR, July 9, 2023, https://www.npr.org/2023/07/09/1186483034/family-exodus-cities-census-data.

9. Matthew B. Ezzell, "'Barbie Dolls' on the Pitch: Identity Work, Defensive Othering, and Inequality in Women's Rugby," *Social Problems* 56, no. 1 (2009): 111–31, https://doi.org/10.1525/sp.2009.56.1.111.

10. Brooke Chambers, "The Stigma of Being Rich," The Society Pages Clippings, September 20, 2017, https://thesocietypages.org/clippings/2017/09/20/the-stigma-of-being-rich/.

11. Rachel Sherman, *Uneasy Street: The Anxieties of Affluence* (Princeton, NJ: Princeton University Press, 2019).

12. Jeffrey M. Jones, "Middle-Class Identification Steady in the U.S.," Gallup, May 19, 2022, https://news.gallup.com/poll/392708/middle-class-identification-steady.aspx.

13. Evita Robinson, "Increase Earnings through Inclusivity," Vrbo Virtual Summit, https://host.expediagroup.com/vrbo/en-us/articles/vrbo-partner-summit/inclusivity.

14. Sara Clemence, "Black Travelers Say Home-Share Hosts Discriminate, and a New Airbnb Report Agrees," *New York Times*, December 13, 2022, https://www.nytimes.com/2022/12/13/travel/vacation-rentals-racism.html.

15. Brian J. McCabe, *No Place Like Home: Wealth, Community, and the Politics of Homeownership* (New York: Oxford University Press, 2016).

16. Brenda Rees, "Beyond Bruce's Beach," *Pomona College Magazine*, June 1, 2023, https://magazine.pomona.edu/2023/summer/beyond-bruces-beach/.

17. McCabe, *No Place Like Home*.

18. Karen Stein, *Getting Away from It All: Vacations and Identity* (Philadelphia: Temple University Press, 2019), 149.

19. Karen Bettez Halnon, "Poor Chic: The Rational Consumptions of Poverty," *Current Sociology* 50, no. 4 (2002): 501–16, https://doi.org/10.1177/0011392102050004002.

20. Stein, *Getting Away from It All*, 110.

21. Shamus Rahman Khan, *Privilege: The Making of an Adolescent Elite at St. Paul's School* (Princeton, NJ: Princeton University Press, 2012).

22. C. Wright Mills, *The Sociological Imagination*, 40th anniversary ed. (New York: Oxford University Press, 2000).

23. Michelle Janning, Tate Kautzky, and Michelle Zhang, "The Pandemic Vacation Home: Media Framing of COVID-19 and Second Home Real Estate Morality Projects," in *More Than Just a "Home:" Understanding the Living Spaces of Families*, ed. Rosalina Pisco Costa and Sampson Lee Blair (Leeds, UK: Emerald, 2024), 15–35.

24. Richard C. Stedman, "Understanding Place Attachment among Second Home Owners," *American Behavioral Scientist* 50, no. 2 (2006): 187–205, https://doi.org/10.1177/0002764206290633.

25. *Mr. Rogers' Neighborhood* Official Website, https://www.misterrogers.org/.

26. Reed, "The 'Je Ne Sais Quoi' of Neighborliness."

Chapter 6

Temporal Boundaries

Sociohistorical and Generational Change in Family Vacation Home Preferences and Practices

I asked Francis how she would classify her Great Lakes Waterfront second home, as I did with every homeowner, providing a list of options that included "vacation home" and "short-term rental," among others. The timing of our conversation was clearly on her mind as she responded, "Well, it's very funny that you should come when you do. We're for the first time thinking we might rent it for a week or two here and there because we can't get out there as much as we used to, but it hasn't happened."

Later in the interview, I asked her how often she and her husband stayed there. She told me a story that showed the variable use of the property over the last several decades:

The first, maybe, sixteen or seventeen years we went probably every other weekend and all the month of August. My husband is okay, but he has a million physical problems. To make a long story short, it is simply easier for him to be here [in the primary residence] than there [in the family vacation home]. I don't know that I would move there, but I would go much more often than we can, actually, than he's comfortable going. The good thing is that our daughter and son-in-law and wonderful little grandson—about to be two—just love being there. So it's being used at this point about what it was in the height of our staying.

When I asked her if she'd use platforms such as Vrbo or Airbnb to rent it out, she said no, that they'd go through a real estate agent who lives in the vacation home community. She added that the whole idea was initiated by her daughter and son-in-law, who said the property is just "sitting out there."

Plus, she noted, the home next door had been used as a short-term vacation rental property for five years, something she had not realized until recently. She concluded our conversation by saying that she and her husband were a bit apprehensive about renting it out, not because of worry over damage to their possessions ("it's not the kind of house that has a lot of stuff that's valuable"), but because of the possibility of disrupting the neighborhood if loud partygoers were to stay there. She was not worried about whether the house would stay in the family, though, because she knew her daughter and son-in-law wanted to keep using it. They just framed the place as something that could also be used to make money.

How people view the value, use, and permanence of a family vacation home as a part of their legacy for future generations differs by age and capacity to stay in the home. Younger generations are increasingly likely to seek job and career success before having children[1] and decreasingly likely to have numerous siblings with whom to divvy up the maintenance and use—or the value—of a vacation home.[2] While younger people have had less geographic mobility compared to older siblings and parents in recent years,[3] it is largely due to financial precarity rather than a desire to settle down. They are also more likely to job-hop[4] and to travel more freely, without the restrictions of health or physical mobility issues. So how do these demographic patterns shape how people view these valuable places? And what happens if different generations of one family have to deliberate about what to do?

It's not easy to talk about money in relation to a place that's been defined as defying connection to the marketplace. Money issues can also lead to family conflict. This process looks different depending what stage a family is at in figuring out what to do with a property: Sell it? Use it? List it on Airbnb? Buy out a sibling or divide up those cherished vacation home possessions six ways?

Property—whether it's land, buildings, or material possessions—makes people draw family boundaries they may not have consciously thought of before, especially at times when a property needs to be divided up but family members are not ready to talk about that process. I recently chatted with an attorney friend of mine who said it baffled her that families argue over small things. She told me a vivid story of a family that had spent thousands of dollars in legal fees in a dispute over who gets a coffee mug. Her job was sometimes made interesting by families who lost a loved one squabbling over items that had no monetary value. Turns out, sentimental value can lead to big arguments and big financial expenditures meant to resolve those arguments. Family vacation homes are both monetarily valuable (as compared to, say, a coffee mug) and sentimentally valuable, filled with memories and memorabilia signifying those memories. They are rich sites for uncovering changing patterns related to money and memorable possessions across generations and from one time period to the next.

When considering social change associated with family vacation homes, we must consider the impact of the COVID-19 pandemic—a time when people were often required to remain at home and when amenity-rich travel destinations and public transportation were shut down. When I attended an in-person hospitality conference in 2022, I made a point to attend sessions on the changing expectations surrounding travel. The message from the conference presentations and discussions was clear: beyond requiring new health and safety standards, COVID-19 had changed travelers' desired vacation expectations. Travelers now want experiences rather than the accumulation of stuff, travel with a greater connection to nature, the ability to be more selective (as a result of people's perceptions that they have less available vacation time), authenticity of place, and respite from Zoom. Being forced to stay at home made people more keenly aware of how they most wanted to get away.

But had COVID-19 fundamentally altered the family vacation home and vacationing in general, or were the trends the experts noticed part of an existing trajectory of changing vacation norms? Here is where having data from before, during, and after COVID-19 lockdowns is particularly valuable. The vacation rental conference I attended in fall 2019, just a few months before the pandemic-induced lockdowns, included sessions with travel experts and homeowners noting the following desires among travelers: experiences rather than souvenirs, oases and refuges away from everyday life (preferably with a connection to outside activities that are unlikely or unavailable at home), ease of arrival and departure (since families have less time than they used to), a connection to the local place where the vacation occurs, and simultaneous being distanced from technology while having access to it for the occasional work email, as discussed in chapter 2.

Upon closer inspection, the list of travelers' desires from pre-COVID bears a striking resemblance to the list of during-COVID expectations and norms, especially when it comes to family travel. Even though some elements of travel are now more explicitly connected to social values and desires for inclusive experiences, expectations for travelers were already changing before the pandemic.

So if family vacation home desires seem similar across time, even taking into account a globally disruptive pandemic, what elements are highlighted differently across property groups? Does the ownership of a family vacation home that is rented to others versus one that is for personal use or both influence homeowners' impressions of changing family vacation desires? The short answer is, not as much as other factors, especially age. The following sections elaborate ways that homeowners across all property groups emphasize similar messages about changing patterns in family vacation homes: that younger family members do not share the same goals (or outcomes) associated with home properties and life stage markers as their parents and grandparents; that experiences matter more than possessions, even as possessions are used to stage an experience; and that attention to values-driven travel and authentic global and local senses of place matter more than in the past.

YOUR KIDS DON'T WANT (AND CAN'T AFFORD) YOUR PROPERTY TAX BILL: AGE AND SENTIMENTALITY ABOUT PLACES

Because they touch on historical changes in family diversity, housing patterns, vacation and leisure preferences, and the sharing economy, family vacation homes are a perfect site in which to examine how today's families actually experience their lives. By focusing on changing structural conditions and cultural values surrounding age and property, this section expands upon the historical patterns introduced in chapter 1 by detailing how adult children look at property—including family vacation homes—differently than their parents and grandparents. But first, I offer a clarification about how I define change across time and generations.

Defining Generational and Sociohistorical Change

Social change comes about in myriad ways, and people of different ages may respond differently or play a greater or lesser role in instigating these changes. Over time, we have seen changes in geographic mobility that result from working from locations other than traditional workplaces, fluctuations in property ownership and mortgage rates, and shifts in the defining markers of adulthood.[5] In news stories, these kinds of changes are sometimes reflected by the use of popular terms attached to people born within a certain set of years, such as a recent *Fortune* news article about thirty-somethings and sixty-somethings that included the phrase, "Boomers hold more housing wealth than any other generation and remain in the properties that millennials and younger generations so desperately want to buy."[6] But what is a generation, really? And does social change that occurs over time (which I call *sociohistorical change*) necessarily demonstrate generational differences that suggest age group boundaries are meaningful?

Yes and no. I use the term *generation* primarily to refer to people in different locations in a family kinship group (e.g., parents and children), not necessarily to the nomenclature associated with groups of people born during the same date range. As demographer Philip Cohen has spelled out, the popular use of generational names such as Gen X or Baby Boomers is meant to point out large historical shifts or to associate social trends with age groups, but its use is problematic because it fails to capture variation within age categories and it creates arbitrary borders between age groups.[7] Case in point: I'm six years younger than one of my brothers and seven years younger than the other. Our oldest brother is a Baby Boomer and my other brother and I are in Gen X, which seems highly problematic given that we grew up in the same household around the same time and that my brothers arguably have more in common with each other than with me. Further, using these generation labels fails to capture the fact that big events (e.g., a recession, the invention of the smartphone, or a global pandemic) affect everyone regardless of when they were born. For example, while my eighty-something-year-old mother got her smartphone around the same time as my twenty-year-old son (around a decade ago), and while they both use these devices dozens of times each day, she is more likely to call a hotel to stay there and my son is more likely to reserve a room using his phone online or via text. Based on this comparison, I could argue that Gen Z uses their smartphones to browse the internet and text more than the Silent Generation, who, despite their assigned generational name, may be more likely to make a phone call. But saying this doesn't necessarily mean it is true exclusively or ubiquitously for everyone in these age groups, and it doesn't necessarily mean their collective generational assignment manifests in predictable ways within our family.

Importantly, there are ways that the year we were born impacts our experiences and attitudes, but lumping years together into discrete generational categories can promote stereotypes and limit the ways we understand historical change. And so, while sociohistorical change at a collective level shows us certain population-level patterns, there may be both similarity across generations (writ large) in terms of access to such change and differences across generations (writ small) about how to respond to it. In any case, I avoid using popular generational terms like Millennials or Gen X. And, because my interviewees skewed older than the general population, I found the most differences between people under and over fifty-five years old, which mirrors recent age differences in housing trends, elaborated below.

AGE AND PROPERTY

The boundary between childhood and adulthood is socially constructed[8] and is experienced differently depending on a variety of life circumstances, including financial stability.[9] Nonetheless, researchers in different fields have identified ages and life stages that carry with them patterned norms and expectations.[10] Over the past several decades, adulthood has come to be defined via life stage experiences and material representations thereof: the completion of school, the establishment of an independent household via leaving the parental home, the establishment of romantic partnerships, full-time employment, the development of independence, responsibility, emotional and cognitive maturity, and self-perception of an adult identity.[11]

Importantly, the capacity to achieve adulthood markers and their accompanying material formations is impacted by structural factors, such as economic shifts and demographic patterns. Homeownership rates are sometimes included in the set of indicators for how various age groups do or do not have access to a valuable resource. Interestingly, homeownership rates have increased since 2016, especially for people under age fifty-five.[12] But this singular measure doesn't sufficiently help us understand the full set of shifting measures that may connote adulthood, nor does it tell the full picture of the challenges of home purchase, especially for younger people. Age can shape someone's likelihood to attain or want to attain a home or a second home.

During the COVID-19 pandemic we saw a continuation of the pattern of "boomerang" kids,[13] a Recession-era pattern where young adults' paths to adulthood were stalled (and relocated back to parents' and guardians' homes) due to economic instability, student loan debt, a dearth of labor market options, and other social factors.[14] Young adults (that is, those under thirty) both pre- and postpandemic are less likely to achieve traditional markers of adulthood, such as marriage, completion of education, moving out of the parental home, or securing a job with a livable wage, as compared to people who were the same age in the mid- to late twentieth century—and this was especially true after the Recession.[15] They are also more likely to live with their parents or others, less likely to buy a house than similarly aged people in the late twentieth century,[16] and if they do achieve these markers at all, do so at later ages and with more support from their parents than in the recent past.[17]

The purchase of vacation homes has dipped in popularity since COVID-19, in part due to a dearth of supply after pandemic-induced buying frenzies.[18] While this is a broader pattern, there are differences in goals associated with vacation home ownership by age. My research shows that today, the inheritance, purchase, and use of a family vacation home by younger generations is more likely to be a way to combine leisure with financial planning and self-use with renting to others. Some of this relates to the structural challenges of being able to afford to maintain and pay taxes or HOA fees on an inherited second home, while some relates to changing cultural values about travel, discussed later.

In chapter 3, I shared part of the conversation I had with Gloria (Personal Property group), who is in her fifties, regarding the condo she shares with her mom and grandma in Tropical Paradise. She noted that unlike the other two women, she would be quick to rent out the place using platforms like Airbnb or Vrbo. I asked her why. She said, "I think it's a wise use of resources and, frankly, if I'm gone someplace and somebody is Airbnb-ing my place, it gives me more resources to do something else I want to do somewhere else." People under fifty-five are interested in vacation homes more than in past, but this is in part because they see them as an investment that can sometimes be rented out.[19] In fact, younger people in urban areas are demonstrating a preference for renting their (expensive) primary residence while owning a vacation home outside of the city. This is because they can't afford a starter home in the locations they work in, so they put their financial investment into a vacation home, then rent it out to earn money that can eventually be used to purchase a primary residence. This is possible only if they're wealthy enough to afford a home at all.[20] This context all demonstrates that the current acquisition and use of family vacation homes is not a monolithic picture reflecting traditional patterns; younger people are increasingly likely to see these properties as useful simultaneously for themselves and others, as desirable for personal memory making and investment, and, interestingly, as a crucial way to save or earn enough money to afford to purchase a primary residence.

Across property categories in my research, age shaped how people viewed the use of the family vacation home: the older the homeowner, the more likely they were to see the property as a permanent marker of adulthood that would be passed along to the next generation (who then are less likely to see it as such). However, some ways in which homeowner age and property groups intersect complicate this finding. For under-fifty-five homeowners in the Investment and Mixed Property groups, there were three key aims to owning a family vacation home: to rent it now in order to meet current financial needs, to be able to use it later in life as a more permanent vacation home, or to be able to sell it in the future to fund a different kind of retirement leisure location. For most over-fifty-five homeowners in the Personal Property group, the aim of owning a family vacation was to use it now for family trips and consider renting it only if aging or health problems prevented them from using the home as often as they had in the past. These individuals in particular expressed the greatest concerns about whether younger generations would want to use the home as much. This was also where conversations about what happens to the property when the current owners are gone were most likely to occur—a topic I return to later in this chapter.

Among older homeowners who reflected on their children's and grandchildren's views on and likelihood to use their vacation homes—especially those in the Personal Property group—a key pattern emerged: these people believed that younger family members do not share the same property-related goals as their parents and grandparents. It is likely that these younger family members worry they can't afford to manage the properties over time, or they see the benefits of renting them out so they can afford to travel to other places. They don't want to be tied down, and if they have interest in the property, they don't want it to be the only place they go for vacations.

Paths to financial stability are still part of the goal of achieving adulthood, but they're less fixed in terms of place and time. Now, adulthood may be signified by some entrepreneurial participation in the sharing economy, or by working across multiple sites or sectors to piece together enough hours, or by trying several jobs before settling on one. It is much less likely to be signified via property ownership. And this is making the assumption that young adults have a choice in such matters, which many do not in a time of economic precarity. Adulthood for younger people today is more likely to be a patchwork quilt of structurally challenging economic stability attempts. This kind of pattern is less prevalent as we move up the age ladder.

Alongside structural barriers to achieving traditional markers of adulthood are shifts in cultural values. Young people want a home but have a hard time affording it. But unlike older generations, they don't want to settle on only one vacation spot. Add to this an increase in diversity of family forms, which is especially pronounced in younger generations, including the increasing age at which young adults first marry or have children.[21] Thus, younger people's propensity to use vacation homes for more than just their use is a result of the interplay between structural conditions and shifting cultural values about families, homes, markers of adulthood, vacations, and the economy. And it's about what it means to vacation in one spot or not.

SEEKING AUTHENTIC EXPERIENCES: GLOBE TREKKING VERSUS STAYING IN ONE PLACE

As my analysis of the webinars and vacation rental and hospitality conferences reveals, values-driven hospitality has become a more frequent demand among travelers, especially when issues like the murder of George Floyd and reports of discriminatory practices in the vacation rental industry are making headlines. Vacation homes—especially those rented to others—have come to be defined not just in terms of activity and landscape amenities, but also in terms of how equitable and inclusive their policies, neighbors, amenities, and decor are. Values-driven travel is what more travelers expect—especially young travelers—and this affects the kinds of places they want to vacation in, visit, or own.

In chapter 4, I noted patterns across homeowner types regarding connection to geographic (local) communities and social (beyond local) communities. Homeowners got involved in the communities where their vacation homes were situated based on their interests, goals, and desire to become engaged in local politics or controversies. Some connected socially with immediate neighbors, while others connected with vacationers who lived in the community but not necessarily next door. Some people also intentionally disengaged from controversial issues in the local community while at their family vacation home as a way to be seen by locals as uncontroversial, to emphasize their removal from the politics and responsibilities of nonvacation life, or because they did not feel entitled to get involved until they had lived there longer. For those who rented their homes to other families, the connection to the local community was primarily seen in terms of how local regulations impacted their property and ensuring they provided visitors enough information, stories, and recommendations for a fun family vacation, all while supporting local businesses. Beyond the geographic local communities of their vacation homes, though, many homeowners demonstrated deep formal and informal commitment to issues such as environmental sustainability, racial reconciliation, and commitment to lessening political divides.

One finding uncovered in the collection of Vrbo Virtual Partner Summit webinars I analyzed is that it is increasingly likely that travelers will pay attention to the significance of place, the intersection of place and global community, and the importance of a travel destination's attention to social values such as environmentalism, social inequalities, and responsibility for preserving local stories and resources.[22] At the same time, travelers are increasingly likely to take steps to disguise their tourist selves to avoid being seen as an outsider,[23] focusing on experiences rather than shopping at tourist traps to bring home trinkets. While they want to escape everyday life, they don't want to stick out as annoying tourists, especially if it makes them look rich and irresponsible. So how do experiences and possessions matter for the family vacation home, especially in terms of variation by age? And how might sociohistorical changes in cultural values surrounding authenticity shape homeowners' desires and actions?

Your Kids Don't Want Your Board Games: Experiences versus Possessions

When I give talks about my research on the social meaning of household possessions, the most common question from audiences is about how parents and children don't want the same thing when it comes to saving and cherishing household items. The biggest conflicts are often about household possessions that some see as rich with meaning and sentimentality and others see as burdensome clutter. Often it is older individuals who see the richness and younger individuals who see the burden.[24] The possessions that characterize these conflicts come in many forms, from a set of dishes that can't go in the dishwasher to a heavy table that is hard to move. At times, they take the form of collections of items that parents think are worth a lot but kids do not. The conflict can center on loyalty and deservedness (e.g., someone feels as if they deserve the china set more than others, because they helped an aging parent with health concerns) or on life stage considerations for adult children (e.g., younger adults are less likely to be able to afford the square footage to store cherished family possessions). Younger people prefer more job mobility and are not "settling down" into traditional family structures as fast or as often as previous generations,[25] and they want less stuff than their parents.[26]

What does the desire to settle down and have possessions have to do with family vacation homes? In today's travel preferences, experiential authenticity is important. Rather than visiting souvenir shops and bringing home a trinket to display in a living room, people (and especially younger people) are now increasingly likely to seek authenticity via the experience of "being local,"[27] whether by participating in hands-on activities that connect them with locals or by finding ways to learn about local cultures. At the hospitality conference I attended, a similar message rang true across sessions: experiencing an authentic local story has become a greater reward for travel than bringing home a physical souvenir, especially since the COVID-19 pandemic.

Possessions—especially too many of them—also matter less for today's homeowners in general.[28] The desire of today's family vacationers to collect authentic experiences across multiple localities, rather than situating memories in one place or bringing home a suitcase full of souvenirs, thus fits into larger social and generational patterns related to people's attachment to possessions. And yet, for family vacation homeowners, it is essential to attach meaning to possessions when enchanting the home, regardless of whether they rent the home to others, use it themselves, or both. Here is where the within-family generational change and broader sociohistorical changes intersect: younger people want fewer of their parents' possessions, and movements to downsize, minimize, and cut back on possessions are powerful parts of our cultural value system.[29] A simple internet search shows thousands of guidebooks, blog posts, and workshops meant to help older generations get rid of their stuff so their kids don't have to deal with it.[30]

When people travel, they take pictures and, more often for younger people, post them on social media. Increasingly, experiences—whether stored in one's memory or shared across Instagram—matter more than possessions, in part because recent cultural values have shifted to focus on concern about mass production and nonbiodegradability.[31] At the same time, older individuals, especially parents, use possessions to stage an experience meant to foster imagined future kinship nostalgia for their children. Family vacation homes are repositories of household possessions—things that must be managed alongside the homes themselves. Younger people's desire to have less stuff comes into conflict with their parents' desire to pass along a property full of memory-rich objects. Especially for the Personal Property group, parents' desire to create imagined future kinship nostalgia for their children using puzzles, old dishes, and kayaks were accompanied by worry that their kids may see the possessions as burdens as they deliberate on how or whether to hold on to the property.

Authenticity and the Balance between Familiar and Exotic

Merriam-Webster's 2023 word of the year was "authentic," meaning "not false or imitation," "true to one's own personality, spirit, or character," and synonymous with the words "real" or "actual."[32] My research shows that homeowners across age categories want to provide or be part of authentic local experiences, balanced with a dedication to global understanding. On the one hand, voices from multiple sites and time periods in my research encouraged homeowners in the Investment and Mixed Property groups to welcome renters from around the world in an authentic way by including local neighborhood stories. A new message in the context of increased general awareness about discrimination and barriers to equity and inclusion faced by people of color was added about inclusivity in vacation rental industry messaging: the 2021 Vrbo Virtual Partner Summit in particular included mention that visitors' stories themselves—especially those from underrepresented groups facing discrimination in the housing, vacation, and leisure industries—sometimes suggested the neighborhood was not particularly welcoming or inclusive.[33] Thus, homeowners need to balance local authenticity and a perspective that allows for diverse global perspectives. In other words, a neighborhood that welcomes vacationers from diverse racial groups and from around the world has to be authentic, but it cannot include the parts of local stories that may be discriminatory against that more diverse set of voices and faces. This is a challenging feat: make visitors feel like insiders in your vacation neighborhood—but keep them away from the ways a local neighborhood may treat them as outsiders. These aims are increasingly present in any kind of vacation neighborhood but are more explicitly packaged by experts as necessary goals for people who rent their homes to others.

Seeking authenticity is at the heart of all of this; "people are looking for credible or sincere performances of everyday life."[34] Travel has become easier over the last several decades, especially after the pandemic lockdowns.[35] But authenticity may be hard to come by. Local cultures that have become more accessible to tourists have embraced commercial possibilities, making a truly authentic local culture ever harder to find. The local story can become staged, even in neighborhoods where locals still live next to vacation rental homes.

And yet, as my observations showed, trying on a new "real" neighborhood to imagine oneself living there is not an uncommon goal for travelers who prefer to stay in vacation rentals, especially among younger travelers who may be figuring out what kind of neighborhood they want to live in when they are able to afford a home. In a sense, they are borrowing several places rather than owning one, due both to preferences and economic barriers.

Vacation spots become desirable when they strike a good balance between the familiar and the exotic, between "wanting to do or be something different and having the reassurance that the comfort of stability and familiarity remain."[36] Family vacation homes can do both, because the activities are different from everyday life (even if done repeatedly over frequent visits) and the experience occurs in a comfortable home that is familiar either because its residents own the place or because it's set up in a way to be familiar to any family that uses it.

Tucked alongside both familiarity and exotic is authenticity: the experience of something "real." In its press release announcing the word of the year, Merriam-Webster noted the elusiveness and increased use of the term "authentic,"[37] which can be applied to an identity, a person, a place, or a culture. People can have an "authentic voice" and restaurants can offer "authentic dishes" from a particular culture or place. The rise of artificial intelligence and fake renditions of reality (which look really real!) has blurred the boundary between fake and real. When it comes to travel, authenticity requires that the experience of place is not simulated. The mountain out the window is really a mountain. The local produce at the supermarket is really local (and really produce). The people who live there actually live there. Of course, the term could be stretched to apply to a family vacation home, too: a real place with one's real family. But in the travel and hospitality worlds, authenticity is usually used when talking about visitors' experiencing a local story without having that story be fabricated, revised, or staged solely for their visit. While we are all audiences in new social settings, authenticity occurs when travelers are in places where local people can (convincingly) act as they normally would.

New travel norms would suggest that collecting authentic local stories from an array of diverse places would give a vacationer a greater understanding—or at least an impression—of global stories. One big takeaway from the conferences I attended was that family connection that occurs during travel is now less about a static place and more about shared experiences collected in diverse locales. The magic or enchantment of the family vacation home is not uniform, but older homeowners, and especially those in the Personal Property group, see enchantment more as a family vacation home that stands still in time as the generations move through it creating memories. For these people, responsible preservation of family requires enchanting one place; it looks like imagined future kinship nostalgia that is placed in a family vacation home.

For younger homeowners, enchantment comes not from repeated use of one place attached to one local set of stories. Rather, it comes in the form of redefining a vacation home as an investment (with rental potential) in a housing marketplace where starter homes are harder to afford. Or it comes in the form of substituting multiple locales for one static locale where they can create memories with a family. One of the important memories to create is an alignment between travel and social good, as people travel in order to "feel part of a family beyond borders," as poet and songwriter Gio Evan's lyrics, shared in chapter 4, convey. For younger families, imagined future kinship nostalgia functions much like it does for older individuals: create memories now that your children will look back on fondly. But for younger families, the memories are not necessarily attached to one place or one set of material possessions that signify "our family vacation home."

Necessarily, money matters in these distinctions: for homeowners of all ages, if financial stability and wealth were a given, it was easier to imagine these ideals. But if the family vacation home was defined as an investment necessary to make ends meet—especially for the Investment Property group—the ideals were not as present in how they talked about the purpose of the home.

It may seem as if finding local stories and valuable global voices are contrasting aims for both travelers and homeowners or hosts. But they point to the same thing. Globe trekking (either literally or by emphasizing the importance of multicultural understanding) by staying in homes in multiple places and staying in a home in one locale both end up enchanting the family vacation, because they turn the space into a place for authentic experience that is removed from everyday life. It's just that one places more emphasis on a physical, static home while the other emphasizes that visiting multiple locations helps a traveler find their place in a more global "home." Hence the popularity of vacation rental homes, now a fixture in the global hospitality industry.

Still, these emphases are always under revision. For under-fifty-five homeowners and older homeowners who talked about their children, it became clear that authenticity and balance between familiarity and exoticism in a static family vacation home may be harder to achieve than in the past. Changing structural conditions that make it harder to maintain a faraway property financially or physically, as well as changing values about honoring multiple localities in travel and leisure pursuits, may mean the popularity of the traditional family-only vacation home is dwindling. Importantly, it's not that younger people don't want community and memories or to honor a local place's story; it's also not that they don't want memorabilia that may help them participate in imagined future kinship nostalgia. It's that they aren't sure memory needs to be wholly connected to the (large amounts of) stuff in one family's vacation home. This helps explain why I saw more interest in Investment and Mixed Property use among younger homeowners in the recruitment process for my interviews.

For family vacation homes, the biggest sociohistorical change in meaning is associated with authenticity. If authenticity means real, then what do we make of places that are enchanted to be removed from the realities of everyday family and work stresses? There are dual realities: an authentic family vacation home self requires removal from the authentic real world. But this sentiment is not as powerful as it used to be. Values are shifting toward a need for global understanding and responsibility to local cultures, an acknowledgment of how inequalities matter in amenity-rich communities, and a disruption to traditional family forms that comes with settling down in one place. As a result, the family vacation home's "realness" must now come with a connection to the realities of other people's and places' everyday realities—and the realness of a family vacation home self can be at odds with the realness of place. This unsettled classification of family vacation homes aligns with changing values and structural conditions that younger people are more likely to espouse and experience.

LEGACY, LOYALTY, AND LOSS: ESTATE AND SUCCESSION PLANNING

Legacy, loyalty, and loss are key elements present at every stage of estate and succession planning—the process of figuring out where your assets (and debts) end up after you die. Estate planning is filled with a desire to preserve a family story,[38] an evaluation of who may or may not deserve an inheritance, and a reckoning with one's own mortality. Figuring out inheritance, even if done in the privacy of an attorney's office using confidential documentation, consists of many social acts. First, people often assess the relationships they have with potential heirs, deliberating over issues like deservedness and the requirement for biological or adoptive kinship. This includes assessing the capacity to give a substantial inheritance to children or grandchildren in the form of property, something that more affluent parents are able to do.[39] Second, decisions that are made are communicated among a group of people with varying degrees of clarity, depending on whether they're written down, easy to find, and classified as a legal will or not. Third, as decisions about inheritance are made, families can come into intense conflict with each other, as in the case of the coffee mug mentioned earlier. Legacy, loyalty, and loss within families are all part of figuring out who gets what—and of who counts as family or not.

Valerie and Morgan shared stories that capture this figuring:

"We have the family cabin that's shared with [my husband's] siblings. There's four of them. . . . One brother is a real pain in the butt when it comes to this piece of property . . . ; he doesn't really want any part of it. And one of my nephews has offered to buy out his share. . . . He has two girls. One is not at all interested in the cabin; the other one is very interested but caused a real family ruckus about two years ago and we ended up, it costs us six hundred bucks to have it appraised, and we weren't real happy about that."

—Valerie, Northwest Woods (Personal Property group)

"We're fortunate that our children like living in the Pacific Northwest, and so they'll use the home, too. It's part of our legacy."

—Morgan, Northwest Oceanside (Personal Property group)

Estate and succession planning about property can be messy, as Valerie's story demonstrates, or it can be tidy, as Morgan's suggests. For family vacation homes, the consideration of an entire property can become a source of excitement, stress, and confusion. What happens when Mom can no longer care for a lake cabin on her own? What should adult children do when parents don't use a vacation home anymore but no children or grandchildren live near the place or want to maintain it? How do you divide a property when those who will inherit it are geographically dispersed and differently available to visit or maintain the property? What role do changing desires for vacations across generations play? In-the-moment goals of creating imagined future kinship nostalgia in a vacation home (for one's own family or others') need to be reviewed and revised when nobody uses or maintains a property. But this was a challenging task for family vacation home owners.

Economizing Enchantment: Family Conversations about Money and Death Are Difficult

As I discussed in chapter 2, emotional conventions about how people believe they should feel in certain interactional contexts are what Arlie Hochschild calls feeling rules, meaning "rules or norms according to which feelings may be judged appropriate to accompanying events."[40] Our inherent understanding of feeling rules is often revealed when others point out that we are violating them: for example, in most families, it would be pointed out that it is crass to bring up financial inheritance while standing around the deathbed of a loved one. A big facet of enchanting the family is to rhetorically or symbolically separate it from the marketplace. So even as norms about who wants a family vacation home and why change across generations, bringing up money or property that will be passed along to others when a family member can't take care of their home anymore, or when a family member passes away, continues to be a difficult thing to do. This was especially likely for homeowners in the Personal Property group.

Willa's (Personal Property group) family vacation home at Northwest Oceanside offers a good example of just how hard talking about money can be, especially in relation to the death of a loved one. She and her nephew co-owned a cabin that Willa's sister and mother had lived in until her mother died. Her sister was "really torn up" about their mom's death, since they had lived together for six years. Her nephew wanted to charge Willa's sister rent, but Willa refused:

> I said, no, no. She's paying her utilities, and that's a help to us, so, no, that will not happen. He made a decision that he wanted out, and so we let him out. Then my sister was there for a year. . . . She got back on her feet, or recovered from the grief, and ended up with a job. It was just like, we've been taking care of this cabin, the only cost is a couple hundred dollars a month to keep it, it's very affordable, so why sell it. That's sort of how it happened.

When I interviewed Faye (Personal Property group) about her vision for the future of her Northern Lake Country home, she reminisced about earlier days, when her children would bring friends to go boating and waterskiing. She segued into memories of how her children—now all married with children of their own—have helped with cabin upkeep and repairs. But she struggled to envision what the future would look like, especially now that she was in her seventies. Would any of her kids want it? Likely not the ones who live several states away. And the son who lives closest has his hands full with work, a spouse who also has a busy career, and kids involved in lots of school activities. In her pondering about the future, she mentioned that the cabin may eventually be rented out using platforms like Airbnb or Vrbo. But she had no desire to manage any of that:

> As I'm able to use it less, that will become okay. So it will be a handing it over and somebody else will be responsible for how that happens. I won't do that. But the way I look at the place is that it's for the family. It's not mine, in that sense. It is for the family. If that's how they want to use it, then that's a way that they can have income coming from it, then that's perfect. . . . It would be harder at the [primary] house, because my underwear is here. It's kind of my place.

Faye had rented out rooms in her primary home for years, mostly to local students or professionals who needed a place to stay for a few weeks at a time. She saw that as her responsibility, since it was entirely her home. The cabin, though—that was the family's, so they'd need to be the ones to decide what to do with it.

I didn't get to talk with Faye's kids about this, but I got a sense from her that this decision was not going to happen anytime soon. The cabin upkeep was enough of a job for her to think about, and making a decision about letting non–family members use it was too much to handle. That would be for the kids to decide. As for her own memory of the place? She reminded me that she had purchased the cabin after her divorce at a hefty price, because she didn't want to lose the connection to it. It wasn't until her estate planning process that she had realized she wanted to keep it so the family could enjoy it with her.

Francis's (Personal Property group) story about her Great Lakes Waterfront home echoed a similar equivocation about the future of her vacation home. Her aging husband's failing health had forced her to consider whether keeping the home exclusively for personal use would be possible much longer. Like Faye, she noted that it would need to be her kids who managed it if it were a vacation rental. In fact, Francis noted that she had just learned that her new next-door neighbors, who are "very nice people," had bought their place with the intention of occasionally renting it out. Francis had noticed different families with young children at that property over the last few years, but it never crossed her mind that it was rented; she figured they were friends of the property owners.

And what about the Investment and Mixed Property groups? Did property inheritance matter differently to them? Truth be told, most of the conversations with these groups took a temporal journey but usually stopped at retirement—even for people with adult children—and these conversations centered on how estate planning connected to financial stability during life stage transitions such as divorce or retirement. The transmission of property to the next generation was symbolically (and perhaps actually) too far down the line in terms of thinking about the value of the vacation property. It was not part of the plan because they intended to use income from renting or selling the property for their own use (which eventually could become what their kids inherited, but this went largely undiscussed). Personal Property group homeowners focused on their own family, especially in terms of imagined future kinship nostalgia and on how their kids and grandkids would look back on today, leading this group to wonder if renting out their home would ruin that possibility or just put a temporal bookend on the memories. But the Investment and Mixed Property group homeowners centered their imagined stories on their own futures and their own financial security during a financially precarious time or as a way to feel secure in retirement. They situated their late-in-life financial standing as important in terms of their children's inheritance, but this was indirectly related to the property.

Marion (Investment Property group), for example, described how the purchase of a property that included a backyard cottage came at a time when she and her ex-husband were near the end of both their marriage and their long-standing pattern of buying and flipping houses together. She was also near retirement age. They had sold a house in a city a few hours away and used the profit to purchase two homes in Wine Country, primarily to be able to retire comfortably in the next ten years. Marion noted that they could have stayed in the city but decided to move away because they "could buy a lot more house over here, even putting money into it, still ending up in a better financial situation for retirement."

Bella (Mixed Property group), who is in her forties and has stayed in her own Eastern Oceanside vacation rental property many times over the years to ensure it was well-maintained, noted, "[T]hat's a huge investment, and it's kind of my retirement plan, so I need to make sure that I can take care of it." What the next generation did with these (largely) investment properties as inheritance was not yet part of the story, which was focused in the present and on the owner's financial well-being. This was true regardless of the age of interviewees' children, grandchildren, nieces, and nephews.

When thinking about the future, most conversations with family vacation home owners—especially in the Personal Property group—noted an imagined future kinship nostalgia for their kids and others who used the properties. It was as if the people who lived in the homes had aged enough to believe there was a sufficient accumulation of fond memories, and they imagined that the next generation would experience the same thing, maybe even staged with the same props. This was all hypothetical, of course, but the imagined future kinship nostalgia was vividly present for current homeowners hoping to preserve the space as a family place. For some in the Personal Property group, the consideration of turning it into a rental was deflected to the next generation.

Ascertaining sentimental value over material possessions and spaces is a necessary and difficult part of figuring out who gets what. For family vacation home owners, imagining the future of the property feels like work. For Faye, defining the space as "the family's" helped her feel okay about avoiding the decision of whether to rent it out in the future. For most other Personal Property group homeowners who purchased a family vacation home so they could create an imagined future kinship nostalgia for their loved ones, the feeling rules suggested that they imagine it as part of inheritance but not name it in terms of actual dollars. Why? To assign the place a pricelessness and timelessness that would make it the backdrop to new memories, carried over to the next generation. Mentioning inheritance attaches a price to a priceless thing. Talking about it all proved difficult, perhaps even taboo, because it brought up their own mortality (or poor health that may lead to decreased use). To talk about money and death would disenchant the family vacation home, so it was avoided by all groups. People in the Investment and Mixed Property groups, while more likely to talk explicitly about financial investment, also enchanted the spaces, if only to rent them to other families. But they stopped their discussion of property value at their own current or future retirement use, rather than delving into questions of death or inheritance.

Places and Objects Are Hard to Divide Up

Inheritance in the form of property is already messy. My research on household objects, like the coffee mug that led to one set of siblings' expensive legal battle, also shows that the monetary value of a place or object may matter less than its sentimental value.[41] But it is the stuff with less value that may also muddy the boundary between those who are and are not entitled to inherit something. Imagine a person passing away, and then imagine that person's neighbor walking over to the grieving children as they plan the funeral. In their conversation, the neighbor says, "You know, your mom said I could have her sewing machine when she died." Of course, this person is not legally part of the deceased woman's family, but something about the item led this neighbor to express her perceived entitlement to it. She would not have done this about money. And the likelihood that the children would allow this neighbor to "inherit" the sewing machine would probably include an assessment of it as a financial asset but also include a deliberation about whether they had any emotional attachment to it. If they didn't, and if it wasn't worth much, it would be more likely that the neighbor would get it.

Carla (Personal Property group) told a story about her and her husband's goal of buying their own vacation home in Northwest Woods, even though her parents already had a place nearby. They were unusual in that, as young people, they wanted to vacation in one spot. But they were doing so as a financial investment for their eventual retirement. She wanted a separate home to call their own: if they stayed at her parents' vacation home, she argued, it wouldn't really feel like a vacation. Further, she noted that it is not easy to divide up a small vacation home into generational sections, in terms of both space and time:

> I have two other sisters and two other brothers, and of course my dad has friends, because he's been here since the '60s, so one of the things we didn't want to have to do is, "Oh, we're going to the cabin this weekend," and my dad say, "Oh, I had so-and-so coming up this weekend." We didn't want to have that sharing battle. We wanted to be able to freely go there anytime we want and not worry about it, and if we want to invite people, then we can invite them, but

we didn't want to have it be a challenge, because that kind of took away from the point.

When families fight over a coffee mug, and spend money on that fight, it is because the possession serves a purpose: to symbolize a personal or family relationship. My interviewees shared stories that led me to conclude that if families can create clear boundaries around who gets access to their stuff and spaces in advance, this can lessen the conflict—or at least delay it until children are faced with a decision about whether they want inherit a property, purchase their own, or vacation at multiple sites with variable local stories. In general because younger people are less inclined to want to imagine their future family vacations as located in static places that require a kind of "settling down," they are also less likely to want to hang onto the possessions they might need to fill these static places. Even in cases like Carla's, having a family vacation home is about simultaneously having a static place to create memories and a malleable place that can be sold for financial stability decades down the road. Or, at the very least, if it is to be a singular place to go with her family, she didn't want it to be defined as anything other than something she and her husband had earned on their own.

CONCLUSION

In general, there were not as many differences between property groups about change over time as there were between age groups. People who invest in and use family vacation homes all want to enchant their spaces so that family memories can be preserved and the properties' connection to the marketplace can be downplayed. But today's younger generations are perhaps more keenly aware of the limitations of this approach, since many have trouble affording one home, let alone two. They are also less interested in fabricating imagined future kinship nostalgia connected to one family vacation home that is never rented to others, due to changing cultural values about wanting fewer possessions, more geographic mobility, and a more global perspective connected to multiple locales. It is also due to the difficulty younger, less well-off families face in affording to buy or maintain a second home. When faced with inheriting or buying a vacation home solely for personal use, young families may not feel that it aligns with their values, or they may be intimidated by the financial cost of preserving such a space over time.

The findings in this chapter reveal three ways that the family vacation home is strategically framed as enchanted by homeowners in terms of temporal boundaries: through sentimentality about places, via authentic experiences, and during estate and succession planning related to family vacation homes. Below, I summarize these findings and how they connect to the over-arching goal of enchanting the family vacation home.

Age and Sentimentality about Places

Young people not only have a harder time affording a starter home, they are also less likely to want to stay in one place for a decades-long career, let alone buy a vacation home that situates their family vacations in one place. Homeowners who rent their vacation homes to others were less visibly concerned about the future of their properties as markers of their children's adulthood status, especially in the case of younger homeowners whose futures filled with grown children and retirement deliberations were decades down the road. Older Personal Property group homeowners, though, recognized that younger family members did not see the vacation home as a place for personal use only, and that it would be likely that the next generation would decide whether to transition the property from personal to investment use.

The Investment Property group connected property ownership more explicitly with a kind of financial stability that marked the achievement of some kind of status, adult or otherwise. This was especially true among younger homeowners and those who needed rental income to afford the mortgage on their primary or second home. But even this group sought as much enchantment as the Personal Property homeowners, who deflected the disenchanting decision of whether to turn their vacation home into a rental to their kids. For both groups—young people who focused on money now to attain increased future benefits and older people who focused on future family use—the end goal was the same: creating an eventual sanctuary apart from the everyday stresses associated with money.

Seeking Authentic Experiences

Across all property groups, there is an increase in dedication to authentic vacationing, especially when compared to decades past. For Personal Property group homeowners, though, the attempts at authenticity were more decidedly focused on within-home family memory making. The scale with familiarity on one side and exoticism on the other tips toward familiarity for the Personal Property group, especially among homeowners who imagine their children using the property for generations to come. For Investment Property group homeowners, renting their places to others entails a focus on exotic local stories that hearken to chapter 3's focus on place history represented in decor. But because it is in a home, an accompanying goal is to provide renters with the creature comforts that signify familiarity. In fact, this familiarity offers a haven to come "home" to while exploring a new neighborhood and community.

Authentic vacations are still framed as escapes from the stresses of everyday work and family life. It's just that these vacation ideals are now centered on experiencing a variety of places and activities rather than a single, static place—something that is especially true today when compared to the past, especially relevant for homeowners who rent out their properties, and especially true for younger people. Enchantment via magical vacations is still the expectation, and experiencing this in homes that line streets with place-based local stories is still valuable. But the experience of renting someone else's vacation home to do this is an increasingly accepted form of enhancing this magic, coupled with just enough of a healthy dose of diverse local realism.

Estate and Succession Planning

The frequency and comfort with which different property groups talked about money as it pertained to the family vacation home varied. Whether the next generation would get a property was most discussed by the Personal Property group, usually when expressing their hope that it would stay in the family (although these homeowners avoided explicit use of the word inheritance or actual dollar amounts and deflected the decision about renting the property out in the future to their children). For homeowners renting their vacation homes to others, the temporal clock usually stopped at their own retirement, meaning they did not extensively discuss the next generation's acquisition of the property that would occur after they are gone.

All families think at least a little about planning for financial stability for themselves and the next generation. Yet it is hard to talk openly about money and death, because it kills the magic associated with a special place. Feeling rules associated with family vacation homes make talking about money seem taboo, especially when it calls to mind either the actual death of an older family member or the figurative death of the dream of the enchanted future of the family vacation home.

* * *

Recently, I caught up with a friend who, after years running a film production and media consulting business, decided to enroll in a graduate program as a way to expand her career options. I'll give this friend the pseudonym Maureen here. It had been two decades since Maureen graduated from college, so she was nervous about going back to school, especially because of the financial strain it would put her under. She had also been renting out her small primary residence for short-term vacationers to supplement her income. In fact, renting out her home, to her, was a creative way to supplement her income and be able to afford the mortgage. During the COVID-19 pandemic, her business slowed down, since she couldn't give talks or travel to filming sites, let alone meet with new clients whose work required in-person assessments of filming locations. Before the pandemic, however, Maureen's travel involved placing all her equipment in her truck and driving to filming sites with her dog, adding a couple of nights of camping vacation to a work trip here and there. She often added these nights as a way to allow for more vacation rentals of her primary residence, since she couldn't stay there if guests were renting it. More rentals meant more income, greater capacity to afford good health insurance and retirement savings, and a great way to be self-reliant as a self-employed businessperson.

During this time, Maureen's mother passed away, leaving her with a house to sell and two storage units' worth of belongings to move across two states and sort through. As the first person in her family to graduate from college, she was glad to have connected with her mom toward the end of her life, giving her mom a chance to say how proud she was of her accomplishments. She moved her mom's possessions to her studio, which was sitting unused during the lockdown.

One of the most captivating stories Maureen told was about a renter who asked whether she and her loved ones should be concerned about the neighborhood, because they were a mixed-race family. They had experienced overt and covert racism in previous vacation rental neighborhoods, so they wondered how this property may or may not differ. My friend's response was to acknowledge the concern and share articles about how the town and its hospitality industry had made strides to be more racially inclusive. She wanted to create a space for this family that would give them pleasant (and safe) memory-making experiences free from discrimination.

As our conversation continued, Maureen also noted that she had a hard time knowing what to do with all her mother's belongings. As a queer woman who lives alone and who has always felt the need to take care of herself, she reminded me that she has been connected to many different types of families besides the one she grew up in, including being involved with partners who have had children and who have needed a lot of care because of illness. And as the oldest daughter, she felt familial pressure to hold onto family possessions, but she had no idea where to put them given the reality of her housing situation: she didn't have room in her primary residence to store items, in part because she didn't have a basement or attic and in part because she had to keep the house tidy enough for her occasional vacation renters. But in deciding to postpone the sorting process, she felt as if she was failing to achieve an idealized goal of memorializing her family story via cherished possessions, even though she was honoring her late mother's admiration by taking on a new educational adventure.

As a busy entrepreneur (and soon-to-be graduate student) she came to a place of "enough is enough," believing that the possessions were holding her back. She wanted to simplify her life and focus on her goals rather than figure out what to do with all her mom's things. Maureen doesn't see it in the cards to have a big family home filled with stuff, so she couldn't bring herself to figure out why anyone would hold onto these things except out of some feeling of obligation. In the end, she donated most of her mother's possessions to a nonprofit that helps women who are unhoused, in abusive relationships, or recovering from addiction set up new homes. She kept a few things—photos, jewelry, and an old quilt—in a couple boxes.

Maureen's multifaceted story calls to mind several topics that matter in my research on family vacation homes: first, the stories of who has these homes are complex and diverse, with some needing to rent out a space in order to afford a primary home and others using the spaces as supplemental income or a hobby, especially among younger generations; second, concerns around racism in amenity-rich neighborhoods are still alive and well, with vacation destination hospitality industry professionals revising their approach to policies and practices to be more inclusive; third, there are generational shifts going on with regard to the meaning and desire to cherish family heirlooms, including the spaces that house them; and fourth, the life stages families go through follow decreasingly linear paths, with real estate choices made reflecting change, innovation, diverse family forms, and piecing together options to attain financial security.

Powerful patterns about how families change over time have been happening for years, evidenced by multiple interviewees' stories and circumstances. Importantly, as urban centers become unaffordable and more dense, younger people who wish to start families have their eye on suburbs or places with space that don't cost as much. Additionally, as the sharing economy grows in use and sector diversification, future understandings of the permanence of work, family structure, and home are being revised. Home-based businesses have been around for decades, but the ways these take shape via innovative entrepreneurial mechanisms showcase not only changing preferences for what a retreat from everyday stresses should look like but also changing means to achieve them. Imagined future kinship nostalgia is still a large attraction of the family vacation home; it's just that it looks different when compared to the past, it occurs in different places, and it is now more likely to be centered on experiences rather than a singular place that comes with a permanent set of responsibilities (and lots of stuff).

As these sociohistorical changes have taken place, ideals about what these life realms ought to offer have, in some ways, remained static. Family vacation homes provide a concrete context in which to witness the story of how families and their dwellings are sites for adaptability and change while at the same time anchoring people into powerful ideals that stand the test of time. They are exotic and they are familiar. Implications for broader understanding of families and sociological insights that apply to all life realms, roles, and relationships coalesce in the conclusion of this book.

NOTES

1. Faranak Safdari-Dehcheshmeh et al., "Factors Influencing the Delay in Child-bearing: A Narrative Review," *Iranian Journal of Nursing and Midwifery Research* 28, no. 1 (2023): 10–19.

2. Pew Charitable Trusts, "The Long-Term Decline in Fertility—and What It Means for State Budgets,," December 5, 2022, https://www.pewtrusts.org/en/research-and-analysis/issue-briefs/2022/12/the-long-term-decline-in-fertility-and-what-it-means-for-state-budgets.

3. Richard Fry, "More Millennials Living with Family Despite Improved Job Market," Pew Research Center, July 29, 2015, https://www.pewresearch.org/social-trends/2015/07/29/more-millennials-living-with-family-despite-improved-job-market/; Cheyenne DeVon, "Starter Homes May Be a Thing of the Past—Millennial and Gen Z Homeowners Plan to Stay Put for Nearly 2 Decades," CNBC, July 12, 2023, https://www.cnbc.com/2023/07/12/gen-z-and-millennial-homebuyers-arent-purchasing-starter-homes.html; Patrick J. Purcell, "Geographic Mobility and Annual Earnings in the United States," *Social Security Bulletin* 80, no. 2 (2020), https://www.ssa.gov/policy/docs/ssb/v80n2/v80n2p1.html.

4. Morgan Smith, "Gen Z and Millennials Are Leading 'The Big Quit' in 2023—Why Nearly 70% Plan to Leave Their Jobs," CNBC, January 18, 2023, https://www.cnbc.com/2023/01/18/70percent-of-gen-z-and-millennials-are-considering-leaving-their-jobs-soon.html.

5. Arnaldo Mont'Alvao, Pamela Aronson, and Jeylan Mortimer, "Uncertainty and Disruption in the Transition to Adulthood during COVID-19," in *Social Problems in the Age of COVID-19*, Vol. 2: *Global Perspectives*, ed. G. W. Muschert et al. (Bristol, UK: Bristol University Press/Policy Press, 2020), 15–26.

6. Sydney Lake, "Millennials Are Replaying Their Parents' Housing Market Journey as First-Time Buyers in Their 30s Flood into an Unaffordable Market," *Fortune*, November 14, 2023, https://fortune.com/2023/11/14/housing-market-affordability-millennials-replaying-boomer-parents-1980s/.

7. Philip N. Cohen, "Generation Labels Mean Nothing. It's Time to Retire Them," *Washington Post*, July 7, 2021, https://www.washingtonpost.com/opinions/2021/07/07/generation-labels-mean-nothing-retire-them/.

8. Gill Valentine, "Boundary Crossings: Transitions from Childhood to Adult-hood," *Children's Geographies* 1, no. 1 (2003): 37–52,https://doi.org/10.1080/14733280302186; Viviana A. Zelizer, *Pricing the Priceless Child: The Changing Social Value of Children* (Princeton, NJ: Princeton University Press, 1994).

9. Sara E. Sandberg-Thoma, Anastasia R. Snyder, and Bohyun Joy Jang, "Exiting and Returning to the Parental Home for Boomerang Kids," *Journal of Marriage and Family* 77, no. 3 (2015): 806–18, https://doi.org/10.1111/jomf.12183; Sharon Sassler, Desiree Ciambrone, and Gaelan Benway. "Are They Really Mama's Boys/Daddy's Girls? The Negotiation of Adulthood upon Returning to the Parental Home," *Sociological Forum* 23, no. 4 (2008): 670–98, https://doi.org/10.1111/j.1573-7861.2008.00090.x.

10. See, for example, Jeffrey J. Arnett, *Emerging Adulthood: The Winding Road from the Late Teens through the Twenties* (Oxford: Oxford University Press, 2014); Frank F. Furstenberg et al., "Growing Up Is Harder to Do," *Contexts* 3, no. 3 (2004): 33–41, https://doi.org/10.1525/ctx.2004.3.3.33; Richard A. Settersten Jr., Timothy M. Ottusch, and Barbara Schneider, "Becoming Adult: Meanings of Markers to Adulthood," *Emerging Trends in the Social and Behavioral Sciences* (2015), https://doi.org/10.1002/9781118900772.etrds0021.

11. Janel E. Benson and Frank F. Furstenberg Jr., "Entry into Adulthood: Are Adult Role Transitions Meaningful Markers of Adult Identity?" *Advances in Life Course Research* 11, no. 3 (2006): 199–224, https://doi.org/10.1016/S1040-2608(06)11008-4.

12. Robert R. Callis, "Rate of Homeownership Higher than before Pandemic in All Regions," US Census Bureau, July 25, 2023, https://www.census.gov/library/stories/2023/07/younger-householders-drove-rebound-in-homeownership.html.

13. Sassler, Ciambrone, and Benway, "Are They Really Mama's Boys/Daddy's Girls?"

14. Ariane Bertogg and Marc Szydlik, "The Closeness of Young Adults' Relationships with Their Parents," *Swiss Journal of Sociology* 42, no. 1 (2016): 40–60, https://doi.org/10.1515/sjs-2016-0003; Karen Fingerman, "Millennials and Their Parents: Implications of the New Young Adulthood for Midlife Adults," *Innovation in Aging* 1, no. 3 (2017): 1–16, https://doi.org/10.1093/geroni/igx026; Anna Walczak, "What Does It Mean to Be an Adult? Adulthood Markers in the Perspective of Emerging Adults," *Emerging Adulthood* 11, no. 6 (2023), https://doi.org/10.1177/21676968231194887.

15. Jonathan Vespa, "The Changing Economics and Demographics of Young Adulthood: 1975–2016," US Census Bureau, April 2017, https://www.census.gov/library/publications/2017/demo/p20-579.html.

16. Laurie Goodman, Jung Hyun Choi, and Jun Zhu, "The 'Real' Homeownership Gap between Today's Young Adults and Past Generations Is Much Larger Than You Think," *Urban Wire* (blog), April 17, 2023, https://www.urban.org/urban-wire/real-homeownership-gap-between-todays-young-adults-and-past-generations-much-larger-you.

17. Hyojung Lee et al., "The Role of Parental Financial Assistance in the Transition to Homeownership by Young Adults," *Journal of Housing Economics* 47 (2020). https://doi.org/10.1016/j.jhe.2018.08.002.

18. Amina Niasse, "U.S. Second Home Sales Slide in Pandemic-Era Vacation Hot Spots," Reuters, October 30, 2023, https://www.reuters.com/markets/us/second-home-sales-slide-pandemic-era-vacation-hot-spots-2023-10-30/.

19. Jessica Guerin, "Who Buys a Vacation Home?" HousingWire, July 11, 2019, https://www.housingwire.com/articles/49537-who-buys-a-vacation-home/.

20. O'Brien Legal, "Rich Millennials Opt for Vacation Properties over Starter Homes," October 9, 2019, https://www.olslaw.com/blog/2019/10/rich-millennials-opt -for-vacation-properties-over-starter-homes/.

21. Philip N. Cohen, *The Family: Diversity, Inequality, and Social Change*, 4th ed. (New York: Norton, 2024).

22. Vrbo Virtual Partner Summit 2021, https://host.expediagroup.com/vrbo/en-us/ articles/vrbo-partner-summit.

23. Karen Stein, *Getting Away from It All: Vacations and Identity* (Philadelphia: Temple University Press, 2019).

24. Michelle Y. Janning, *The Stuff of Family Life: How Our Homes Reflect Our Lives*, (Lanham, MD: Rowman and Littlefield, 2017).

25. Belle Siricord, "Why More Millennials and Gen Zs Are Opting to Delay Settling Down or Not Settling Down at All. I'm One of Them," *Medium*, November 15, 2023, https://medium.com/@bellesiricord/why-more-millennials-and-gen-zs-are -opting-to-delay-settling-down-or-not-settling-down-at-all-0a966d8c7f2f.

26. Michelle Y. Janning, *Love Letters: Saving Romance in the Digital Age* (New York: Routledge, 2018).

27. Stein, *Getting Away from It All*, 72.

28. Chip Colwell, "Too Much Stuff: Can We Solve Our Addiction to Consumerism?" *Guardian*, November 28, 2023, https://www.theguardian.com/environment /2023/nov/28/too-much-stuff-can-we-solve-our-addiction-to-consumerism.

29. Joshua N. Hook et al., "Minimalism, Voluntary Simplicity, and Well-Being: A Systematic Review of the Empirical Literature," *Journal of Positive Psychology* 18, no. 1 (2023): 130–41, https://doi.org/10.1080/17439760.2021.1991450.

30. See, for example, Patricia Marx, "A Guide to Getting Rid of Almost Everything," *New Yorker*, February 21, 2022, https://www.newyorker.com/magazine/2022 /02/28/a-guide-to-getting-rid-of-almost-everything-decluttering.

31. Amy Clarke, "We've Been Collecting Souvenirs for Thousands of Years. They Are Valuable Cultural Artefacts—but What Does Their Future Hold?" *Conversation*, October 12, 2022, https://theconversation.com/weve-been-collecting-souvenirs-for -thousands-of-years-they-are-valuable-cultural-artefacts-but-what-does-their-future -hold-189449.

32. Merriam-Webster, "Word of the Year 2023," November 27, 2023, https://www .merriam-webster.com/wordplay/word-of-the-year.

33. Evita Robinson, "Increase Earnings through Inclusivity," Vrbo Virtual Partner Summit, https://host.expediagroup.com/vrbo/en-us/articles/vrbo-partner-summit /inclusivity.

34. Stein, *Getting Away from It All*, 67.

35. Stein, *Getting Away from It All*.

36. Stein, *Getting Away from It All*, 145.

37. Merriam-Webster, "Word of the Year 2023."

38. Janning, *Love Letters*.

39. Lee et al., "The Role of Parental Assistance."

40. Arlie Hochschild, *The Managed Heart: Commercialization of Human Feeling*, (Berkeley: University of California Press, 2020), 59.

41. Janning, *Love Letters.*

Conclusion

Family Vacation Homes, Enchantment, and the Sociological Imagination

ENCHANTMENT

Just before a global pandemic shut the world down, vacation rental companies were hosting in-person events for homeowners eager to rent their vacation homes to others. One such event was the 2019 Vrbo Partner Summit in Scottsdale, Arizona. A video overview of the event aired just after the summit on the company's Facebook page.[1] In the video, homeowners shared what their favorite experiences were from their three days together, including networking with other homeowners and getting creative ideas to stage a home. Particularly captivating were two comments by homeowners in the video:

"You find that they [guests] become part of your family."

"We gave them food out of our garden. . . . [T]hey became more like our family—you know—than just hotel guests."

In these comments by vacation home owners, guests who stay at their vacation rental properties are framed as family members.

As I began this research several years ago and shared ideas with my students at the time, one student told me his family's family vacation home story. They never rented this vacation home out, and his grandparents were wary of the possibility of doing so. In his family, his grandparents were at the age where they could no longer take care of the property alone. His parents, aunts, and uncles were thus deliberating about what was going to happen. They asked the grandkids (including him) what they thought. These conversations were not new: for several years his family circled around the sensitive subjects of the bodily ability of the grandparents currently maintaining the property (as well as his parent's abilities), barriers of access among siblings resulting from differing geographic distance to the property, and varying levels of desire among the younger generations to keep it. As a twenty-two-year-old about to head into the next phase of his life far away from anyone in his family, he had no desire to inherit the property even though he loved going there as a child. He shared that every family conversation avoided the topic of money—what the home may be worth, how it may be part of an equitable inheritance, how busy it may make the family's accountants, whether it may impact individual financial standing, and how much it may cost in the future to maintain it and pay the property taxes. That stuff was no fun to talk about, he said. What was fun to talk about? All of the activities, amenities, natural beauty, and connectedness that is part of family gatherings at the vacation home. Importantly, he said that he thought they should list it as a vacation rental until the family figures out what to do with it, although he would not be able to help maintain it if asked. His grandparents didn't like that idea.

I've been told dozens of stories like this as I've done the research for this book. This student's family is different from the homeowners featured in the Vrbo video, since his family is not renting out the place to anyone. But both the video clips and his story represent changing patterns associated with the idea of a family vacation home, patterns that point to an acknowledgment of shifting family forms, altered ideals for vacations, and new economies where family and vacation interactions take place (especially for younger generations) alongside long-standing visions of retreat from the stresses of everyday life (for everyone).

The previous chapters contain evidence that homeowners differ across the Investment, Mixed, and Personal Property groups in terms of experiencing labor and leisure, defining family boundaries, connecting to neighborhood and community, deliberating about moral claims to property, and changing desires based on age. But despite property group differences, these two scenarios—like a lot of other findings I shared in the previous chapters—tell a similar story: if your vacation home is a business, you have to frame it as a place for family; if your vacation home is not a business but you need to figure out financial stuff, you have to frame it as a place for family. The most powerful cultural message impacting all types of property owners and their families is this: the family vacation home is to be enchanted. It is to be artificially removed from the marketplace, separated from parts of life that are impersonal or hard to talk about, and focused on affective connection and memory making among people defined to be family.

THE SOCIOLOGICAL IMAGINATION

Arriving at the aforementioned conclusion requires the use of the sociological imagination: seeing both the individual family story and the broader sociohistorical context when we try to understand any social phenomenon related to families.[2]

How might this work? Interestingly, my findings point to the astute recognition by homeowners that the current sociohistorical context—including places where there is controversy surrounding second homes—is one filled with structural inequalities by race and class, alongside environmental degradation and political divides. The family vacation home owners in my research understand the broader context beyond their family, and emphasize their dedication to remedying these social ills as they talked about their activism, philanthropy, and global lens on inequality. But they do not often explicitly situate their own family vacation home biography in these larger sociohistorical patterns. To do so would mean going against the powerful cultural value of enchanting the family vacation home. It is supposed to be a place of retreat from hard social things. And if they do place their individual property in the larger political story, it is usually because their use of the property as an enchanted place is threatened by outside forces.

In contrast, many property owners in my research also have a hard time seeing beyond their own family when they talk about their specific family vacation home, including the hard things associated with the property. For these people, the framing of the challenge is centered on idiosyncratic family dynamics (e.g., our children dishonor us by not coming often enough and instead propose renting it out; I want to be more financially responsible than my parents by creatively using my property). Left out of these stories is a recognition of broad sociohistorical patterns that shape individual choices: younger people feeling less connected to possessions and less affinity for singular vacation spots with singular purposes, definitions of "home" varying by age, and time periods and groups especially susceptible to financial precarity.

In the first instance, people possess half of the sociological imagination: recognizing sociohistorical context but not telling their story as part of it. In the second instance, people possess the other half of the sociological imagination: recognizing the importance of their story but not situating it in a larger sociohistorical context.

This may seem like a selective or strategic use of the sociological imagination. But I believe what is really going on is this: the cultural value of enchanting the family vacation home leads to both responses. Enchanting the family vacation home disallows recognition of the harsh world of structural inequalities and market forces that constrain individual choice; it disallows framing it as anything other than about the intimate and emotionally fulfilling story of family. This powerful cultural value makes us ignore the ways our individual stories are part of an acknowledged structural reality, and it makes us ignore structural conditions that shape our individual family stories. To

enchant is to define the family vacation home as private and just about family relationships. This can make us artificially overindividualize some things
(my kids don't want it) or underindividualize other things (I'm not part of
the problem or solution relating to structural inequalities taking shape in my
neighborhood).

SOCIOLOGICAL TAKEAWAYS

There are several sociological takeaways that this research uncovers besides
the power of cultural values to influence people's willingness to see the connection between their individual family stories and larger social patterns.
First, formal classifications for groups of people may or may not tell the story
of (a) variability within those classifications, (b) how the boundaries between
the classifications are socially defined and symbolically enacted, and (c) what
people *actually do*. My introduction of three property groups that emerged
from my data—Investment, Mixed, and Personal—that differ from formal
homeowner classifications may mean my findings are not easily able to be
mapped onto research and regulatory projects, but it also means I capture the
fluidity and subjectively defined attitudes and behaviors of people in terms
of how they actually live their lives. Classification that can capture variation
is crucial across many social science research endeavors.

Second, because social actors become more aware of their desires and
circumstances when they are shaken up, large-scale social disruption such
as a global pandemic can highlight timeless and stable social patterns at
the same time (and because) those patterns are disrupted. I almost gave up
on this multiyear project because COVID-19 interrupted it. I figured that
all things relating to families, homes, and vacations had changed forever.
But then I discovered that the trajectory of what families were doing (and
what vacationers were wanting) had started well before 2020. The pandemic
induced a widespread collective realization that the home is a contradictory
site of haven (protecting people from a virus) and a place of stress (too much
time at home and juggling all the blurry life realms was hard). Postlockdown,
people wanted to regain their sense of adventure, reunite with people they
hadn't seen in a long time, and get control over their environments. This
enhanced consciousness about the implications of place, social connection,
and autonomy meant that people were better able to see how their individual
stories were implicated in a collective story. Thus, while it didn't entirely disrupt patterns related to homes, families, and vacations that had started earlier,
the pandemic offered an interruption and an opportunity to home in on what
cultural values were really important, and it honed people's capacity to use
their sociological imaginations, whether they knew they were doing so or not.

Third, the value of retreat from things that are hard seems to remain a strongly held cultural value, even though it is impossible to attain. One outcome of the pandemic has been to double down on the need for a respite. If it can't be found in our homes, maybe it can be found at work. If it can't be found in either realm, maybe we need to find other spaces that give us what we need. Family vacation homes by definition are meant to offer respite. They are distanced from the stress of a primary residence and the paid work world, they are an adventure and yet a haven, and they offer people control over their environment. However, their capacity to fully offer a retreat, as my research shows, is an illusion.

Fourth, structural inequality is interwoven with, and often supported by, cultural value systems that seem universal but are not equally accessible. Property ownership is still a significant factor in determining who has wealth and privilege, but it also determines who gets to enact strong cultural values such as enchanting the family. Having privilege allows people greater capacity to escape structural realities that point out that privilege in an unequal system. Ultimately, regardless of property group and stance on vacation property regulation, entitlement is framed as something connected to property ownership. Vacation home owners across property groups believe that it's their right to do with their property what they'd like, perhaps including using it to make money. This belief is supported by a powerful cultural value that suggests enchanting the family is the ultimate goal, and that it is best achieved via private property.

Fifth, emotions are important to study sociologically. Consumption of properties and their furnishings, even if rented, is a form of care that intersects families and the marketplace. Consumption acts as a symbolic language through which buyers make connections to others, as many of the authors introduced in chapter 1 articulated. Thus, enchanting a family vacation home by playing up the emotional connection of family life is done via acts and places that have a price tag attached. Whether via ritual (reunions at the cabin), rhetoric (talking about how this place is all about love and memories), or object (a family photograph in a seashell-lined frame), people turn a market-driven good into a family-focused memory in the name of love.

Sixth, leisure ought to be a more popular and serious area of study for sociologists. Sociologists study paid work more than they study leisure. Sociologists Cathy Stein Greenblat and John H. Gagnon offer a few reasons for this, suggesting that paid work has been defined as a more serious area of study within sociology than leisure and that leisure does not focus as much on social problems or disorder as compared to other subfields. There is also a bias in the discipline "against studying persons who are enjoying themselves."[3] They elaborate: "Far more prestige has been attached to the analysis of problems, conflicts, and traumas than to analyses of joys, harmonies, and elation. Perhaps it is felt that there are moral risks associated with studies of the ostensibly pleasurable domains in which the objects of scrutiny and the observers are in danger of having a good time."[4]

But of course the study of family vacation homes and other tourism and leisure experiences, as Greenblat and Gagnon suggest, highlights the relationship between work and leisure in advanced industrial societies, reveals coping patterns people seek in stressful lives, and points out the role of migration and identity management as people move from place to place or culture to culture or group to group. Importantly, family vacations are voluntary, where the migration is not compulsory, as it would be in forced migration. And, as my research reveals, the study of family vacation homes also reveals unequal access to leisure (and housing), strategies used to navigate the sharing economy and collaborative consumption, and patterns surrounding values about the artificial distinction between the priceless magic of family and the priced reality of the marketplace. Thus, even research on people in privileged positions enjoying themselves sheds light on larger cultural values and systems of inequality. And in my opinion, it's also quite okay to study people enjoying themselves because that, too, is part of the human condition.

Finally, and most importantly, despite being a specific type of place, the family vacation home is a helpful site for understanding broad patterns related to families. Historian John Gillis noted this about ideals and realities among families:

> The prophets of family decline bemoan the gap between the ideal and reality, cynics take it as proof of the hypocrisy of contemporary society, and both assume that sometime in the near or distant past things were different, that there was a time when home and family were all they were meant to be. But just when was this golden age? You will search in vain for a time when people found it possible to realize in the families they lived with all the values they wished to live by, when people felt wholly at home in their places of residence.[5]

Gillis wrote this nearly thirty years ago. Since then, and despite continuing rhetoric in certain pockets of our social world that advocate for a return to some kind of traditional nostalgic past version of family life, people are more likely to recognize that there may not have been such thing as a golden age for families and that, if it did exist, it may have been quite bad for some groups, especially women, LGBTQIA+ people, people of color, and people in financially precarious circumstances. The home is still defined as a haven removed from the harsh realities of other, more public life realms, but now more than ever, we see how this is an inaccurate definition. It is an ideal rather than a reality to say that home is distinct from other realms that are defined as harsh, public, or unsafe. In fact, to do so perpetuates social inequalities that have disallowed certain groups from achieving a haven for generations. It also perpetuates artificial ideals that don't reflect how people actually live their work and family lives. So people increasingly recognize that the world is filled with inequality and hardship, including pain found in homes and families and including structural patterns that make it challenging for people without privilege to escape those hardships. At the same time, people across all social groups still yearn for respite, retreat, and the capacity to remove oneself from painful things.

The family vacation home serves to innovatively manage the mismatch between ideal and reality. Families know that home life is stressful, that challenges are not reserved just for the harsh worlds of work and other public realms. And they know the realities of their past family stories may be fraught, trauma filled, or painful. And yet we work hard to try to shelter ourselves and future generations in our families from all of this. And not everyone has the financial resources to do this, or to do it without some other kind of entrepreneurial mechanism in place, such as renting the property out to others for a fee.

The definition of family has become more inclusive compared to even a decade ago, demonstrated in national surveys and among homeowners I interviewed and within the other data sites in my research. Yet as families change and as the structure of who counts as a family gets more flexible, the ingredients of what families are supposed to do seems to have remained relatively stable: the idealized family persists as an enchanted private haven meant to socialize children, protect people from the harsh worlds of politics and the economy, offer emotional support, and exclude strangers and market forces that signify an impersonal set of transactions. In other words, despite the fact that families are not at all removed from the economy, politics, media, and other institutions, and despite greater recognition of this in people's minds, families are meant to be enchanted. Love, emotional support, and trust are the priceless goods that people are meant to get from their family. This pricelessness—now more precarious in a world where life realm boundaries are increasingly blurry and where home stresses are more acknowledged by scholars and the public at large—extends to other spaces and places of family life: namely, we search for enchantment in family vacation homes. But we do so in ways that blur families and the marketplace even as we try to keep these separate.

As municipalities continue to deliberate about whether their community is tourism based, amenable to part-time visitors, open to the sharing economy, or fiercely protective of homeowners who live there year-round, it will be important to have in mind these realities that my research uncovers: the increasing desire for fluidity of ownership and use over time by homeowners and the strategic-yet-understandable framing of properties as enchanted family places by homeowners. If we can include rigorously analyzed qualitative data and stories alongside numbers and maps included in policy deliberations, and if we recognize that sometimes groups that seem very different are actually pointing to the same powerful cultural values, then we will be better able to create the best version of family vacation homes in supportive and sustainable neighborhoods and communities.

* * *

A recent animated television ad from Airbnb opens with a family of three settling into a hotel room bed together at the same time, closing the curtains on the early evening light streaming into the room. The narrator says, "When you share a hotel room with your kid, you also share a bedtime with your kid." The room is then shown magically folding into a two-story home with an upstairs bedroom where the child is sleeping and a downstairs living room where the parents are situated, with the voiceover saying, "But if you get an Airbnb you get to pick your own bedtime." The parents grab drinks and open the curtain, revealing a vista of the Eiffel Tower and fireworks bursting over a Parisian skyline—familiar because it's a home, exotic because it allows for romance in a faraway place that couldn't happen if the parents had to go to bed before dark.[6] The family vacation home—ours or someone else's that we borrow for a fee—offers a lot to meet the current needs of families. Despite debates about whether they ought to be used by owners or others, the outcome is quite similar: families seek new and authentic experiences that remove them from everyday stress at the same time they offer familiarity and comfort—a magical combination.

The family vacation home is a site filled with complexity and contradiction. It is a place and a set of experiences. It is a collection of concrete objects and a backdrop for elusive memories. It is imagined and realized. It is exotic and familiar. It is the past and the imagined future. It is a symbol of achievement and a symbol of immense social inequality. It is preserved as somehow separate from other life realms and yet is interwoven intimately with them. It is enchanted and yet very real.

NOTES

1. Vrbo Partners, "Summit 2019 | Scottsdale, AZ," Facebook, November 11, 2019, https://www.facebook.com/watch/?v=560415408108868.

2. C. Wright Mills, *The Sociological Imagination*, 40th anniversary ed. (New York: Oxford University Press, 2000).

3. Cathy Stein Greenblat and John H. Gagnon, "Temporary Strangers: Travel and Tourism from a Sociological Perspective," *Sociological Perspectives* 26, no. 1 (1983): 90, https://www.jstor.org/stable/1389161.

4. Stein and Gagnon, "Temporary Strangers," 90.

5. John R. Gillis, *A World of Their Own Making: Myth, Ritual, and the Quest for Family Values* (Cambridge, MA: Harvard University Press, 1996), 21.

6. Airbnb, "Bedtime" (advertisement), YouTube, January 20, 2024, https://www.youtube.com/watch?v=1STa1vWPCmo.

Appendix

METHODOLOGICAL NOTES

My methodological approach to this study on family vacation homes is decidedly qualitative, with particular attention to uncovering meanings, stories, and subjective experiences that point to broader patterns when analyzed systematically. To research how vacation and investment property ownership and use may shape current understandings of families, I conducted homeowner interviews and surveys, supplemented by a review of research and practice related to the topic, field observation and mapping in homeowner neighborhoods, participant observation at hospitality conferences and public meetings about housing regulations, and content analysis of news stories, lifestyle television shows, and instructional webinars for vacation rental owners.

I have three methodological goals: (1) incorporating diverse data sets gathered over time that include a variety of people and places that appropriately capture the family vacation home story (a multimethod approach to data, analytic technique, sample, and site); (2) ensuring that my interpretations are consistent with how other researchers may interpret them and that I'm capturing the realities of people's lives (attention to reliability and validity, especially with regard to the property group classifications I use in this research); and (3) honoring the subjective meaning making among the voices included in the research without imposing my biases or risking breaches in confidentiality (ethical considerations). Below I detail my work toward reaching the three aforementioned goals.

MULTIMETHOD APPROACH TO DATA, ANALYTIC TECHNIQUE, SAMPLE, AND SITE

I aimed for methodological triangulation throughout this project, with each new data element that was added across several years of data collection increasing my confidence that the patterns uncovered in this book are substantiated. Also important for my project is the capacity to bridge findings that appeared before COVID-19 and those that emerged after 2020, a task made possible by implementing similar analytic techniques across data that I collected between 2017 and 2022. Doing this allowed me to show that most patterns relating to enchantment and imagined future kinship nostalgia were already part of a temporal trajectory that had started prepandemic and that is still present today, with the pandemic serving as an important interrupter—not a total disrupter—of these patterns. As I aimed for consistency across analytic techniques and interpretation of findings, I also tailored my analysis to the type of data being analyzed.

Interviews, Surveys, and Tours of Homes and Neighborhoods

In order to understand how homeowners defined and used their properties, I conducted phone and in-person interviews and surveys of fifty-six homeowners in the United States who own forty-five properties across fourteen states (and one site outside the United States) that are used for family or personal getaways (their own, or to rent to other families using property management companies or platforms such as Airbnb and Vrbo, or both). The interviews lasted between one and three hours each and were fully transcribed before analysis. Fifteen of the interviews were conducted on the phone. I recruited people for my interviews via blasts on social media and my website for participation in an interview and survey study about second homes. When I began doing interviews across the United States, I also contacted people I knew in each area to ask them to share a call for participation in their professional and personal networks. As I started the recursive process of finalizing my research question, I narrowed the rest of the focus on vacation home use specifically, rather than on second homes that may be used as long-term rentals or other corporate enterprises such as timeshares. While these additional interviews provided a helpful way to understand the second home investment property marketplace beyond vacation and leisure uses, and beyond properties that owners have full control over, they are excluded from analysis here because they have less to do with my research question surrounding the social and material dimensions of vacationing and family memory making.

The groups of people I'm studying, as I discuss in chapter 1, are not representative of the US population, although they are geographically dispersed, wide-ranging in age and income level, and varied in experiences relevant for my research. The homeowners whose voices are included in this research do not represent a random sample of people who are supposed to capture an average set of experiences across a wide swath of the population; rather, they are people who already fit into an unusual group with specific experiences. Just as an archaeologist would not dig random holes every tenth mile across

South Dakota to happen to find dinosaur bones, I did not create a random sample. I did my digging strategically, seeking the places and people who would be most likely to be able to talk about the topic I'm studying, and I used my own personal and professional network to do so. Because second home owners are not necessarily a population that is easy to access, I relied on nonprobability sampling techniques.

The properties of the interviewees could be considered second homes regardless of their classification as a separate dwelling or building (that is, they could be a room or ADU in the same location as a primary residence) and regardless of their size, value, or legal status as either a vacation home or investment property. These were subjectively defined. But they had to be physically locatable and tangibly constructed (in other words, they could not be vacation homes that existed entirely in the minds of their possessors). Homeowners did not necessarily need to reference the phrase "family vacation home" in our conversations, but the way they used the properties needed to suggest that a significant portion of the property's use was dedicated to their own or other families' vacations or personal leisure time. If it was for their own vacation time, the property needed to be in a different location than the primary residence. The interviews included in my analysis focused on twelve properties in the Investment Property group, seven in the Mixed Property group, and twenty-six in the Personal Property group; these property groups are defined in the next section. The relatively lower number of interviewees included in the first two groups is complemented by research findings about investment property use in other data included in my project. Among homeowners who owned property beyond the primary residence (that is, a vacation home, or a separate dwelling used to rent out to others, or both), and excluding RVs, property values ranged from $90,000 to $1.2 million, with a median home value (as reported by homeowners) of $225,000. Everyone in the study had enough equity in their homes that they could yield a sizable amount if they sold them, although the people who no longer carried a mortgage on any property were in a much less precarious financial position as compared to some others.

The homeowners I interviewed were between twenty-eight and seventy-nine years old and identified predominantly as heterosexual, with a handful of exceptions. Two-thirds (thirty-seven of fifty-six) of the interviewees were women. The interviewees represented a wide array of political views, from very conservative to very liberal. All but three interviewees identified as white, with an additional two people identifying partners as members of other racial-ethnic groups. The annual income ranges skewed toward middle- and upper-income brackets, including two people earning less than $20,000 a year, three people earning between $20,000 and $50,000, nine people earning between $50,000 and $100,000, and the rest earning more than six figures annually in their households. The ones with higher incomes were disproportionately likely to have their home mortgages fully paid off. Thirteen homeowners among the top income group had a third, or sometimes fourth, property besides their primary residence and the vacation home that was the focus of the interviews. Thirty-four interviews were conducted with individuals; eleven were conducted with pairs of family members, with most of these married partners and one of them a mother-daughter pair. Each person or pair of people answered the same questions in roughly the same order, with some variation if people offered stories that led to a request for clarification or elaboration. This means the interviews were semistandardized. Responses did not differ in substantive ways based on whether an interview was conducted with one or two people, and people who interviewed in pairs seemed to have very little disagreement and very high levels of comfort answering honestly in front of each other. The questions I asked were not about highly sensitive information such as relationship conflict, violence, or financial hardship that families sometimes have trouble talking about. Arguably, the interviews took more of a conversational form than a standardized formal form, which allowed for plenty of stories and meanderings but also led to an analysis that was centered more on what inductively emerged from the conversations rather than any kind of deductive hypothesis testing.

In the interviews, I asked people to tell me about their families and to recount the story of the home purchase, what type of property or space it is (e.g., ADU, condo, portion of primary residence), how they'd classify it from among a list of options that included "vacation home" and "short-term rental," who uses the home and when, where the home is located, and whether anyone but them manages the property. I then asked about the neighborhood and community in terms of how other properties are used, regulations, controversies, and property values. (The accompanying survey asked about their incomes and individual property values.) I inquired about whether they think of themselves differently in their vacation home as opposed to their primary residence, what activities they do, what labor is involved, and how any objects or furnishings or material aspects of the home have emotional significance. Included in the interview was also a set of questions asking them to describe their impression of the positive or negative impact of their own and others' second homes on social and economic conditions of the host community and neighborhood, as well as their ties to local residents and goings-on. I also asked everyone how they'd define "home."

I was physically invited into sixteen of the vacation homes and visited the neighborhoods where a dozen additional homes were located without going into the homes. For the rest, I located pictures on real estate valuation websites and online maps. Most of the neighborhoods were places I had not visited before, so I thought of my note-taking and mapping as my "rental car ethnography," which other researchers have identified as a "windshield survey," a research tool used to get a sense of a neighborhood's condition, age, aesthetics, activity, visibility of people, and types of shops and amenities.[1] This note-taking allowed me to get a more vivid image of the physical and social neighborhood characteristics that homeowners described.

Employing data analytic cycles outlined by Johnny Saldaña,[2] I analyzed the homeowner interview transcripts using several code-mapping steps and tools, with the help of Dedoose qualitative software.[3] As is typical in semistandardized interview analysis, I started with the broad topics I asked about, turning them into codes that could be broken down into subcodes. I then revised and/or complemented these with new codes that emerged in a recursive process. My codes were at times about straightforward attributes—homeowner and location characteristics, for example. Other codes were more about magnitude—to what degree people thought vacation homes were good or bad for a community, for example. But descriptive codes that turned into analytic codes (that is, codes that showed some causal relationships or thematic connections) represented the bulk of the analysis. This included codes about how people did or did not feel comfortable talking about the property in financial terms, for example, which then connected to the conceptual framework of enchantment (which I initially coded as "pricelessness"). The process of revisiting codes, adding to them, refining them, and connecting them to existing theoretical conceptualizations included rigorous attention to defining the three property groups I use in my analysis (Investment, Mixed, and Personal), which I defined based on multiple rounds of coding and which I elaborate below when I discuss reliability and validity. In terms of what may count as a "finding" throughout this book, I included patterns among property groups that showed up in either several interviewee transcripts, or across more than one data source, or both. In some cases, if a topic or experience was raised by multiple property owners in one property group and not others, thus situating it as unique to one group, I noted it as a finding that demonstrated group differences. In other words, findings showed up as patterns that connected groups of people as having something in common, or they showed up as ways to distinguish one group's experiences from another's by virtue of an experience existing only within one group. If a group's experience differed across data sites, I noted the inconsistency and noted substantive reasons why this may have happened.

As part of my research, I also conducted interviews and surveys with a dozen stakeholders in positions connected to vacation home and family tourism markets and communities (e.g., real estate, lending, tourism, hospitality, community organizing, city government, property management, and home construction). These were all conducted in person. While I did not conduct as thorough and systematic analysis of their responses as I did for

the homeowners, their voices are included in the book as context and cor-
roboration for claims made by people in other parts of my research or ways
to connect homeowner experiences to larger issues in sectors connected to
family vacation homes.

Participant Observation

Along with interviews and surveys, I conducted participant observation
research across multiple sites to understand what's going on with family
vacation homes. This included in-person research as a participant observer
at a vacation rental conference in 2019 and at a hospitality conference in
2022. I don't name the organizations sponsoring these events in the book
because they were not free and open to the public. I had to pay to participate.
I disclosed to the vacation rental conference organizers that while I do own
a second property (which was a requirement for registration), I do not have
any vacation rental listings. I disclosed to the hospitality conference organizers that I am writer and researcher and not a hospitality business owner. The
vacation rental conference was aimed at homeowners who list their homes on
the company's online platform and who want to network with others and find
ways to have successful businesses by doing this. The hospitality conference
was about resources, tools, and design items for hospitality industry professionals in the hotel, restaurant, cruise ship, spa, and vacation sectors.

My participant observation also included field notes from two public city
council meetings in August and November 2017 in my town—Walla Walla,
Washington—which was undergoing revision to short-term rental regulations
in 2017 after months of controversy, political organizing by groups represent-
ing opposing sides, and study of the issue by city and county employees. I
name the site here because the meetings were free and open to the public.
Walla Walla has just under thirty-five thousand residents, a sizable Hispanic
or Latino population (23.6 percent), and a median household income of
$58,179.[4] The short-term rental regulation deliberations ended in the creation
of a set of ordinances that allow for two types of vacation rentals where the
home is the primary residence of the owner: rooms (including detached spaces
or ADUs) rented with the owner present or rental of the entire dwelling.[5]

At each of these events or sets of events, I took copious notes in hand-
written and digital form, using whatever writing method allowed me to be
the least distracting to other participants. I also gathered publicly available
documents at all sites, which included meeting and session agendas as well
as advertisements for products used in vacation rentals and in the hospitality
industry broadly. In all three field sites, I disclosed my role as a researcher
to meeting hosts or organizers and to anyone engaged in substantive conversation with me. I took vigorous notes to ensure accuracy of quotes, drew

maps and noted my observations about visual goings-on and types of people attending, and used the same initial broad codes and multiple-round coding technique that I did for the interviews, but instead of using an online platform I used only pen-and-paper coding of text and added codes that pertained only to the field sites.

Participant observation in these sites helped me understand how entities beyond families were framing (a) the definition of vacations and families based on people's views about private property and community, (b) how the sharing economy is shaping current housing debates, and (c) the role of politics and the marketplace in issues that are centered on social and emotional connections between people in families on vacation. It also helped me situate homeowner stories in politics and the marketplace.

Content Analysis

In addition to consulting social scientific, tourism, and real estate writing as part of a thorough review of research and practitioner literature, I conducted systematic content analysis of specific types of texts relating to family vacation homes. The datasets used came from video and transcripts of ten free and publicly accessible episodes of HGTV series about vacation properties aimed at families that aired in 2018 and 2019 (*Log Cabin Living*, *Lakefront Bargain Hunt*, and *Beachfront Bargain Hunt*), text from free and publicly accessible summer 2020 news articles about vacation home controversies during COVID-19 in amenity-rich vacation communities, and six free and publicly accessible instructional webinars aimed at vacation homeowners from the 2021 Vrbo Virtual Partner Summit.[6] These content analyses—all done using pen-and-paper color-coding methods rather than a qualitative analysis program on a computer—provided ways to understand the production of stories about the vacation home marketplace in media forms, the role of the pandemic in shaping local residents' views about visitors, and the impact of the pandemic and increased racial tension on strategies for homeowners who want to create a successful vacation rental business with their homes. Like the participant observation elements of my research, the content analyses involved the same type of coding process as other data analyses in this project, which then helped me contextualize and update findings that emerged from homeowner interviews.

RELIABILITY AND VALIDITY: PROPERTY
GROUP CLASSIFICATION

Imagine a local property owner in your neighborhood who wants to switch their home's rental designation from long-term rental (say, a twelve-month lease) or medium-term rental (between thirty days and twelve months) to short-term vacation rental (less than thirty continuous days) using platforms such as Airbnb and Vrbo. This person used to live in town but now lives in another part of the country. They are visiting for a month to fix up the property after the previous tenants damaged it. In the future they may move back to this house, but right now they're not sure about their career trajectory. They know that, according to federal law, they can only stay in the house for a couple weeks, since it is technically an investment property and not a vacation home. They also know that according to local ordinances, the home has to be designated as their principal residence (or portion of it). They believe that surely their month-long stay will be fine because they are working on home repairs. This is no vacation. But they're not exactly blasting this news wide and far. Now imagine this person also wants to place a tiny home in the driveway so they can either rent it out as a second vacation spot or stay in town even if vacationers are renting their house. But the municipal ordinances disallow an ADU to be rented out on the same property as another vacation rental unless full utilities are paid on the unit. This set of expenses for two dwellings, along with any licenses, would eat up nearly a third of any earnings made on vacation rental bookings. Confused yet? This is a lot of complexity for a pair of small homes on a small lot in a residential neighborhood! This is a story happening in my community, and it is not an uncommon scenario for people who rely on rental incomes to be financially stable or to make their retirement accounts healthier. It will be intriguing to see what happens with this property, including how neighbors talk about it.

It's fair to say that the people included in my research varied in small and large ways when compared with formal classificatory rules and categories, as elaborated throughout the book. This became apparent as I gathered data about what people *actually* did with their properties. In my interviews, very few people talked at length about their property's official legal classification, unless it was part of their assertions about the fairness or unfairness of short-term rental regulations in the area. In these cases they had studied local ordinances thoroughly. Among most of my interviewees, there was some talk of tax distinctions between their primary and second homes, state differences in taxation, and some tax deductions associated with maintenance or remodeling, but not much else. It was more common for people to just brush off the topic by saying their accountants knew more about it than they did. Among the people I observed at the vacation rental conference, though, regulations at federal, state, and local levels were on the tips of everyone's tongues.

Formal Property Group Classifications

Before I delve into my property group classifications, I want to elaborate on the formal federal property classifications for second homes in the United States. Recall from chapter 1 that I formed different property ownership categories based on what emerged from my research (discussed later in this appendix), but it's important to know how these properties are viewed by formal institutions and organizations such as the government or mortgage lending agencies.

According to the IRS and several stakeholders included in my research, a home is a vacation home if you rent it out fourteen or fewer days per year. In this case, you can deduct real estate taxes and mortgage interest in the same way you could do with a primary residence (with caps at local, state, and federal levels). You don't have to pay taxes on any income that comes from fourteen or fewer days of rentals per year, and the house is considered your personal residence. With more than fourteen days rented out, the house becomes a rental house or investment property, and you have to report the income to the IRS, but you also get to deduct rental expenses. These deductions depend on how many days per year you (or sometimes your family) use the property as compared to the number of days you rent it to others. If your personal use exceeds fourteen days per year, tax deductions get more mathematically complex.

The IRS defines what counts as "a day" in its "Topic No. 415, Renting Residential and Vacation Property" document:

A day of personal use of a dwelling unit is any day that the unit is used by:

- You or any other person who has an interest in it, unless you rent your interest to another owner as their main home and the other owner pays a fair rental price under a shared equity financing agreement
- A member of your family or of a family of any other person who has an interest in it, unless the family member uses it as their main home and pays a fair rental price
- Anyone under an agreement that lets you use some other dwelling unit
- Anyone at less than fair rental price[7]

Despite digesting the IRS website, reading numerous books, viewing several webinars, and sifting through countless news articles, I did not become an expert on real estate law, city zoning, or taxation across the multiple sites where I conducted interviews or where homeowners at the conference rented their properties. Instead, I noticed that traditional markers of formal economic exchange such as prices, taxes, and receipts seemed to matter less than perception, rhetorical strategy, and meaning making. This is not to say that policies and regulations and legal classifications of homes don't matter; rather, as numerous findings across the varied data included in this research reveal, why people do what they do may not be easily apparent to them, and actions and the impact of powerful cultural values are certainly not always a result of following rules or laws. This is the focus of the book, rather than a study of precise policy abiding.

Property Group Classifications Use in This Research

Social researchers aim to have their research be replicable and to have their findings be consistent if other researchers look at the same data. This can be challenging, especially if two people are interpreting the same television show scene or interview transcript. To reach the conclusions I did in this book, I implemented thoughtful *inter-coder reliability* checks throughout, regardless of whether I collected the data alone or research assistants did the data collection and analysis. This means that for the interview and content analyses, I worked with research assistants to see if what I was interpreting from the qualitative data was the same as what they were interpreting. (One research assistant also conducted one homeowner and one stakeholder interview to get more familiar with the questions.) Depending on the specific data, this entailed periodic check-ins at beginning, middle, and end points of coding, with conversations leading to code revisions along the way. Because each coding process went through at least three iterations of code mapping, there were plenty of opportunities to check in to see if the findings that were emerging from the data were visible across a few different researchers. Some of the findings from these subsets of this project have been presented at conferences or published as research articles, in which my coauthors and I elaborated methods details.[8]

The coding that required the most depth and rigor in terms of inter-coder reliability was the creation of the three property group classifications based on interviewee responses to my questions: Investment, Mixed, and Personal. Using time spent in the home, the types of people who stay there, and the formality of exchange (if any) with people who stay there, these three groups emerged via a coding process that included ten iterations of cross-checking with a research assistant and across other data elements over eighteen months of analysis to see if the clustering of property owners into these three groups made sense. Property owners were first divided into five groups based on their current use of the properties, with the first group always renting out the spaces to others for a formal fee, the second group mostly doing so but infrequently (less than four short visits a year), the middle group spending about half the time there and renting it out the other half, the fourth group mostly allowing family to stay but occasionally (less than four short visits a year) renting it out formally or informally, and the last group only allowing family and close friends to stay (and never for a formal fee). As the coding transpired, it became apparent that groups 1 and 2 had a lot in common in terms of time, people, and formality; that groups 4 and 5 also had this in common; and that group 3 remained uniquely situated between the extremes. So three groups emerged based on their current use:

- Investment is primarily rented out most of the year, primarily to strangers, and primarily via formal fee structures.
- Personal is primarily used for personal or family use, rarely in exchange for a small fee or informal exchange such as gifts or labor.
- Mixed is halfway between these.

Because I did not use existing property classifications (such as those defined by the IRS), this meant that the groups I use also represented an exercise in validity: are these true findings that capture the realities of participants (internal validity) and that realistically represent the experiences of others outside of the study (external validity)? To the latter point, the participant observation research I did at the hospitality and vacation rental conferences, as well as the webinar content analysis, led me to the finding that the biggest differences among property owners fall precisely along the boundaries between the groups I use as a new way of classifying property ownership and use, even as the boundaries between them may shift over time for any individual property owner.

The hardest part of all of this research was ensuring that the property group categories I'm drawing (a) make sense, (b) are represented in the data, and (c) reflect the realities of people not included in my research but who may fit into the categories. This is about representativeness of my samples, to be sure, but it's also about validity—making sure I'm measuring variables in a way that captures the reality for which they are a proxy—and reliability—making sure that other people who may study my data find the same patterns and organize the qualitative data in similar ways. Because the property group classifications emerged from people's actual experiences as reflected across several different types of data, and because I went through numerous reliability and validity checks with several research assistants, I feel confident that the three property groups I propose—Investment, Mixed, and Personal—reflect how families actually live their lives with regard to family vacation homes.

RESEARCH ETHICS

To strike the right balance between data and stories, and to honor the subjective voices of people involved in all parts of my research, I paid a lot of attention to ethics, with particular focus on two issues: bias and confidentiality. My project, importantly, was approved by the Whitman College Institutional Review Board at every stage of the research process, with an original approval in 2017 (approval number 16/17–38), and amendments in 2018, 2019, and 2022 that reflect added data sources and analyses.

Recognizing *bias* (I have values that could shape how I go about this research) and *positionality* (I have identities that could shape what happens in this research) helped me to practice researcher *reflexivity* (I should examine my bias and positionality as they may impact this research). Whichever way it is framed, my role as a researcher is part of the research story.

I am not a robot. One of the gifts of being a human is that I assuredly have opinions about property, vacations, families, and community. As a sociologist, I gravitate toward projects that help uncover what's really going on in society so that we can eradicate social ills, including inequalities and injustices. My job in this project is to ensure that my views and values—while informing my interest and access to people willing and able to talk to me about family vacation homes—are not what ultimately lead me to my findings. I also have to recognize that some of the patterns I uncover may not feel very flattering to people I interviewed and observed, which makes me anxious. But as a sociologist, I value the uncovering of patterns that occur across a group of individuals even if they conflict with certain individual people's experiences or desires to be seen in a certain way. Truth be told, I find myself somewhere in the middle of a whole sea of opinions relating to the topic of family vacation homes, at times feisty alongside friends who are proud of their vacation rental business and at other times feeling compelled to agree with other friends who lament old ways of vacationing, being in a family, or being neighborly. I've stayed in family vacation homes that my extended family have, and I've stayed in short-term vacation rentals. I am sure that people with strong opinions about their properties and their communities will read this book and get upset with some of the findings, or at least get frustrated that not everyone shares their views. But I do not intend to reflect my views in the findings. I'd like to think that the value guiding my research more than anything else is curiosity. This is what allows me to go into any conversation or field site with an open mind, not assuming what I'd find and not being disappointed if what I find surprises me or conflicts with a view I or others close to me may hold. I found myself uninterested in agreeing or disagreeing with people's bold opinions, focusing instead on asking questions about why they held those opinions. And when I was worried if my values were shaping the data story that I saw unfolding, I had invaluable research assistants whose interpretations offered checks along every step of the research process.

When it comes to positionality, of course the fact that I'm a relatively affluent and well-connected, property-owning white woman with gray hair matters. That probably affected who was willing to talk with me or, if they were willing, what they were willing to disclose. These traits, alongside the fact that I have close family members with enough resources to have vacation properties that I get to visit, and alongside the fact that during the research process I owned an investment property that I rented to long-term tenants, assuredly make me not representative of the US population. But, alas, these characteristics do make me more like the kinds of people who are prototypical family vacation home owners. This means that as I carried out the interviews and ventured into field sites, I didn't have to work very hard to fit in. I didn't have to radically shift my affect, appearance, wardrobe, conversational style, or disclosure of my own characteristics. It means I'm in (or could pass for being in) the culture of people who make up most of what I'm studying. It means I didn't have to work hard to build trust among those who agreed to participate in my research. In this sense, I have access; I have insider status. Case in point: I could access the 2019 vacation rental conference because I owned a second property at the time, which allowed me to register for the conference in the first place, and talk about this property with vendors and participants. While I disclosed that I was a researcher and also did not rent my second home out as a vacation rental (that would have been a conflict of interest, since I could have financially benefited from conference goings-on), just owning this property gave me entrée into the entire conference and several conversations therein.

But I am not completely like the homeowners in my study, since I do not own a second home used for vacations for me or anyone else, since many of the property owners I include in the research are more affluent than I am, and since most of the people included in my research are not sociologists or involved in university or college settings. And I'm generally not an outdoor enthusiast and I don't particularly like skiing or hunting or swimming in lakes or oceans, which makes it a little harder to relate to stories about nature-based amenities in vacation spots. All of this is to say that I acknowledge my positionality and how it may have affected my research. But I don't think it lessens the value of what I've found, and it definitely allowed me access to stories and observations that informed my findings.

Confidentiality is the second ethical issue among many that matter for any sociological project. Here I focus my attention on ways I aim to protect the identities of people participating. When I talk about the book with people who participated in this research, I tell them that they may recognize their own story, but they shouldn't recognize anyone else's. There are people for whom, if their names or locations are included in my research, it may be possible for readers to identify who they are. So I don't name locations. Some of this is because I interviewed clusters of people who live in the same towns, and their responses would clue others in about their identities. Given my focus on patterns that are more about families than they are about specific sites, excluding these names works. Besides, thinking of pseudonyms for people can be a creative process: I based all pseudonyms in the book on places I have lived throughout my life that do not match up with where the interviewees reside: street names, landmarks, city names, and even state or region names. That's why, for instance, there are people named Red, Woody, and Minnie in my research (I grew up in a Minnesota town called Redwood Falls). For any participant observation findings, I de-identify people to focus on group patterns.

In terms of the sites where interviewees own family vacation homes, I clustered the properties into eleven fictitiously named regions that made sense given similarities of amenities, climate, geographic location, and landscape—mostly to give the reader an idea of the types of views out windows and activities people may enjoy: Tropical Paradise, Western City, Western Desert, Western Mountain, Northwest Woods, Northwest Oceanside, Wine Country, Northern Lake Country, Great Lakes Waterfront, Eastern Woods, and Eastern Oceanside. People who live in these areas may live in the same town or city, or they may not. For example, Northwest Woods may be anywhere in Washington, Oregon, Idaho, and Montana. I kept RVs and Portables as a separate category. While using fake place names disallows findings that may show idiosyncratic experiences, regulations, or events associated with a particular location (or even a particular state), it allows for a heightened chance of keeping interviewee identities confidential (especially since some people from the same neighborhood are interviewed).

Despite my inclusion of publicly accessible named television shows, webinars, and municipal regulation meetings in my collection of data elements, the focus of my research is not on regulations and site-specific patterns. It is on patterns that may transcend location and organization. In this sense, my work is similar to the type of conceptual and empirical understandings that sociologist Matthew Desmond defines as relational ethnography, which "takes as its scientific object neither a bounded group defined by members' shared social attributes nor a location delimited by the boundaries of a particular neighborhood or the walls of an organization but rather processes involving configurations of relations among different actors or institutions."[9]

While I do "bound" groups by property use in this study, I do so only based on the processes involved in their use. I find it helpful to describe my book as a story about memory making and the enchantment of family vacation homes that happen to take place in a lot of specific sites and that connect to some specific organizations, but that those sites and organizations are not the story here. The findings revealed in this research point to larger patterns about families and the real estate marketplace that transcend specificity of place, just as any fairy tale is supposed to do.

NOTES

1. University of Kansas Center for Community Health and Development, "Section 21. Windshield and Walking Surveys," Community Tool Box, https://ctb .ku.edu/en/table-of-contents/assessment/assessing-community-needs-and-resources/ windshield-walking-surveys/main.

2. Johnny Saldaña, *The Coding Manual for Qualitative Researchers*, 3rd ed. (Los Angeles: SAGE, 2016).

3. Dedoose Version 9.0.17, cloud application for managing, analyzing, and presenting qualitative and mixed method research data (2021), https://www.dedoose.com.

4. US Census Bureau, "QuickFacts: Walla Walla city, Washington," https://www .census.gov/quickfacts/fact/table/wallawallacitywashington/PST045222.

5. City of Walla Walla, "Short-Term Rental FAQ," https://www.wallawallawa.gov /government/development-services/short-term-rental-faq.

6. Vrbo Virtual Partner Summit 2021, https://host.expediagroup.com/vrbo/en-us/ articles/vrbo-partner-summit.

7. US Internal Revenue Service, "Topic No. 415, Renting Residential and Vacation Property," https://www.irs.gov/taxtopics/tc415.

8. Michelle Janning, Tate Kautzky, and Michelle Zhang, "The Pandemic Vacation Home: Media Framing of COVID-19 and Second Home Real Estate Morality Projects," in *More than Just a "Home": Understanding the Living Spaces of Families*, edited by Rosalina Pisco Costa and Sampson Lee Blair (Leeds, UK: Emerald, 2024), 15–35; Michelle Janning, Hannah Bashevkin, and Nate Raphael, "Investment in 'Home:' Second Properties, Lifestyle Television, and the Production of Family Spaces in the Marketplace," 2018; Michelle Janning and Nate Raphael, "Won't You Be My Neighbor? Short-Term Rentals, Vacation Homes, and the Perception of Neighborhood Impact," 2019.

9. Matthew Desmond, "Relational Ethnography," *Theory and Society* 43 (2014): 547, https://doi.org/10.1007/s11186-014-9232-5.

References

Airbnb. "Bedtime" (advertisement). YouTube, January 20, 2024. https://www.youtube.com/watch?v=1STa1vWPCmo.

Aries, Elizabeth. "Task and Expressive Roles in Groups." In *Men and Women in Interaction: Reconsidering the Differences*, 24–44. Oxford: Oxford University Press, 1996.

Arnett, Jeffrey J. *Emerging Adulthood: The Winding Road from the Late Teens through the Twenties.* Oxford: Oxford University Press, 2014.

Atkinson, Rowland, and Keith Jacobs. *House, Home and Society.* London: Red Grove Press, 2016.

Barton, Kelly. "Leading the Way with Safety." Vrbo Virtual Partner Summit. https://host.expediagroup.com/vrbo/en-us/articles/vrbo-partner-summit/safety (accessed June 1, 2022).

Batcho, K. I., and S. Shikh. "Anticipatory Nostalgia: Missing the Present Before It's Gone." *Personality and Individual Differences* 98 (2016): 75–84. https://doi.org/10.1016/j.paid.2016.03.088.

Beck, Julie. "Trick-or-Treating Isn't What It Used to Be." *Atlantic*, October 31, 2018.

Benjamin, Esme. "Finding Ourselves: How Travel Shapes Identity." Full-Time Travel. https://www.fulltimetravel.co/ftt_inspirations/finding-ourselves-travel-and-identity/ (accessed December 10, 2023).

Benson, Janel E., and Frank F. Furstenberg Jr. "Entry into Adulthood: Are Adult Role Transitions Meaningful Markers of Adult Identity?" *Advances in Life Course Research* 11, no. 3 (2006):199–224. https://doi.org/10.1016/S1040-2608(06)11008-4.

Bericat, Eduardo. "The Sociology of Emotions: Four Decades of Progress." *Current Sociology* 64, no. 3 (2016): 491–513. https://doi.org/10.1177/0011392115588355.

Bertogg, Ariane, and Marc Szydlik. "The Closeness of Young Adults' Relationships with Their Parents." *Swiss Journal of Sociology* 42, no. 1 (2016): 40–60. https://doi.org/10.1515/sjs-2016-0003.

Blumer, Herbert. *Symbolic Interactionism: Perspective and Method.* Berkeley: University of California Press, 1969.

Bourdieu, Pierre. *The Field of Cultural Production.* Cambridge: Polity Press, 1993.

———. "The Forms of Capital." In *Handbook of Theory of Research for the Sociology of Education*, edited by John Richardson, 46–58. Westport, CT: Greenwood, 1986.

Boykin, James H. *Investing in a Vacation Home for Pleasure and Profit.* Mason, OH: Thomson South-Western, 2006.

Callis, Robert R. "Rate of Homeownership Higher than before Pandemic in All Regions." US Census Bureau, July 25, 2023. https://www.census.gov/library/stories/2023/07/younger-householders-drove-rebound-in-homeownership.html.

Chambers, Brooke. "The Stigma of Being Rich." The Society Pages Clippings (website), September 20, 2017. https://thesocietypages.org/clippings/2017/09/20/the-stigma-of-being-rich/.

Chaplin, Davina. "Back to the Cave or Playing Away? Gender Roles in Home-from-Home Environments." *Journal of Consumer Studies and Home Economics* 23, no. 3 (1999): 181–89. https://doi.org/10.1046/j.1365-2737.1999.00109.x.

Cheung, Wing-Yee, Erica G. Hepper, Chelsea A. Reid, Jeffrey D. Green, Tim Wildschut, and Constantine Sedikides. "Anticipated Nostalgia: Looking Forward to Looking Back." *Cognition and Emotion* 34, no. 3 (2020): 511–25. https://doi.org/10.1080/02699931.2019.1649247.

City of Walla Walla. "Short-Term Rental FAQ." https://www.wallawallawa.gov/government/development-services/short-term-rental-faq (accessed January 23, 2024).

Clapham, David. *The Meaning of Housing: A Pathways Approach*. Bristol, UK: Policy Press, 2005.

Clarke, Amy. "We've Been Collecting Souvenirs for Thousands of Years. They Are Valuable Cultural Artefacts—but What Does Their Future Hold?" *Conversation*, October 12, 2022. https://theconversation.com/weve-been-collecting-souvenirs-for-thousands-of-years-they-are-valuable-cultural-artefacts-but-what-does-their-future-hold-189449.

Clemence, Sara. "Black Travelers Say Home-Share Hosts Discriminate, and a New Airbnb Report Agrees." *New York Times*, December 13, 2022. https://www.nytimes.com/2022/12/13/travel/vacation-rentals-racism.html.

Cohen, Philip N. *The Family: Diversity, Inequality, and Social Change*. 4th ed. New York: Norton, 2024.

———. "Generation Labels Mean Nothing. It's Time to Retire Them." *Washington Post*, July 7, 2021. https://www.washingtonpost.com/opinions/2021/07/07/generation-labels-mean-nothing-retire-them/.

Collins, Caitlyn, Liana Christin Landivar, Leah Ruppanner, and William J. Scarborough. "COVID-19 and the Gender Gap in Work Hours." *Gender, Work and Organization* 28, no. S1 (2021): 101–12. https://doi.org/10.1111/gwao.12506.

Colwell, Chip. "Too Much Stuff: Can We Solve Our Addiction to Consumerism?" *Guardian*, November 28, 2023. https://www.theguardian.com/environment/2023/nov/28/too-much-stuff-can-we-solve-our-addiction-to-consumerism.

Cooley, Charles H. *Human Nature and the Social Order*. New York: Scribner's, 1902.

Coontz, Stephanie. *The Way We Never Were: American Families and the Nostalgia Trap.* New York: Basic Books, 1993.

Coppock, John Terence, ed. *Second Homes: Curse or Blessing?* Oxford: Pergamon, 1977.

Csernyik, Rob. "The Professional Airbnb Landlord Class Is Simply the Worst." *Globe and Mail*, December 2, 2023. https://www.theglobeandmail.com/business/commentary/article-the-professional-airbnb-landlord-class-is-simply-the-worst/.

Cuba, Lee, and David M. Hummon. "A Place to Call Home: Identification with Dwelling, Community, and Region." *Sociological Quarterly* 34, no. 1 (1993): 111–31. https://www.jstor.org/stable/4121561.

Davis, Fred. *Yearning for Yesterday: A Sociology of Nostalgia.* New York: Free Press, 1979.

Desmond, Matthew. "Relational Ethnography." *Theory and Society* 43 (2014): 547–79. https://doi.org/10.1007/s11186-014-9232-5.

de Visé, Daniel. "What Is the 'Sandwich Generation'? Many Adults Struggle with Caregiving, Bills and Work." *USA Today*, November 17, 2023. https://www.usatoday.com/story/money/2023/11/17/sandwich-generation-helping-parents-children/71590330007/.

DeVon, Cheyenne. "Starter Homes May Be a Thing of the Past—Millennial and Gen Z Homeowners Plan to Stay Put for Nearly 2 Decades." CNBC, July 12, 2023. https://www.cnbc.com/2023/07/12/gen-z-and-millennial-homebuyers-arent-purchasing-starter-homes.html.

Deem, Rosemary. "Women, the City and Holidays." *Leisure Studies* 15, no. 2 (1996): 105–19. https://doi.org/10.1080/026143696375657.

Dijst, Martin, Martin Lanzendorf, Angela Barendregt, and Leo Smit. "Second Homes in Germany and the Netherlands: Ownership and Travel Impact Explained." *Tijdschrift voor Economische en Sociale Geografie* 96, no. 2 (2005):139–52. https://doi.org/10.1111/j.1467-9663.2005.00446.x.

Dolgon, Corey. *The End of the Hamptons: Scenes from the Class Struggle in America's Paradise.* New York: New York University Press, 2006.

Donelson, Sophie. "Designing for Families." Vrbo Virtual Partner Summit. https://host.expediagroup.com/vrbo/en-us/articles/vrbo-partner-summit/design-with-purpose (accessed June 1, 2022).

Drake, Bruce. "Another Gender Gap: Men Spend More Time in Leisure Activities." Pew Research Center, June 10, 2013. https://www.pewresearch.org/short-reads/2013/06/10/another-gender-gap-men-spend-more-time-in-leisure-activities/.

Durkheim, Émile. *The Elementary Forms of Religious Life*, translated by Carol Cosman. Oxford: Oxford World Classics, 2008.

Durlauf, Steven N. "*Bowling Alone*: A Review Essay." *Journal of Economic Behavior and Organization* 47 (2002): 259–73. https://doi.org/10.1016/S0167-2681(01)00210-4.

Epp, Amber M., and Linda L. Price. "The Storied Life of Singularized Objects: Forces of Agency and Network Transformation." *Journal of Consumer Research* 36, no. 5 (2010): 820–37. https://doi.org/10.1086/603547.

Evan, Gio. "Viaggiate." Track 18 on *Mareducato*. Polydor, Universal Music Italia, 2021.

Ezzell, Matthew B. "'Barbie Dolls' on the Pitch: Identity Work, Defensive Othering, and Inequality in Women's Rugby." *Social Problems* 56, no. 1 (2009): 111–31. https://doi.org/10.1525/sp.2009.56.1.111.

Fingerman, Karen. "Millennials and Their Parents: Implications of the New Young Adulthood for Midlife Adults." *Innovation in Aging* 1, no. 3 (2017): 1–16. https://doi.org/10.1093/geroni/igx026.

Flognfeldt, Thor, and Even Tjørve. "The Shift from Hotels and Lodges to Second-Home Villages in Mountain-Resort Accommodation." *Scandinavian Journal of Hospitality and Tourism* 13, no. 4 (2013): 332–52. https://doi.org/10.1080/15022250.2013.862440.

Freud, Sigmund. "The Uncanny." In *The Complete Psychological Works*, vol. 27. London: Hogarth Press, 1955.

Fry, Richard. "More Millennials Living with Family Despite Improved Job Market." Pew Research Center, July 29, 2015. https://www.pewresearch.org/social-trends/2015/07/29/more-millennials-living-with-family-despite-improved-job-market/.

Furstenberg, Frank F., Sheela Kennedy, Vonnie C. McLoyd, and Ruben G. Rumbaut. "Growing Up Is Harder to Do." *Contexts* 3, no 3 (2004): 33–41. https://doi.org/10.1525/ctx.2004.3.3.33.

Gallent, Nick. *Second Homes: European Perspectives and UK Policies*. Ashgate, UK: Routledge, 2005.

Gayatri, Maria, and Mardiana Dwi Puspitasari. "The Impact of COVID-19 Pandemic on Family Well-Being: A Literature Review." *Family Journal* 31, no.4 (2022): 606–13. https://doi.org/10.1177%2F10664807221131006.

Giddens, Anthony. *Modernity and Self Identity: Self and Society in the Late Modern Age*. Cambridge: Polity Press, 1991.

Gillis, John R. "Gathering Together: Remembering Memory Through Ritual." In *We Are What We Celebrate: Understanding Holidays and Rituals*, edited by Amitai Etzioni and Jared Bloom, 89–103. New York: New York University Press, 2004.

———. *A World of Their Own Making: Myth, Ritual, and the Quest for Family Values*. Cambridge, MA: Harvard University Press, 1996.

Goffman, Erving. *The Presentation of Self in Everyday Life*. Scotland: Doubleday, 1959.

Goldberg, Emma. "Here's What We Do and Don't Know about the Effects of Remote Work." *New York Times*, October 10, 2023. https://www.nytimes.com/2023/10/10/business/remote-work-effects.html.

Goodman, Laurie, Jung Hyun Choi, and Jun Zhu. "The 'Real' Homeownership Gap between Today's Young Adults and Past Generations Is Much Larger Than You Think." *Urban Wire* (blog), April 17, 2023. https://www.urban.org/urban-wire/real-homeownership-gap-between-todays-young-adults-and-past-generations-much-larger-you.

Green, Jeffrey E. "Two Meanings of Disenchantment: Sociological Condition vs. Philosophical Act—Reassessing Max Weber's Thesis of the Disenchantment of the World." *Philosophy and Theology* 17, no. 1/2 (2005): 51–84. https://doi.org/10.5840/philtheol2005171/24.

Greenblat, Cathy Stein, and John H. Gagnon. "Temporary Strangers: Travel and Tourism from a Sociological Perspective." *Sociological Perspectives* 26, no. 1 (1983): 89–110. https://www.jstor.org/stable/1389161.

Grose, Jessica. "The Sandwich Generation Is Getting Squished." *New York Times*, November 2, 2022. https://www.nytimes.com/2022/11/02/opinion/sandwich-generation.html.

Guerin, Jessica. "Who Buys a Vacation Home?" HousingWire, July 11, 2019. https://www.housingwire.com/articles/49537-who-buys-a-vacation-home/.

Guttentag, Daniel. "Airbnb: Disruptive Innovation and the Rise of an Informal Tourism Accommodation Sector." *Current Issues in Tourism* 19, no. 12 (2015): 1192–217. https://doi.org/10.1080/13683500.2013.827159.

Hall, C. Michael, and Dieter K. Muller. *Tourism, Mobility, and Second Homes: Between Elite Landscape and Common Ground.* Clevedon, UK: Channel View Publications, 2004.

Halnon, Karen Bettez. "Poor Chic: The Rational Consumptions of Poverty." *Current Sociology* 50, no. 4 (2002): 501–16. https://doi.org/10.1177/0011392102050004002.

Hochschild, Arlie. *The Commercialization of Intimate Life: Notes from Home and Work.* Berkeley: California University Press, 2003.

———. "Emotion Work, Feeling Rules, and Social Structure." *American Journal of Sociology* 85, no. 3 (1979): 551–75. https://www.jstor.org/stable/2778583.

———. *The Managed Heart: Commercialization of Human Feeling.* Updated, with a new preface. Berkeley: University of California Press, 2012.

———. "The Time Bind." *WorkingUSA* 1, no. 2 (1997): 21–29. https://doi.org/10.1163/17434580-00102006.

Hochschild, Arlie, and Anne Machung. *The Second Shift: Working Families and the Revolution at Home.* New York: Penguin, 2012.

Hoffman, Lily M., and Barbara Schmitter Heisler. *Airbnb, Short-Term Rentals and the Future of Housing.* New York: Routledge, 2021.

Honig, Bonnie. "Difference, Dilemmas, and the Politics of Home." *Social Research* 61, no. 3 (1994): 563–97. https://www.jstor.org/stable/40971048.

Hoogendoorn, Gijsbert, and Gustav Visser. "Focusing on the 'Blessing' and Not the 'Curse' of Second Homes: Notes from South Africa." *Area* 47, no. 2 (2015): 179–84. https://www.jstor.org/stable/24811767.

Hook, Joshua N., Adam S. Hodge, Hansong Zhang, Daryl R. Van Tongeren, and Don E. Davis. "Minimalism, Voluntary Simplicity, and Well-Being: A Systematic Review of the Empirical Literature." *Journal of Positive Psychology* 18, no. 1 (2023): 130–41. https://doi.org/10.1080/17439760.2021.1991450.

Host Rooster. "Journey through Time: The Fascinating History of Vacation Rentals." November 1, 2023. https://hostrooster.com/insights/journey-through-time-the-fascinating-history-of-vacation-rentals/.

Huang, Youqin, and Chengdong Yi. "Second Home Ownership in Transitional Urban China." *Housing Studies* 26, no. 3 (2011): 423–47. https://doi.org/10.1080/02673037.2011.542100.

Illouz, Eva. *Cold Intimacies: The Making of Emotional Capitalism.* Cambridge: Polity Press, 2007.

———. *Consuming the Romantic Utopia: Love and the Cultural Contradictions of Capitalism*. Berkeley: University of California Press, 1997.

———. *Why Love Hurts: A Sociological Explanation*. Cambridge: Polity Press, 2013.

Institute for Social Capital. "Putnam on Social Capital—Democratic or Civic Perspective." https://www.socialcapitalresearch.com/putnam-on-social-capital -democratic-or-civic-perspective/ (accessed January 10, 2024).

Jaffee, Daniel. *Brewing Justice: Fair Trade Coffee, Sustainability, and Survival*. Updated ed. Berkeley: University of California Press, 2014.

Janhunen, Sari, Maija Hujala, and Satu Pätäri. "Owners of Second Homes, Locals and Their Attitudes towards Future Rural Wind Farm." *Energy Policy* 73 (2014): 450– 60. https://doi.org/10.1016/j.enpol.2014.05.050.

Janning, Michelle Y. *Love Letters: Saving Romance in the Digital Age*. New York: Routledge, 2018.

———. *The Stuff of Family Life: How Our Homes Reflect Our Lives*. Lanham, MD: Rowman and Littlefield, 2017.

Janning, Michelle, Hannah Bashevkin, and Nate Raphael. "Investment in 'Home:' Second Properties, Lifestyle Television, and the Production of Family Spaces in the Marketplace." Presentation at the Annual Meeting of the Pacific Sociological Association, Long Beach, CA, March, 2018.

Janning, Michelle, Tate Kautzky, and Michelle Zhang. "The Pandemic Vacation Home: Media Framing of COVID-19 and Second Home Real Estate Morality Projects." In *More Than Just a "Home": Understanding the Living Spaces of Families*, edited by Rosalina Pisco Costa and Sampson Lee Blair, 15–35. Leeds, UK: Emerald, 2024.

Janning, Michelle, Julian Landau, Jess Lilly, Ruby Matthews, and Kaia Roast. "Coming Home to College: Living Arrangements and Perceptions of Adulthood for U.S. College Students during COVID-19." *Cogent Social Sciences* 8, no. 1 (2021): 1–20. https://doi.org/10.1080/23311886.2022.2045453.

Janning, Michelle, and Nate Raphael. "Won't You Be My Neighbor? Short- Term Rentals, Vacation Homes, and the Perception of Neighborhood Impact." Presentation at the Annual Meeting of the Pacific Sociological Association, Oakland, CA, March, 2019.

Janning, Michelle, and Helen Scalise. "Gender and Generation in the Home Curation of Family Photography." *Journal of Family Issues* 36, no. 12 (2013): 1702–25. https://doi.org/10.1177/0192513X13500964.

Jones, Jeffrey M. "Middle-Class Identification Steady in the U.S." Gallup, May 19, 2022. https://news.gallup.com/poll/392708/middle-class-identification-steady .aspx.

Kamin, Debra. "Home Appraised with a Black Owner: $472,000. With a White Owner: $750,000." *New York Times*, August 18, 2022. https://www.nytimes.com /2022/08/18/realestate/housing-discrimination-maryland.html.

Khan, Shamus Rahman. *Privilege: The Making of an Adolescent Elite at St. Paul's School*. Princeton, NJ: Princeton University Press, 2012.

Kliger, Gili. "Keeping the Score." Aeon, November 10, 2022. https://aeon.co/essays/ give-and-take-how-gift-giving-forges-society-and-ourselves.

Kohn, Kari. "Boardinghouses of Yesterday and What They Mean for Today." NYU Marron Institute of Urban Management, December 30, 2013. https://marroninstitute .nyu.edu/blog/boardinghouses-of-yesterday-and-what-they-mean-for-today.

Korver-Glenn, Elizabeth. "Compounding Inequalities: How Racial Stereotypes and Discrimination Accumulate across the Stages of Housing Exchange." *American Sociological Review* 83, no. 4 (2018): 627–56. https://doi.org/10.1177 /00031224187817.

Lake, Sydney. "Millennials Are Replaying Their Parents' Housing Market Journey as First-Time Buyers in Their 30s Flood into an Unaffordable Market." *Fortune*, November 14, 2023. https://fortune.com/2023/11/14/housing-market-affordability -millennials-replaying-boomer-parents-1980s/.

Lasch, Christopher. *Haven in a Heartless World: The Family Besieged*. Rev. ed. New York: Norton, 1995.

Lee, Hyojung, Dowell Myers, Gary Painter, Johanna Thunell, and Julie Zissimopoulos. "The Role of Parental Financial Assistance in the Transition to Homeownership by Young Adults." *Journal of Housing Economics* 47 (2020): 101597. https://doi.org /10.1016/j.jhe.2018.08.002.

Levin, Yuval. "'The Upswing' Review: Bowling Alone No More?" *Wall Street Journal*, October 9, 2020.

Marotta, Mario. "A Disenchanted World: Max Weber on Magic and Modernity." *Journal of Classical Sociology* (2023). https://doi.org/10.1177/1468795X231160716.

Marx, Patricia. "A Guide to Getting Rid of Almost Everything." *New Yorker*, February 21, 2022. https://www.newyorker.com/magazine/2022/02/28/a-guide-to -getting-rid-of-almost-everything-decluttering.

Mauss, Marcel. *The Gift: The Form and Reason for Exchange in Archaic Societies*. Translated by W. D. Halls. New York: Norton, 2000.

Mayol-García, Yerís. "Pandemic Brought Parents and Children Closer: More Family Dinners, More Reading to Young Children." US Census Bureau, January 3, 2022. https://www.census.gov/library/stories/2022/01/parents-and-children -interacted-more-during-covid-19.html.

McCabe, Brian J. *No Place Like Home: Wealth, Community, and the Politics of Homeownership*. Oxford: Oxford University Press, 2016.

McIntyre, Norman, Daniel Williams, and Kevin McHugh, eds. *Multiple Dwelling and Tourism: Negotiating Place, Home, and Identity*. Wallingford, UK: CABI Publishing, 2006.

Mead, George Herbert. *Mind, Self, and Society from the Standpoint of a Social Behaviorist*. Chicago: University of Chicago Press, 1967.

Merriam-Webster. "Word of the Year 2023." November 27, 2023. https://www .merriam-webster.com/wordplay/word-of-the-year.

Miller, Daniel. *The Comfort of Things*. Cambridge: Polity Press, 2008.

———. *Stuff*. Cambridge: Polity Press, 2010.

Milligan, Melinda J. "Interactional Past and Potential: The Social Construction of Place Attachment." *Symbolic Interaction* 21, no. 1 (1998): 1–33. https://doi.org/10 .1525/si.1998.21.1.1.

Mills, C. Wright. *The Sociological Imagination*. 40th anniversary ed. New York: Oxford University Press, 2000.

Mont'Alvao, Arnaldo, Pamela Aronson, and Jeylan Mortimer. "Uncertainty and Disruption in the Transition to Adulthood during COVID-19." In *Social Problems in the Age of COVID-19*, Vol. 2: *Global Perspectives*, edited by G. W. Muschert, K. M. Budd, D. C. Lane, and J. A. Smith, 15–26. Bristol, UK: Bristol University Press/Policy Press, 2020.

Mooi-Reci, Irma, and Barbara J. Risman. "The Gendered Impacts of COVID-19: Lessons and Reflections." *Gender and Society*, 35, no. 2 (2021). https://doi.org/10.1177/08912432211001305.

Mr. Rogers' Neighborhood Official Website. https://www.misterrogers.org/ (accessed January 22, 2024).

Nadeem, Waqar, Mari Juntunen, Farid Shirazi, and Nick Hajli. "Consumers' Value Co-creation in Sharing Economy: The Role of Social Support, Consumers' Ethical Perceptions and Relationship Quality." *Technological Forecasting and Social Change* 151 (2020): 1013. https://doi.org/10.1016/j.techfore.2019.119786.

Neal, Zachary P. "Community." *Oxford Bibliography of Sociology*. https://www.oxfordbibliographies.com/display/document/obo-9780199756384/obo-9780199756384-0080.xml.

Niasse, Amina. "U.S. Second Home Sales Slide in Pandemic-Era Vacation Hot Spots." Reuters, October 30, 2023. https://www.reuters.com/markets/us/second-home-sales-slide-pandemic-era-vacation-hot-spots-2023-10-30/.

Nippert-Eng, Christena E. *Home and Work: Negotiating Boundaries through Everyday Life*. Chicago: University of Chicago Press, 1996.

Norris, Michelle, and Nessa Winston. "Second-Home Owners: Escaping, Investing or Retiring?" *Tourism Geographies* 12, no. 4 (2010): 546–67. https://doi.org/10.1080/14616688.2010.516401.

O'Brien Legal. "Rich Millennials Opt for Vacation Properties over Starter Homes." October 9, 2019. https://www.olslaw.com/blog/2019/10/rich-millennials-opt-for-vacation-properties-over-starter-homes/.

Paris, Chris. *Affluence, Mobility and Second Home Ownership*. Abingdon, UK: Routledge, 2010.

Park, Lisa Sun-Hee, and David Naguib Pellow. *The Slums of Aspen: Immigrants vs. the Environment in America's Eden*. New York: New York University Press, 2011.

Parker, Kim, and Rachel Minkin. "Views of Different Family Living Arrangements." In *Public Has Mixed Views on the Modern American Family* (report). Pew Research Center, September 14, 2023. https://www.pewresearch.org/social-trends/2023/09/14/views-of-different-family-arrangements/.

Pasquale, Ashley. "Home Staging Techniques to Appeal to Families." Seattle Staged to Sell, September 15, 2021, https://www.seattlestagedtosell.com/home-staging-techniques-to-appeal-to-families/.

People ACCIONA. "Does Gender Inequality Persist Also in Our Leisure Time?" July 28, 2022. https://people.acciona.com/diversity-and-inclusion/gender-inequality-leisure/.

Pew Charitable Trusts. "The Long-Term Decline in Fertility—and What It Means for State Budgets." December 5, 2022. https://www.pewtrusts.org/en/research -and-analysis/issue-briefs/2022/12/the-long-term-decline-in-fertility-and-what-it -means-for-state-budgets.

Pew Research Center. "IV: Family." In *The Decline of Marriage and Rise of New Families* (report), November 18, 2010. https://www.pewresearch.org/social-trends /2010/11/18/iv-family/.

Polanyi, Karl. *The Great Transformation: The Political and Economic Origins of Our Time*. 2nd ed. Boston: Beacon Press, 2001.

Psychology Today. "Affective Forecasting." https://www.psychologytoday.com/us/ basics/affective-forecasting (accessed January 5, 2024).

Pugh, Allison. *The Last Human Job: The Work of Connecting in a Disconnected World*. Princeton, NJ: Princeton University Press, 2024.

Purcell, Patrick J. "Geographic Mobility and Annual Earnings in the United States." *Social Security Bulletin*, 80, no. 2 (2020). https://www.ssa.gov/policy/docs/ssb/ v80n2/v80n2p1.html.

Putnam, Robert. *Bowling Alone*. New York: Simon and Schuster, 2000.

Reed, Tiffany Owens. "The 'Je Ne Sais Quoi' of Neighborliness." Strong Towns, October 10, 2023. https://www.strongtowns.org/journal/2023/10/10/the-je-ne-sais -quoi-of-neighborliness.

Rees, Brenda. "Beyond Bruce's Beach." *Pomona College Magazine*, June 1, 2023. https://magazine.pomona.edu/2023/summer/beyond-bruces-beach/.

Ritzer, George. *Enchanting a Disenchanted World: Continuity and Change in the Cathedrals of Consumption*. 3rd ed. Los Angeles: Pine Forge Press/SAGE, 2009.

Robbins, Roberta A. Davilla, and A. Frank Thompson. *Communicating Finances in the Family: Talking and Taking Action*. Solana Beach, CA: Cognella Academic Publishing, 2020.

Robinson, Evita. "Increase Earnings through Inclusivity." Vrbo Virtual Partner Summit. https://host.expediagroup.com/vrbo/en-us/articles/vrbo-partner-summit/ inclusivity (accessed June 1, 2024).

Rollero, Chiara, and Norma de Piccoli. "Place Attachment, Identification and Environment Perception: An Empirical Study." *Journal of Environmental Psychology* 30, no. 2 (2010): 198–205. https://doi.org/10.1016/j.jenvp.2009.12 .003.

Rose, David. *Enchanted Objects: Innovation, Design, and the Future of Technology*. New York: Scribner, 2014.

Rudrum, Sarah, Elisabeth Rondinelli, Jesse Carlson, Lesley Frank, Rachel K. Brickner, and Rebecca Casey. "When Work Came Home: Formation of Feeling Rules in the Context of a Pandemic." *Emotion, Space, and Society* 42 (2022): 1–9. https://doi .org/10.1016/j.emospa.2021.100861.

Rugh, Susan Sessions. *Are We There Yet? The Golden Age of American Family Vacations*. Lawrence: University Press of Kansas, 2008.

Safdari-Dehcheshmeh, Faranak, Mahnaz Noroozi, Fariba Taleghani, and Soraya Memar. "Factors Influencing the Delay in Childbearing: A Narrative Review." *Iranian Journal of Nursing and Midwifery Research* 28, no. 1 (2023): 10–19.

Saldaña, Johnny. *The Coding Manual for Qualitative Researchers*. 3rd ed. Los Angeles: SAGE, 2016.

Sandberg-Thoma, Sara E., Anastasia R. Snyder, and Bohyun Joy Jang. "Exiting and Returning to the Parental Home for Boomerang Kids." *Journal of Marriage and Family* 77, no. 3 (2015): 806–18. https://doi.org/10.1111/jomf.12183.

Sassler, Sharon, Desiree Ciambrone, and Gaelan Benway. "Are They Really Mama's Boys/Daddy's Girls? The Negotiation of Adulthood upon Returning to the Parental Home." *Sociological Forum* 23, no. 4 (2008): 670–98. https://doi.org/10.1111/j.1573-7861.2008.00090.x.

Schor, Juliet. After the Gig: How the Sharing Economy Got Hijacked and How to Win It Back. Berkeley: University of California Press, 2020.

Scott, Susie. *Making Sense of Everyday Life*. Cambridge: Polity Press, 2009.

Senior, Jennifer. *All Joy and No Fun: The Paradox of Modern Parenthood.* New York: Ecco, 2014.

Settersten, Richard A. Jr., Timothy M. Ottusch, and Barbara Schneider. "Becoming Adult: Meanings of Markers to Adulthood." *Emerging Trends in the Social and Behavioral Sciences* (2015). https://doi.org/10.1002/9781118900772.etrds0021.

Sherman, Rachel. *Uneasy Street: The Anxieties of Affluence.* Princeton, NJ: Princeton University Press, 2019.

Siricord, Belle. "Why More Millennials and Gen Zs Are Opting to Delay Settling Down or Not Settling Down at All. I'm One of Them." *Medium*, November 15, 2023. https://medium.com/@bellesiricord/why-more-millennials-and-gen-zs-are-opting-to-delay-settling-down-or-not-settling-down-at-all-0a966d8c7f2f.

Smaliukiene, Rasa, Lai Chi-Shiun, and Indre Sizovaite. "Consumer Value Co-creation in Online Business: The Case of Global Travel Services." *Journal of Business Economics and Management* 16, no. 2 (2015): 325–39. http://dx.doi.org/10.3846/16111699.2014.985251.

Smith, Morgan. "Gen Z and Millennials Are Leading 'The Big Quit' in 2023—Why Nearly 70% Plan to Leave Their Jobs." CNBC, January 18, 2023, https://www.cnbc.com/2023/01/18/70percent-of-gen-z-and-millennials-are-considering-leaving-their-jobs-soon.html.

Snowden, Brandi, and Nadia Evangelou. "Racial Disparities in Homeowner Groups." National Association of Realtors, March 3, 2022. https://www.nar.realtor/blogs/economists-outlook/racial-disparities-in-homeownership-rates.

Sowersby, Shauna. "Shelton Residents Push Back against Proposed Taylor Shellfish Oyster Farm in Oakland Bay." *Olympian*, November 12, 2023. https://www.theolympian.com/news/politics-government/article281260723.html.

Stedman, Richard C. "Understanding Place Attachment among Second Home Owners." *American Behavioral Scientist* 50, no. 2 (2006): 187–205. https://doi.org/10.1177/0002764206290633.

Stein, Karen. *Getting Away from It All: Vacations and Identity.* Philadelphia: Temple University Press, 2019.

Sternheimer, Karen. "The Sharing Economy Paradox." *Everyday Sociology Blog*, December 3, 2015. https://www.everydaysociologyblog.com/2015/12/the-sharing-economy-paradox.html.

Strong Towns. "About Strong Towns." https://www.strongtowns.org/about (accessed November 15, 2023).

Swidler, Ann. *Talk of Love: How Culture Matters.* Chicago: University of Chicago Press, 2001.

Tjørve, Even, Thor Flognfeldt, and Kathleen M. Calf Tjørve. "The Effects of Distance and Belonging on Second-Home Markets." *Tourism Geographies* 15, no. 2 (2013): 268–91. https://doi.org/10.1080/14616688.2012.726264.

Torres, Emilio, and J. Santos Dominguez-Menchero. "The Impact of Second Homes on Local Taxes." *Fiscal Studies* 27, no. 2 (2006): 231–50. https://www.jstor.org/stable/24439994.

Tuan, Yi-Fu. *Space and Place: The Perspective of Experience.* Minneapolis: University of Minnesota Press, 1977.

Tuedio, James. "Ambiguities in the Locus of Home: Exilic Life and the Space of Belonging." In *Homes in Transformation: Dwelling, Moving, Belonging*, edited by Hanna Johansson and Kirsi Saarikangas, 284–310. Helsinki: Finnish Literature Society, 2009.

Urry, John. *Sociology beyond Societies.* London: Routledge, 2000.

US Census Bureau. "QuickFacts: Shelton city, Washington." https://www.census.gov/quickfacts/fact/table/sheltoncitywashington/PST045222 (accessed January 23, 2024).

———. "QuickFacts: Walla Walla city, Washington." https://www.census.gov/quickfacts/fact/table/wallawallacitywashington/PST045222 (accessed January 23, 2024).

US Government Accountability Office. "The Affordable Housing Crisis Grows While Efforts to Increase Supply Fall Short." October 12, 2023. https://www.gao.gov/blog/affordable-housing-crisis-grows-while-efforts-increase-supply-fall-short.

US Internal Revenue Service. "Topic No. 415, Renting Residential and Vacation Property." https://www.irs.gov/taxtopics/tc415 (accessed January 10, 2024).

University of Kansas Center for Community Health and Development. "Section 21. Windshield and Walking Surveys." Community Tool Box. https://ctb.ku.edu/en/table-of-contents/assessment/assessing-community-needs-and-resources/windshield-walking-surveys/main (accessed January 10, 2024).

Valentine, Gill. "Boundary Crossings: Transitions from Childhood to Adulthood." *Children's Geographies* 1, no. 1 (2003): 37–52. https://doi.org/10.1080/14733280302186.

Van Patten, Susan R., and Daniel R. Williams. "Problems in Place: Using Discursive Social Psychology to Investigate the Meanings of Seasonal Homes." *Leisure Sciences* 30 (2008): 448–64. https://doi.org/10.1080/01490400802353190.

Velsey, Kim. "Upstate Buyers Are Too Rich for Airbnb Now." *Curbed* (blog), October 30, 2023. https://www.curbed.com/2023/10/upstate-new-york-rich-buyers-airbnb.html.

Vercel, Kelcie L. "Feels Like Home: How Home Stagers Construct Spatial Rhetorics to Persuade Homebuyers." *Consumption Markets and Culture* 24, no. 6 (2021): 545–74. https://doi.org/10.1080/10253866.2021.1891894.

Vespa, Jonathan. "The Changing Economics and Demographics of Young Adulthood: 1975–2016." US Census Bureau, April 2017. https://www.census.gov/library/publications/2017/demo/p20-579.html.

Vrbo. "According to Vrbo Data, Taking a 'Flexcation' Is the Latest Family Travel Trend." https://www.vrbo.com/vacation-ideas/explore-vrbo/travel-trends/according-to-vrbo-data-taking-a-flexcation-is-the-latest-family-travel-trend (accessed January 23, 2024).

———. "Cabin in Rockbridge." Facebook, January 23, 2024. https://www.facebook.com/100064955641000/posts/7077655112273867.

———. "Only Your People" (advertisement). YouTube. https://www.youtube.com/watch?v=nAcwMLsSsGo (accessed July 2022).

———. "Vrbo Releases 'Only Your People' Creative Campaign" (press release). July 25, 2022. https://www.vrbo.com/media-center/press-releases/2022/vrbo-releases-only-your-people-creative-campaign.

Vrbo Partners. "Summit 2019 | Scottsdale, AZ." Facebook November 11, 2019. https://www.facebook.com/watch/?v=560415408108868.

Vrbo Virtual Partner Summit 2021. https://host.expediagroup.com/vrbo/en-us/articles/vrbo-partner-summit (accessed June 1, 2022).

Walczak, Anna. "What Does It Mean to Be an Adult? Adulthood Markers in the Perspective of Emerging Adults." *Emerging Adulthood* 11, no. 6 (2023). https://doi.org/10.1177/21676968231194887.

Walmsley, Laurel. "Young Families Continued to Leave Cities Last Year—but at a Slower Pace." NPR, July 9, 2023. https://www.npr.org/2023/07/09/1186483034/family-exodus-cities-census-data.

Washington State University Carson College of Business. "How the Sharing Economy Is Transforming Business." November 9, 2023. https://onlinemba.wsu.edu/blog/how-the-sharing-economy-is-transforming-business.

Waters, Michael. "The New Family Vacation." *Atlantic*, December 18, 2023. https://www.theatlantic.com/family/archive/2023/12/large-multigenerational-family-vacation-parents-relatives/676382/.

Weber, Max. *Max Weber on the Methodology of the Social Sciences*. Translated by Edward A. Shils and Henry A. Finch. Glencoe, IL: Free Press, 1949.

———. *The Protestant Ethic and the Spirit of Capitalism: The Complete Text—Inclusive of Notes*. Translated by Talcott Parsons. N.p.: Pantianos Classics, 1905.

Wigert, Ben, Jim Harter, and Sangeeta Agrawal. "The Future of the Office Has Arrived: It's Hybrid." Gallup, October 9, 2023. https://www.gallup.com/workplace/511994/future-office-arrived-hybrid.aspx.

Young, Iris Marion. *Intersecting Voices: Dilemmas of Gender, Political Philosophy, and Policy*. Princeton, NJ: Princeton University Press, 1997.

Zelizer, Viviana A. *Pricing the Priceless Child: The Changing Social Value of Children*. Princeton, NJ: Princeton University Press, 1994.

———. *The Purchase of Intimacy*. Princeton, NJ: Princeton University Press, 2005.

Zerubavel, Eviatar. "Lumping and Splitting: Notes on Social Classification." *Sociological Forum* 11, no. 3 (1996): 421–33. https://www.jstor.org/stable/684894.

Zillman, Claire. "Women Are Worse than Men at Using Their Vacation Time." *Fortune*, May 23, 2017. https://fortune.com/2017/05/23/vacation-time-women-take-less/.

Index

Washington (state): land use politics
example in, 119–21; Walla Walla, 48,
129, 130, 144, 202
wealth. *See* income; privilege;
socioeconomic status
Weber, Max: on disenchantment, 16–17,
19; on ideal type, 36

Williams, Daniel, 13

Zelizer, Viviana, 17, 56, 104
zoning and land use, 5–6, 24, 115–16,
127, 133, 144; Washington state
example of conflicts around, 119–21

About the Author

Michelle Janning is professor of sociology and Raymond and Elsie Gipson DeBurgh Chair of Social Sciences at Whitman College. Her research focuses on the sociology of families, with emphasis on the material and spatial dimensions of family life. She is a frequent speaker and commentator in news media about contemporary families and home design and the author of several books, including *The Stuff of Family Life: How Our Homes Reflect Our Lives* (Rowman & Littlefield, 2017), *Love Letters: Saving Romance in the Digital Age* (2018), and *A Guide to Socially Informed Research for Architects and Designers* (2023).

www.ingramcontent.com/pod-product-compliance
Lightning Source LLC
Chambersburg PA
CBHW032347280326
41935CB00008B/484